THE CHARISMATIC FIGURE AS MIRACLE WORKER

by

David Lenz Tiede

Published by

SOCIETY OF BIBLICAL LITERATURE

for

The Seminar on the Gospels

DISSERTATION SERIES, NUMBER ONE

1972

THE CHARISMATIC FIGURE AS MIRACLE WORKER

by

David Lenz Tiede
Luther Theological Seminary
2375 Como Avenue West
St. Paul, Minnesota 55108

Ph.D., 1970
Harvard University

Advisor:
Helmut Koester

Copyright © 1972

by

The Society of Biblical Literature

Second Printing 1973

ISBN 0-88414-010-5

Library of Congress Catalog Card Number: 72-87359

Printed in the United States of America

Printing Department, University of Montana
Missoula, Montana 59801

CONTENTS

iii

53373

ABBREVIATIONS

BZNW = Beiheft zur Zeitschrift für die neutestamentliche Wissenschaft und die Kunde der älteren Kirche.

CBQ = Catholic Biblical Quarterly

EvTh = Evangelische Theologie

F.Gr.Hist. = Felix Jacoby, Die Fragmente der Griechischen Historiker. Leiden: E.J. Brill, 1957ff.

FRLANT = Forschungen zur Religion und Literatur des Alten und Neuen Testaments.

HTR = Harvard Theological Review

IG = Inscriptiones Graecae

JBL = Journal of Biblical Literature

JQR = Jewish Quarterly Review

JTS = Journal of Theological Studies

NT = Novum Testamentum

NTS = New Testament Studies

PGM = Karl Preisendanz. Papyri Graecae Magicae; Die Griech-Zauberpapyri, vol. I, 1928, vol. II, 1931.

PW = A. Pauly-G. Wissowa. Real-Encyclopädie der klassischen Altertumswissenschaft. 1894ff.

RAC = Reallexicon für Antike und Christentum. Hsg. v. Th. Klauser. 1941ff.

RGG = Die Religion in Geschichte und Gegenwart, third edition, 1957ff.

SIG = Sylloge Inscriptionum Graecarum. Ed. W. Dittenberger, editio tertia. Leipzig, 1915-1924.

SVF = Johannes von Arnim. Stoicorum Veterum Fragmenta. Stuttgart: B.G. Teubner, 1964 (second edition). [First edition 1921-1924.]

TDNT = Theological Dictionary of the New Testament (trans. by G.W. Bromiley). Grand Rapids: Wm. B. Eerdman's, 1964ff. Vols. I-VI.

Th.R.= Theologische Rundschau

ThWNT = Theologisches Wörterbuch zum Neuen Testament, bgr.
v. G. Kittel, hg. v. G. Friedrich. Stuttgart: W. Kohlhammer
1933ff. Vols. I-VIII.

TU = Texte und Untersuchungen zur Geschichte der altchristlichen
Literatur.

ZNW = Zeitschrift für die neutestamentliche Wissenschaft
und die Kunde der älteren Kirche

ZThK = Zeitschrift für Theologie und Kirche

CHAPTER ONE: THE DIVINE WISE MAN

A. The Problem of Aretalogies

There appears to be no unified picture of what constituted an aretalogy in the ancient world. Nilsson is probably correct in insisting that "there is no justification for speaking of a literary genre" since poetry and prose are interchangeable.[1] The term "aretalogy" is itself relatively rare in antiquity [cf. LXX Sirach 36:14 (19) = הוד in Heb.; Manetho the Astrologer (c. IV A.D. pseudonymous collection) 4:444-477],[2] yet it has proved to be a helpful descriptive term for correlating a variety of oral and semi-literary traditions in which the ἀρεταί of a god or illustrious man are recounted. The function of such "aretalogical" traditions may be broadly described as propagandistic recitations of praise, but more precise distinctions as to form, content, and propagandistic intent must be made before the particular thrust of a given "aretalogical" formulation can be assessed. Although this is not primarily a study of the classification of such traditions, it appears necessary to offer a schema for distinguishing certain kinds of material that have been

---

[1]Martin P. Nilsson, Geschichte der Griechischen Religion, Band II (München, 1961), p. 228.

[2]Cf. O. Crusius, "Aretalogi," PW II, pp. 670-672. It is worth noting that the term occurs in Sirach outside of the contexts that have been frequently called "aretalogical": cf. Sirach 24 and 43.

1

frequently called "aretalogies."

One relatively pure type of aretalogy can be noted in passing, since it is only of indirect significance for this study, that is, the so-called aretalogy of the self-proclamations of Isis. The inscriptions from Cyme and Ios together with a citation of an inscription from "Nyssa in Arabia" preserved by Diodorus Siculus (Bibl. Hist. 1.27.3) provide ample evidence of a well-wrought form in which Isis is quoted as reciting her own virtues.[3] Since the terms ἀρετή and ἀρεταλογία are never used in those texts, the ambiguity that results from using a Greek cognate could be avoided by merely calling the form a recitation of self-praise.

The form, nevertheless, is distinct. The most obvious characteristic is the constant repetition of first person pronouns. In the three inscriptions which document the form, 81 of 91 clauses begin with ἐγώ. All of the other clauses have some form of the first person pronoun and the ἐγώ εἰμι formula occurs 24 times. The phrasing is clipped and contains no elaboration as to how Isis accomplished her praiseworthy deeds.

The content is also consistent. Isis identifies herself by her place in the family of the gods and by her

---

[3]The Greek texts are printed in full in W. Peek, Der Isishymnus von Andros und verwandte Texte (Berlin, 1930). A. Deissmann, text and translation of the Ios inscription in Light from the Ancient East (New York, 1927), pp. 138-140 W.L. Knox reprints the Cyme inscription in "The Divine Wisdom," JTS 38 (1937), pp. 230-231.

role as ruler of the heavens and of earth and as legislator of all helpful human ordinances. It is also noteworthy that although these recitations of the praise of Isis probably originated in a context where an Isis cult or Isis-Sarapis cult was being established in competition with other religions,[4] Isis does not present herself as a healer or miracle worker, although she is viewed this way in other contexts, nor as a model of virtue to be imitated. She praises herself as the one who instituted and preserves order in the world.

The formal consistency of the "Isis aretalogy" has provided a precise control by which the self-predications of God in II Isaiah and the self-praises of Wisdom in Sirach 24 have been evaluated.[5] It may now be possible to press such comparisons even further in the light of the recent study of these praises of Isis as expressive of the Egyptian ideology of kingship.[6] Furthermore, the variety of ways in which the ἐγώ εἰμι formula is used in these inscriptions provided one of Bultmann's basic controls for describing the usages of this formula in the Gospel of

---

[4]Cf. A.D. Nock, Conversion (London, 1961), pp. 40-41.

[5]Cf. Hans Conzelmann, "Die Mutter der Weisheit," Zeit und Geschichte, Dankesgabe an Rudolf Bultmann, ed. Erich Dinkler (Tübingen, 1964), pp. 225-234. H. Ringgren, Word and Wisdom (Lund, 1947), W.L. Knox, op. cit., pp. 230-237.

[6]Jan Bergman, Ich bin Isis: Studien zum memphitischen Hintergrund der griechischen Isisaretalogien (Acta Universitatis Upsaliensis, Historian Religionum #3; Uppsala, 1968).

John[7] and has furnished a backdrop for discriminating among
the several uses of the ἐγώ εἰμι formula in early Christian
and gnostic literature.[8] Without becoming embroiled in the
complex questions of the theological significance of such
ἐγώ εἰμι formulations, it may be germane to note that recent
attempts to delineate a miracle source behind the Gospel of
John appear agreed on excluding the typical ἐγώ εἰμι
formulations from that source.[9] This observation merely
reenforces the premise that the "Isis aretalogy" represents
a particular style of propaganda which must not be confused
with other "aretalogical" modes.

This study is focused upon two other kinds of traditions
which have been called aretalogical. Although all of these

---

[7]Rudolf Bultmann, Das Evangelium des Johannes (Abt. II
of Kritisch-exegetischer Kommentar über das Neue Testament,
founded by H.A.W. Meyer; Göttingen, 1941, 19th edition 1968),
pp. 167-168. Cf. also E. Schweizer, Ego Eimi ... Die
religionsgeschichtliche Herkunft und theologische Bedeutung
der Johanneischen Bildreden, zugleich ein Beitrag zur
Quellenfrage des vierten Evangeliums (FRLANT, n.s. #38, entire
series #56; Göttingen, 1939). Raymond E. Brown, The Gospel
according to John (Anchor Bible vol. I; New York, 1966),
especially pp. 533-538. Helmut Koester, "One Jesus and Four
Primitive Gospels," HTR 61 (1968), especially pp. 221-223.

[8]Cf. A.J. Festugière, "À propos des arétalogies d'Isis,"
HTR 42 (1949), p. 221, note 40. H. Koester, "One Jesus and
Four Gospels," op. cit., pp. 221-223. George W. MacRae,
"The Ego-proclamation in Gnostic Sources," The Trial of Jesus
(Studies in honour of C.F.D. Moule, ed. E. Bammel, Studies
in Biblical Theology, Second Series #13; London, 1970),
pp. 122-134.

[9]Even Robert T. Fortna, The Gospel of Signs (Society
for New Testament Studies, monograph series #11; Cambridge,
1970), whose reconstructed source is very extensive, follows
Bultmann and Haenchen in suggesting that the source does
not use the ἐγώ εἰμι formula with any revelatory force.

forms of praise share a propagandistic function, it is vital
to the methodology of this essay to demonstrate that the
origins of the following two traditions are discrete. The
discussion of the aretalogies of the divine wise man and of
the miracle worker requires much more elaboration than this
section on the problem of aretalogies permits. But in what
sense are such traditions concerning wise men and miracle
workers aretalogies?

In the case of the traditions about the wise man, the
recitation of his ἀρεταί appears to have been an important
facet of the propaganda of the Hellenistic philosophical
schools. In their attempt to describe "the genesis, fortunes,
and consequences of an ancient type of biographical writing
called aretalogy."[10] Hadas and Smith submit a preliminary
definition which appears to be an adequate statement of the
cultivated description of the wise man: "a formal account
of the remarkable career of an impressive teacher that was
used as a basis for moral instruction."[11] The specificity of
this kind of aretalogy is clearly seen in the qualification
by Hadas and Smith that "the effective catalyst for
aretalogy ... is the Platonic image of Socrates"[12] with the
further observation that "it is the aretalogy of Socrates,

---

[10]Moses Hadas and Morton Smith, Heroes and Gods (New
York, 1965), p. 3.

[11]Ibid. This definition is too specific, however, to
encompass the range of material that has been elsewhere
called aretalogical.

[12]Ibid., p. 17.

implied, or even premised, in Plato that doubtless became
the model for an independent literary genre."[13]

Although the existence of such an "independent literary
genre" may be doubtful, the cultivation of images of heroes
or athletes of virtue (ἀρετή) was a vital aspect of the
moral teaching of the philosophical schools. Clearly Hadas
and Smith are correct that the picture of Socrates as a
paradigm of virtue had a profound effect upon the way the
images of Diogenes and Zeno, not to mention Heracles, were
drafted in the Hellenistic period. The recitation of the
lives, words, and deeds of such charismatic giants of the
past for the purpose of ethical instruction constitutes the
"aretalogy" of the divine wise man.

The aretalogy of the miracle worker has often been
treated as a natural vulgarization of philosophical traditions. The variable is seen as the level of credulity
present in a given situation.[14] No doubt the use of
miraculous motifs in Hellenistic propaganda did vary with
the level of scientific knowledge, but a much more basic
ideological conflict existed in the Hellenistic world with
both sides competing for the allegiances of men: i.e. the
schools against the cults.

R. Reitzenstein provided a major breakthrough on this
question in 1906 in his study Hellenistische Wundererzählungen.

_____

[13]Ibid., p. 58.

[14]Cf. Ibid., p. 62 and R. Grant, Miracle and Natural
Law (Amsterdam, 1952), pp. 61-86.

He demonstrated that the ἀρεταλόγοι must be treated as the prophets of Oriental cults who were flooding the empire with new, specifically religious currents. It is impossible to account for this phenomenon against a Greek, particularly Greek philosophical, background alone.[15] The cultic setting of this kind of aretalogy and its separation from the schools can be demonstrated, for example, by the new valence that the term ἀρετή assumes. In the fourth century B.C., Isyllus of Epidaurus related a miracle of Asclepius beginning and ending with the words: τόδε σῆς ἀρετῆς τοὖργον and τιμῶν σὴν ἀρετήν .[16] The citation from Isyllus is instructive because it documents a particular kind of cultic recitation in which the miracles of Asclepius document his ἀρετή . In this connection, the term has a particular connotation: ἀρετή is the power to work wonders. Thus the miraculous manifestations become identified with the ἀρεταί of Asclepius so that one who is healed is said to have "seen the greater ἀρεταί of the god" (SIG 1172) and the crowd that witnesses another healing "rejoices because the ἀρεταί are still alive" (IG 14.966). It should be noted that the term ἀρετή does not appear in the famous Epidauran inscriptions

---

[15]Cf. R. Reitzenstein, Hellenistische Wundererzählungen (Darmstadt, 1963: reprint from 1906), p. 12. Cf. also, O. Crusius, "Aretalogoi," PW II, 670-672 (1896). W. Aly, "Aretalogoi," PW Supplement VI, 13-15 (1935).

[16]IG IV^2,1, no. 128, 57-79. Cf. text and translation in E.J. & L. Edelstein, Asclepius (Baltimore, 1945: Institute of the History of Medicine, Johns Hopkins Univ, Second Series, II) I #295, pp. 143-145.

8

describing the healings performed at the shrine by Asclepius, but the citation from Isyllus and the inscriptions show that those who were testifying to such miracles were bearing witness to Asclepius' ἀρεταί.[17] Thus it is not inappropriate to refer to the extended and detailed Epidauran account of the healings as an "aretalogy" of Asclepius.

This specialized use of the term ἀρετή is, therefore, the basis for speaking of the miracle accounts as "aretalogies," and it also militates against the combination of such traditions with those where the ἀρεταί of a hero of the philosophical schools are recited. The special connotation of the term ἀρετή is crucial.

An excellent additional example of this usage can be found in Oxyrhynchus Papyrus 1381 where the writer, a devotee of the Egyptian Asclepius, Imhotep, hesitates in his assigned task of describing the mighty deed (διηγεῖσθει τὰς δυνάμεις) of the god or divine physician (cf. note 17) out of concern for his mortal inability to describe the undying power (ἀρετή) of Imhotep (cf. lines 40-47). Falling ill as a punishment for this procrastination, he is miraculously

---

[17]Cf. edition of R. Herzog, Die Wunderheilungen von Epidaurus (Leipzig, 1931: Philologus, Supplement Band 22, Heft 3). The critical Greek text is also included in E.J. and L. Edelstein,Asclepius I, op. cit., #423, pp. 231-237. Cf. also Pausanius 2.27.3. Asclepius is once regarded as a god, again as a hero, and again as a "divine man.", but as L. Bieler, ΘΕΙΟΣ ΑΝΗΡ (Wien, 1935-1936, 2 vols), pp. 104-106, vol. II, shows, Asclepius was increasingly regarded in the Hellenistic world as having displayed "divine power" in his healings.

healed by Imhotep. The writer's mother, a witness of the miracle, attempts to describe it (μηνύειν ἀρετήν) to him, but the writer interrupts with his hymn in praise of the manifestation of miraculous power (ἐπιφανεία δυνάμεως) .[18]

Such recitation of the miraculous activity of the central figure of the cult was by no means limited to the Asclepius traditions. One of the crucial texts for establishing the aretalogy of the recitation of miracles comes from Strabo's description of the worship of Sarapis. In book 17, page 801 of his geography, Strabo tells of the temple of Sarapis in Canobus "which is honored with great reverence and produces cures (θεραπεία) so that even the most reputable men believe" (καὶ τοὺς ἐλλογιμωτάτους ἄνδρας πιστεύειν). Although the text is uncertain, the next sentence which describes the cult functionaries probably read: συγγράφουσι δέ τινες καὶ τὰς θεραπείας, ἄλλοι δὲ ἀρετὰς τῶν ἐνταῦθα ἀρεταλογίων. This difficult reading seems to explain the range of variants best, including one MS which reads τερατολογίων instead of ἀρεταλογίων ,[19] and the sense of it may be that "certain scribes record the healings while others record the ἀρεταί as recited by the local aretalogists." At any rate, it demonstrates the cultic context in which miracles are recorded and again points up the immediate connection

---

[18]Cf. The Oxyrhynchus Papyri, XI, ed. with translation and notes by B.P. Grenfell and A.S. Hunt (London, 1915).

[19]Cf. discussion and literature cited by O. Crusius, op. cit., p. 670.

between the attestation of miracles and the recitation of
the ἀρεταί of the god.

Outside of the specific context of the ἐγώ εἰμι
"aretalogy," Isis was also praised for miraculous healings.

Diodorus of Sicily relates that Isis is credited with
bringing the arts of healing to men and once she attained
immortality, she took pleasure in miraculously healing
(παραδόξως ὑγιάζεσθαι) those who incubate themselves in her
temple (Bibl. Hist. 1.25.2-7). In this text it is clear
that such claims are exerted in competition with Greek
cults with the intent that Isis will be shown superior to
the whole world by her healings: ἀποδείξεις δὲ τούτων
φασὶ φέρειν ἑαυτοὺς οὐ μυθολογίας ὁμοίως τοῖς Ἕλλησιν,
ἀλλὰ πράξεις ἐναργεῖς· πᾶσαν γὰρ σχεδὸν τὴν οἰκουμένην
μαρτυρεῖν ἑαυτοῖς, εἰς τὰς ταύτης τιμὰς φιλοτιμουμένην διὰ
τὴν ἐν ταῖς θεραπείαις ἐπίφανείαν. [They claim to produce
proofs which are not legends like the Greeks have but
manifest demonstrations, for almost the whole world supports
them by revering her honors because of the miracle of her
healings.]

Two Delian inscriptions from about the first century
B.C. indicate that Isis worship was attended by a func-
tionary specifically called an ἀρεταλόγος . Although the
precise duties are not spelled out, it appears from one of
the inscriptions that the office was an official appointment
(ἀρεταλόγος κατὰ πρόσταγμα : IG 11.4.1263) and from the
second that at least one of the office holders also
functioned as a dream interpreter (ὀνειροκρίτης καὶ ἀρεταλόγος:

<u>IG</u> 11.4.2072). In order to establish more precisely what the content of the "aretalogist's" recitation might have been, further study is needed of the relationship between the recitation of the self-praise of Isis and the propagandistic retelling of the miraculous cures that Isis performs in dreams. For the present purpose, however, the fact that an "aretalogist" can be identified as a "dream interpreter" appears to suggest that he functioned as a proclaimer of miraculous phenomena.[20]

This hypothesis receives support from the way in which the Latin writers can refer to those who tell fantastic and teratological stories as "aretalogists," apparently giving a pejorative connotation to the title while still preserving its sense as referring to the one who relates the miracles. In his Egyptian satire (15), Juvenal describes Ulysses, telling an incredible story about cultic observances, as a <u>mendax</u> <u>aretalogus</u> (line 16). As long as such recitations were only regarded as entertainment, cultured Romans could enjoy them. Thus Suetonius describes the lavish banquets of

---

[20]Cf. Reitzenstein, <u>Hellenistische Wundererzälungen</u>, <u>op</u>. <u>cit</u>., pp. 9-10, where he observes that in antiquity visions and dreams belonged to the miraculous in that they display the intervening activity and power of the god. Such a definition of miracle is also an operating premise of this study. Dramatic displays of supernatural power whether in healings, control of nature or ability to predict the future all belong within such a functional definition of miracle. On the other hand, when divination is based upon a rationalized approach such as was the case with Stoic prognostication which was based on a physical theory, there was no expectation of divine intervention and thus nothing "miraculous" about the art.

Augustus, including details on the entertainers: "music and actors, or even strolling players from the circus, and especially storytellers" (aretalogus: Augustus 74). But the title is not complimentary when applied to an author who professes seriousness. Porphyrion (early third century A.D.) in his commentary on Horace (I.1,120) describes Plotius Crispinus as a student of philosophy and poet who was so voluble (tam garrule) that he was called an aretalogus. Although the term aretalogus is missing, Terence appears to know the double valence of ἀρετή: virtus when in Adelphi 535 (based on Menander) he has Syrus brashly claim: "I make you a god with him, I recite your virtues" (virtutes narro).

Thus the role of the aretalogist as a propagandist who recites the incredible deeds of the god on behalf of the cult appears established, and the antipathy of educated Romans to this kind of preaching is attested by the condescending connotation of the word aretalogus. The precise content might vary from healings, to visions, to other demonstrations of divine power (θεῖα δύναμις) , as the ancient concept of miracle was not restrictive (cf. footnote 20). Yet the peculiar use of the term ἀρετή , the appointed task of the aretalogist as an interpreter of dreams, and the intimate connection between the recording of healings and the recitation of ἀρεταί make it probable that the content of the narrations of the ἀρεταλόγοι more closely approximated the aretalogy of Asclepius, i.e. the healing accounts from Epidauros, than the self-praises of Isis.

If this specific aretalogy of the miracle worker is once established, then it is possible to identify particular features such as vocabulary and form more closely. Thus the remark of H.D. Betz that "the concept of δύναμις (τοῦ θεοῦ) belongs to the technical vocabulary of the aretalogy"[21] is helpful and cogent when it is quite clear that he is speaking of the aretalogy of the miracle worker. But the distinction between such accounts and those which focus on the moral virtues of the heroes of the philosophical traditions must not be blurred by an appeal to the "aretalogy" as a genre which encompasses both of these phenomena.

---

[21]Hans Dieter Betz, "Eine Christus-Aretalogie bei Paulus (2 Kor 12, 7-10)," ZThK 66 (1969), p. 300, n. 69.

B. The Pythagorean "Divine Men"

Prior to the time of Socrates, diverse conceptions
of the "divine man" were already current. E.R. Dodds
has shown that alongside more ancient Greek depictions
of the θεῖος ἀνήρ, the figure of the shaman grew in
popularity as a contrasting image of divine presence.[22]
Such individuals as Abaris, Aristeas of Proconnesus,
Epimenides, Pherecydes, and Zalmoxis were remembered
in colorful legends which rehearsed their teratological
exploits. Even Plato cited a story about Epimenides,
calling him a θεῖος ἀνήρ, although this reference indicates
more about the vitality of such popular legends than about
Plato's conception of divine presence.[23]

The significance for this study of the pre-Socratic
figure of the shaman comes into focus in the persons of
Pythagoras and Empedocles. The case of Pythagoras is
particularly difficult because of the paucity of historically
trustworthy sources. On the basis of the third and fourth
century A.D. biographies of Pythagoras by Porphyry and
Iamblichus in which many of the earlier traditions about the
hero are pulled together, it first appears that beginning

---

[22]E.R. Dodds, The Greeks and the Irrational (Berkeley and
Los Angeles, 1951: Sather Classical Lectures, Vol. 25), pp.
135-146.

[23]Cf. Kern, "Epimenides," PW VI (1909), pp. 173-178.

with Pythagoras, a new image of the divine man was forged

out of the combination of the figure of the popular miracle

worker or shaman, the image of the divine philosopher, and

the idealized portrait of the practical statesman.[24] From

this perspective, Pythagoras may be regarded as the proto-

type of the synthetic Hellenistic "divine man". Such

a view enables Windisch to make his intentionally provocative

statement:

> "die Jesusüberlieferung steht nach Form und Gehalt
> der Pythagoraslegende erheblich näher als der
> Geschichte oder Legende eines 'jüdischen Messias.'
> Jesus ist, religionsgeschichtliche gesprochen, eher
> 'Pythagoras' als 'Barkochba'." [25]

Recent gospel criticism and studies of the traditions

about Pythagoras demand much more precision from that

statement. Which Jesus tradition and which Pythagoras

tradition are comparable? Read in this light, the pre-

Porphyry accounts of the Pythagorean "divine men" are in

significant disagreement as to the basis of their exalted

status.

Particularly significant is the evidence that has been

---

[24]Cf. Hans Windisch, Paulus und Christus (Leipzig,
1934: Untersuchungen zum Neuen Testament, hsg. von H.
Windisch, Heft 24). O. Weinreich, "Antikes Gottmenschentum,"
N. Jahrbuch für Wissenschaft und Jugendbildung 2 (1926),
pp. 633-651. Hans von Leisegang, "Der Gottmensch als Archetypus,"
Eranos-Jahrbuch XVIII (1950: Sonderband für C.G. Jung, hsg.
von Olga Fröbe Kapteyn), pp. 9-45. L. Bieler, op. cit., vol.
I, p. 16.

[25]Windisch, op. cit., p. 60.

compiled by Werner Jaeger, E.R. Dodds, and Walter Burkert
which shows that the Pythagoreans were themselves deeply
divided over the interpretation of their founder so that
Pythagoras the shaman is remembered in a circle of followers
quite removed from the Pythagorean scientists who cultivate
the reputation of their hero as a mathematician and
physicist.[26]

The importance of this schism within Pythagoreanism
must be underlined. Even if Pythagoras was able to unite
the roles of shaman and scientist in his person,[27] his
followers apparently viewed him as functioning either in
one of these capacities or in the other. While an author
like Dicaearchus may have mixed the teratological and
scientific traditions quite uncritically in his effort to
praise Pythagoras as the ideal of the practical life (cf.
note 26), it remained for Porphyry and Iamblichus to attempt
to synthesize this diverse material in order to create their
full-blown image of Pythagoras as a divine man.

---

[26]Cf. Werner Jaeger, "On the Origin and Cycle of the
Philosophic Ideal of Life," Aristotle, trans. by Richard
Robinson (Oxford, 1948), Appendix II, pp. 426-461, especially
451-461 where Jaeger argues that it was left to the Peripatetic
Dicaearchus (c. 300 B.C.) to bring the divergent cycles of
tradition about Pythagoras together in his attempt to portray
Pythagoras as a lawgiver and founder of states. Dodds, op. cit.,
pp. 143-145. Walter Burkert, Weisheit und Wissenschaft (Nürnberg,
1962: Erlanger Beiträge zur Sprach- und Kunstwissenschaft, 10),
pp. 98-150. Cf. the review of Burkert by J.S. Morrison, Gnomon
37 (1965), pp. 344-354. Cf. also W.K.C. Guthrie, A History
of Greek Philosophy (Cambridge, 1962), vol. I, pp. 146-181.

[27]Burkert, op. cit., pp. 86-202, argues against such a
possibility, suggesting that later interpretations made
the historical shaman Pythagoras into a scientist.

Additional evidence of divergent images of Pythagoras
can be gleaned from pre-Porphyry witnesses. Diogenes
Laertius (8:36) cites the accusation of the skeptic Timon
(3rd century B.C.) that Pythagoras had a propensity for
a beguiling skill with words (Πυθαγόρην τε γόητας ἀποκλίναντ'
ἐπὶ δόξας θήρῃ ἐπ' ἀνθρώπων, σεμνηγορίης ὁαριστήν). But
when the same passage of Timon is later cited by Plutarch
(Numa 65), it is placed after a discussion of Pythagoras'
ability to stop an eagle in mid-flight, his golden thigh
and other marvelous contrivances and deeds (τερατώδεις
μηχανὰς αὐτοῦ καὶ πράξεις), thus clearly referring to
Pythagoras' miraculous power rather than his rhetorical skill.

Diogenes Laertius also includes a stray piece of tradition
(ἄλλο τι περὶ Πυθαγόρου: 41) which he found in the highly
questionable source, Hermippus (3rd century B.C.),[28] to the
effect that when Pythagoras crawled out of a subterranean
cave he claimed to have been in Hades (cf. Diog. Laert. 8:21).
Upon telling of his experiences in the assembly, they
believed him to be divine (ἐπίστευον εἶναι τὸν Πυθαγόραν
θεῖόν τινα).

---

[28]Frank W. Walbank, Oxford Classical Dictionary (Oxford,
1949), p. 419, argues that "Hermippus deliberately falsified
history, revelling in sensationalism, particularly in death
scenes." Josephus, however, disagrees violently with this
assessment, calling Hermippus the most distinguished
(ἐπισημότατος) of the historians of Pythagoras who is always
careful (περὶ πᾶσαν ἱστορίαν ἐπιμελῆς: Contra Ap. I 162-165).
But Josephus is out to show that Pythagoras "who excelled
all other philosophers by his wisdom and piety" imitated
the Jews, which opinion he cites Hermippus as attesting.

The citation from Hermippus demonstrates that as early as the third century B.C. the claim that Pythagoras was divine was clearly thought by some to rest upon the accounts of his supernatural feats. Yet compared with the other material in Diogenes Laertius 8, this emphasis on the authenticating significance of a teratological display is singular. Furthermore, Hermippus' use of pathetic embellishment ("they were so affected that they wept and wailed") stands in contrast to the more sober and rational treatments of Pythagoras the philosopher.

Another striking example of the cultivation of the image of Pythagoras as a shaman or miracle worker can be found in the Marvelous Tales (ΙΣΤΟΡΙΑΙ ΘΑΥΜΑΣΙΑΙ) of a writer of the second century B.C. named Apollonius. Apollonius tells of the miraculous deeds of a series of six great shamans, including Epimenides, Aristeas of Proconnesus, Hermotimus of Clazomenae, Abaris, Pherecydes, and Pythagoras.[29] In addition to the tale of Epimenides' long sleep, Apollonius adds that not a few other miracles (ἄλλα οὐκ ὀλίγα παράδοξα) are attributed to him. He relates that two of these figures had temples built to them and that Aristeas was worshipped as a hero (ὡς ἥρωϊ). Pythagoras comes at the end of the list, "not refraining from the miracle working of his

---

[29]Cf. Appendix I, p. 317 for chapters I-VI of the text of Apollonius. Cf. also the critical edition of O. Keller, Rerum Naturalium Scriptores Graeci Minores, vol. I: Paradoxographi Antigonus, Apollonius, Phlegon, Anonymus Vaticanus (Lipsiae: Teubner, 1879).

predecessor Pherecydes" (τῆς Φερεκύδου τερατοποιίας οὐκ
ἀνέστη). Apollonius then lists six of Pythagoras' miraculous
acts.

Here is a clear attempt to correlate Pythagoras to the
famous charismatic miracle workers of great antiquity. The
primary mode of authentication is the recitation of the
miraculous acts of the hero, although Apollonius does know
of Pythagoras' "previous labors in mathematics and numbers."
A fragment of Aristotle quoted in Iamblichus' Life of
Pythagoras (31) appears to provide an explicit statement of
the contrasting philosophical viewpoint on the divinity of
Pythagoras. Iamblichus cites Aristotle as an authoritative
source for the Pythagorean doctrine of the three kinds of
rational animals (λογικὸν ζῷον): τὸ μέν ἐστι θεός, τὸ
δ' ἄνθρωπος, τὸ δὲ οἷον Πυθαγόρας. Such a formula ought
not be quoted as evidence of the antiquity of Iamblichus'
theology of Pythagoras since Iamblichus has aggregated
diverse pieces of tradition into one image. This is, rather,
evidence of the antiquity of a particular view of Pythagoras
as the divine philosopher whose rational excellence elevates
him above human status (cf. Lucian, Alex. 4: σοφὸς ἀνὴρ καὶ
τὴν γνώμην θεσπέσιος).

The historical Pythagoras may have still eluded us.
But the contrast between the philosophical and paradoxographical
traditions authenticating the "divine Pythagoras" corresponds
to the division that has been identified between the

Pythagorean scientists and the ascetic religious order of
Pythagoreans.[30]

In the case of Empedocles, alleged to have been a pupil
of Pythagoras (Diog. Laert. 8:54), it may be possible to
assert more unequivocally that he did unite the roles of
shaman and scientist in his own person. Dodds made the
noteworthy observation that many of Empedocles' more
teratological statements were part of his scientific
poem On Nature.[31] But Dodds also cautioned against
accepting Jaeger's judgment that Empedocles was "a new
synthesising type of philosophical personality",

> "... since any attempt to synthesise his religious and
> his scientific opinions is precisely what we miss in him.
> If I am right, Empedocles represents not a new but a
> very old type of personality, the shaman who combines
> the still undifferentiated functions of magician and
> naturalist, poet and philosopher, preacher, healer, and
> public counsellor. After him these functions fell
> apart; philosophers henceforth were to be neither poets
> nor magicians; indeed, such a man was already an anachronism
> in the fifth century."[32]

Further evidence that this combination of roles was personal
and not a new philosophical synthesis is found in the contrasting
views of the basis of Empedocles' reputation for divinity.
Heraclides, a fourth century B.C. author whom Diogenes
Laertius himself knows as a "collector of absurdities"

---

[30]Cf. Leisegang, op. cit., p. 22. Jaeger, op. cit., p. 455.

[31]Cf. Dodds, op. cit., pp. 145-146.

[32]Ibid., p. 146.

(παραδοξολόγος: Diog. Laert. 8:72), is apparently Diogenes'
primary source for material on Empedocles. Heraclides
describes Empedocles as a physician (ἰητρός) and diviner
(μάντις: Diog. Laert. 8:61-62), quoting Empedocles as calling
himself an immortal god, no longer mortal (θεὸς ἄμβροτος,
οὐκέτι θνητός). He heightens the account of Empedocles
curing the woman in a trance (cf. 8:60-61, 69), to a story
of sending a dead woman away alive (8:67), and he tells an
elaborate tale of Empedocles being called to heaven so that
he had earned the right to receive sacrifice, since he was
now a god (γεγονὼς θεός: 8:68). Diogenes also cites a
second hand tradition that Empedocles had the power "to
bewitch" (γοητεύειν: 8:59); but as with Pythagoras, such a
word may be interpreted merely as "to beguile," i.e. a reference
to rhetorical skill.

Although less well attested in Diogenes Laertius, there
is additional support for this less paradoxographical option
for understanding Empedocles. His gifts as a rhetor and poet
are praised by Aristotle (Diog. Laert. 8:57); Satyrus knows him
as a physician and orator (58) and the Epicurean Lucretius
treats Empedocles as a metaphysician and poet when he says:
"the poems of his divine mind (divini) utter a loud voice and
declare illustrius discoveries, so that he seems hardly to
be born of mortal stock" (de rerum natura I:729ff). The
citation of an Epicurean, of course, suggests a very particular
understanding of divinity which can be distinguished from
that of the other philosophical schools, and the poetic

tone should not be ignored. But the point to be observed
here is that Empedocles' reputation as a poet was sufficiently
untainted by the accounts of his miraculous performances that
even the Epicureans who disdained all teratological displays
could speak of him as divine.[33]

Detailed study of the traditions about Pythagoras and
Empedocles, such as the material collected in Diels-Kranz,[34]
would make the description of the differing types of treatment
of these charismatic figures more precise. Even this brief
survey, however, demonstrates that in the hands of the
paradoxographers such as Hermippus and Heraclides such
traditions take on a particular tendency of authenticating
the claim that these figures were divine by pointing to their
supernatural acts and thus correlating them to the charismatic
miracle workers of the pre-Socratic shaman type, while
diverging significantly from more rational and philosophical
evaluations. Apparently Diogenes Laertius was more dependent
upon sources of a paradoxographical tendency for his

---

[33]Cf. A.D. Nock, "Deification and Julian," Journal of
Roman Studies 47 (1957), pp. 115-123, especially p. 120.
A.D. Nock's review of Henry G. Meecham, The Epistle to Diognetus
(Manchester, 1949: "Publications of the University of
Manchester," No. CCCV; "Theological Series," No. VII),
Journal of Religion 31 (1951), pp. 214-216. A.D. Nock,
"Soter and Euergetes," The Joy of Study: Studies in honor of
F.C. Grant, ed. Sherman E. Johnson (New York, 1951), pp. 127-
141. Nock cautions against reading the language of divinization
too literally in praise formulations, and his advice is
particularly in order in the case of the poet Lucretius.
Nevertheless, such language does reflect the high regard that
Lucretius had for Empedocles as a scientific poet, without
regard to his role as a shaman.

[34]Hermann Diels, Die Fragmente der Vorsokratiker, 7.
Auflage, hsg. v. Walther Kranz (Berlin, 1954).

description of Empedocles than he was for Pythagoras.[35]

From the second century B.C. onward, it is easy to document the growing interest in paradoxography. Such figures as Nigidius Figulus (first century B.C.), Anaxilaus of Larissa (first century B.C.), and Numenius of Apamea (second century A.D.) are known for their knowledge of the abstruse. A growing number of marvelous tales about Pythagoras and his disciples figured prominently in this literature,[36] and Porphyry and Iamblichus used such sources, apparently without reservation.[37] Further study is needed to clarify the precise intent of making such collections of amazing things, but even our quick review of the work of Apollonius (cf. note 29 above) suggests that such writers represent a serious point of view.[38]

The significance of the development of Pythagorean traditions is most directly seen when another figure named Apollonius, Apollonius of Tyana, is brought into view. Like Pythagoras, whom he apparently sought to imitate, the historical Apollonius of Tyana is an elusive figure. Perhaps like Empedocles,

---

[35]Cf. R.D. Hicks, Diogenes Laertius (Loeb edition, 1925), vol. II, p. 340, note a.

[36]Cf. R. Grant, p. 62. Note the skepticism with which this literature is viewed by W. Jaeger, Early Christianity and Greek Paideia (London, 1961), p. 55.

[37]A helpful and critical list of the sources identified in Porphyry's Life of Pythagoras is found on pp. 105-106 in Hadas and Smith, op. cit. Cf. I. Levy, Recherches sur les sources de la légende de Pythagore (Bibliothèque de l'école des hautes études sc. re. 42; Paris, 1926).

[38]Cf. R. Grant, op. cit., p. 62, where he cites a Chassang (Histoire du roman) to the effect that it is not necessary to suppose that Antonius Diogenes took his own work seriously, although Porphyry did.

Apollonius dramatically united popular cultic and philosophical traditions in his person, anticipating in the first century A.D. and, in part, helping to create the image of the miracle working philosopher that was current in a later period. For the purposes of this study, however, it is only necessary to point up the tension between those sources that present him as a miracle worker and those which portray him as a philosopher.

The Gordian knot of the sources of Apollonius of Tyana resists hasty cutting; but on the basis of external witnesses and clear evidence of redaction within Philostratus' Life of Apollonius, it seems safe to assert that early traditions about the activity of Apollonius as a miracle worker were incorporated into subsequent accounts of his life which were apologetically intended to depict him as a philosopher. Since solid and extensive work has been done to support this hypothesis,[39] a brief recitation of some of

---

[39]Cf. Reitzenstein, pp. 39-54. An excellent bibliography is found in K. Gross, "Apollonius von Tyana," RAC I (1950), pp. 529-533. A classic work also deserves mention: F.C. Baur, Apollonius von Tyana und Christus (Tübingen, 1832: reprinted from the Tübinger Zeitschrift für Theologie). The reader should also be advised of the work of G. Petzke, Die Traditionen über Apollonius von Tyana und das Neue Testament (Studia ad Corpus Hellenisticum Novi Testamenti, #1; Leiden, 1970). This study, which only reached me as I was preparing my manuscript for the typist, fills a great gap in scholarship on Apollonius and promises to provide much more viable controls on this literature. On hasty review, Petzke's study appears to support the basic methodological approach to the Apollonius material that has been advocated in this chapter, but Petzke's analysis is much more extensive and refined by a comprehensive approach to the texts. Any reader who wishes to pursue the problems of the redaction of the Life of Apollonius beyond the introductory level of the discussion in this chapter, should begin with Petzke's book.

the critical evidence will suffice.

Apollonius' reputation as a wizard and magician is longstanding. When Lucian of Samosata seeks to discredit another self-styled follower of Pythagoras, Alexander the (false) prophet, he argues that Alexander is completely unlike Pythagoras, "a wise man of more than human intelligence" (σοφὸς ἀνὴρ καὶ τὴν γνώμην θεσπέσιος) , but Alexander was an apt disciple of a pupil of Apollonius of Tyana, "one of those quacks that give assurances of enchantments and inspired incantations and charms for love affairs, visitations on enemies, discoveries of buried treasures, and inheritances of estates" (γόης τῶν μαγείας καὶ ἐπῳδὰς θεσπεσίους ὑπισχνουμένων καὶ χάριτας ἐπὶ τοῖς ἐρωτικοῖς καὶ ἐπαγωγὰς τοῖς ἐχθροῖς καὶ θησαυρῶν ἀναπομπὰς καὶ κλήρων διαδοχάς : Alex. 4-5).[40] In the magical papyri, the name of Apollonius of Tyana is attached to a spell, further attesting his popular reputation as a wizard (PGM XI a).

Dio Cassius reports that Caracalla was a great admirer of quacks and magicians to the point that he built a temple in honor of Apollonius, "who was a perfect example of a charlatan and magician" (ὅστις καὶ γόης καὶ μάγος ἀκριβὴς

---

[40]It is dangerous to assume that Lucian's high praise of Pythagoras is fully sincere, note how he has his tongue in his cheek when he describes a follower of Pythagoras, Arignotus as "a man of superhuman wisdom" (ἀνὴρ δαιμόνιος τὴν σοφίαν: The Lover of Lies 32). In both cases, however, Lucian is appealing to the image of the "divine wise man", which will be discussed in the next section of this study, in order to ridicule the vulgar conception of the divine miracle worker.

ἐγένετο : Dio Cass. 78.18.4; cf. 67.18.1). Finally, the
lost work of Moiragenes (second century A.D.) of four books
on Apollonius of Tyana was probably one of the earliest
systematic treatments of him and appears from the testimony
of Origen (Contra Cels. 6.41) and Philostratus (Life of
Ap. 1.3) to have presented him as a magician and wizard.

In his discussion of the redactional stages of Philostratus' Life of Apollonius, Reitzenstein has argued
convincingly that the earliest stratum of that work was
probably a recitation of the marvelous acts of magic and
supernatural power of Apollonius, a collection similar in
content to that of Moiragenes.[41] At least two stages of
subsequent redaction can be clearly identified, both of which
qualify the thrust of the miracle material.

Philostratus himself claims that he is editing the
unliterary work which he attributes to Damis, a disciple of
Apollonius (1.3; 1.19; 7.28). The account of Damis is
clearly constructed with an eye to opposing the view of
Apollonius set forth by Euphrates, a pupil of Apollonius
who is repeatedly treated as the arch enemy and held in
particular disdain for his love of money and his charges that
Apollonius was a wizard which Euphrates made in order to
improve his own position (cf. 1.13; 2.26; 5.33; 5.37-39;
6.7; 6.13; 6.28; 7.9; 7.36; 8.3; 8.7; Cf. also the
Epistles of Apollonius 1-8, 14-18, 50-52, and 60).
Reitzenstein is probably correct that this polemic reflects

_____

[41]Reitzenstein, p. 40.

a struggle between the followers of Apollonius (frequently called the companions of Damis: (τοὺς ἀμφὶ τὸν Δάμιν: 1.40: οἱ περὶ Δάμιν 2.7 & 29) and the followers of Euphrates (cf. 6.28 in particular.)[42] At least, the consistent criticism and response to Euphrates' charges against Apollonius provide evidence that the work attributed to Damis aimed to show Apollonius as a philosopher, not a mere quack.[43]

Philostratus clearly found the work of Damis suitable to his taste and accepted the task of editing it with particular attention to style (1.3). At several points, his own attempts to curb the tendency of the material are obvious, particularly as he elaborates the intention of Damis to show that Apollonius was not a wizard but a divine philosopher. Among the more transparent examples is 7.39 where Philostratus obviously feels constrained to interpret a tradition that appears magical in Damis' account (see previous note).

---

[42]Reitzenstein, p. 46.

[43]The study of the evolution of this tradition is, however, very complex. Whatever intentions of Damis or Philostratus appear demonstrable, the fact that they both preserved immense amounts of miraculous material is still the most obvious feature of their accounts. But as in the Gospel of Mark where miracles comprise an amazing proportion of the whole, recent scholarship has demonstrated that the miracles are theologically controlled, so the massive collection of the miracles of Apollonius is conditioned first by the need to defend him against the charges of Euphrates, then by Philostratus' desire to depict him systematically as a philosopher. Such observations need much more elaboration before some of the very knotty texts can be satisfactorily handled: cf. 7.38 where Damis is reported to have first grasped the fact that Apollonius was divine when he saw him perform a miraculous escape from a fetter. (cf. 8.13). Cf. Petzke, op. cit., p. 69.

Philostratus also takes care to explain how prognostication differs from wizardry (5.12, cf. 4.44). Perhaps less obvious, but deserving of careful study, are the cases where secondary expansions display editorial reworking of Apollonius traditions, as in 1.9, for example, where a miracle story has been reworked into a story about a philosopher-physician.[44] All such modifications of the tradition are part of Philostratus' stated purpose of recounting the "habits of wisdom, by means of which he (Apollonius) attained the recognition of one who is supernatural and divine":

τῆς σοφίας τρόποις, ὑφ' ὧν ἔφαυσε τοῦ δαιμόνιός τε καὶ θεῖος νομισθῆναι : 1.2).

As with Pythagoras and Empedocles, therefore, Apollonius is described as divine, but once more it is possible to observe a divergence of opinion and a tension between those who think his miracles are the primary means of authenticating his divinity and those who see his wisdom as a philosopher as demonstrating his supernatural character. Perhaps the most precise statement of this difference of opinion comes from Jerome, when speaking of Apollonius, "whether he was a magician, as popular tradition has it, or a philosopher, as the Pythagoreans present him" (sive ille magus, ut vulgus loquitur, sive philosophus, ut Pythagorici tradunt: Ep. 53.1).

Thus the late works of Philostratus and Porphyry

_____

[44]Cf. the comments on this text in Hans Dieter Betz, "Eine Christus-Aretalogie bei Paulus", op. cit., p. 295.

combine diverse materials about Apollonius and Pythagoras
to create composite pictures of them as divine men, and the
historical accuracy of those images is very difficult to
assess. Perhaps further study will demonstrate that these
literary pieces from the Pythagorean tradition are merely
additional examples, similar in their pre-literary phases
to the growth process of the Christian gospels, of the way
competing Hellenistic conceptions of divine presence can
eventually be merged. For the present, however, their
complexity eliminates them as a viable control for
describing the interplay between the forms and religious
functions of various gospel materials. Rather than explain
a complexity by a conundrum, more clearly delineated
traditions must be isolated with which gospel materials
may be compared.

C. The Ideal Wise Man after Socrates

In order to clarify the debate in the later
Hellenistic world as to who is truly a "divine man", it is
necessary to begin with Plato. Such a starting point is not
dictated merely by the natural predilection of classicists
but by the specific contribution Plato made to later
philosophical thought in his depiction of Socrates as the
ideal wise man. It is not important for our purposes to
attempt to determine to what degree Plato's image of
Socrates is historically accurate compared with that of
Xenophon or Aristophanes, since it is the continuing
influence of the idealization that is focal. In the light
of extensive scholarly discussion of this point,[45] it is
possible to deal directly with a few crucial texts,
omitting a lengthy justification of the position.

Plato does not refer to Socrates or himself as θεῖος,
and he ironically calls statesmen who have no rational
understanding and are thus on a level with enthusiastic
prophets and soothsayers θεῖοι ἄνδρες (Meno 99 B-D). Yet
he is able to depict the true philosopher in terms of
those same traditional religious myths as being the one
who is truly inspired (ἐνθουσιάζων : Phaedrus 249 D), and he

---

[45]This view is something of a commonplace in secondary
literature, but it might be helpful to point to a few
authors whose use of it have directly influenced this
study. H. Windisch, op. cit., pp. 27-40. M. Hadas and
M. Smith, op. cit., passim. Martin Hengel, Nachfolge und
Charisma (BZNW; Beiheft 34; Berlin, 1968).

clearly regarded the δαιμόνιον of Socrates in a religious
light (θεῖόν τε καὶ δαιμόνιον : Apol. 31 C; μαντικὴ ἡ τοῦ δαιμονίου
... τὸ τοῦ θεοῦ σημεῖον : Apol. 40 A-B; τὸ εἰωθὸς σημεῖον τὸ
δαιμόνιον : Euthydemus 272 E). Thus Plato is reshaping the
traditional picture of the divine man in his depiction of
Socrates as the ideal philosopher without completely
rejecting the traditional religious overtones of that
picture. Further evidence of this link with traditional
religion is the organization of the subsequent philosophical
schools as θίασοι.

The conception that Plato has of the "divine statesman",
which figures prominently in the Republic and Laws, also
reflects the modification of the traditional concept of the
"divine man". As Windisch states it:

> "Es ist eine neue Fassung dieses Typos, die wohl aus
> dem Begriff des 'göttlichen' Staatsmannes entwickelt
> ist; auch hier kein Korybanth und Inspirierter, gleich-
> wohl Träger des reinen Geistes, der mit dem Nomos
> identisch ist, ja wohl geradezu als Inkarnation des
> Nus zu betrachten."[46]

The view of the statesman as a law unto himself (νόμος ἔμψυχος)
was destined to have a powerful influence on the hellenistic
ideal of kingship,[47] but Plato contributed to the concept by
insisting that the ruler had no ecstatic gift of divinity
but was divine in so far as he imitated the philosopher who
truly displayed the divine. Plato's divine statesmen are

---

[46]H. Windisch, op. cit., p. 33.

[47]Cf. A.R. Anderson, "Heracles and His Successors,"
Harvard Studies in Classical Philology (1928), pp. 7-58.
E.R. Goodenough, "The Political Philosophy of Hellenistic
Kingship, "Yale Classical Studies I (1928), pp. 55-102.

32

philosophers (θείῳ δὴ καὶ κοσμίῳ ὅ γε φιλόσοφος ὁμιλῶν
κόσμιός τε καὶ θεῖος εἰς τὸ δυνατὸν ἀνθρώπῳ γίγνεται : the
lover of wisdom by keeping company with the divine and
orderly becomes himself divine and orderly in so far as it is
possible for man, Republic VI. 500.C-D). Plato does admit
the theoretical possibility that one could be born so
divinely gifted that this orderly route of philosophical
training and learning of the "divine necessities" (arithmetic,
geometry, and astronomy: Laws VII 818-822) could be by-
passed, but eliminates it as practically impossible (Laws
875 C).

Plato did not write a biography of Socrates, but he
created an idealization which greatly affected subsequent
portrayals of the saints of the philosophical tradition.
This is the import of the statement of Hadas and Smith that
"it is the aretalogy of Socrates, implied, or even premised,
in Plato that doubtless became the model for an independent
literary genre."[48] Furthermore it was the death of
Socrates that acted as the catalyst for this idealization,
as can be documented in Plato's autobiographical epistle
(VII 325B-326B) where he credits the death of Socrates with
his own "change of direction." (To refer to Plato's
experience as a "conversion" is perhaps something of an
overstatement; yet, as Nock states, "adhesion to Socrates

---

[48]Op. cit., p. 58.

somehow meant giving your soul to him.")[49]

Particularly in the trial and death scenes in the Apology and the Phaedo, it is the person of Socrates that stands out, even more than the doctrines discussed. Socrates is the paradigm of moral virtue whose incessant quest for the good is cut short by a martyrdom at the hands of tyrants. Yet he calmly conducts his own·defense and faces death with complete tranquility. As Hadas and Smith observe, "the account of Socrates' last moments is surely the second most compelling passion in all literature."[50]

Although his martyrdom provided the impetus for thrusting Socrates into the role of the ideal divine philosopher, other facets of his portrayal by Plato were crucial for completing the image. Socrates was poor on account of his service of the god (ἐν πενίᾳ μυρίᾳ εἰμι διὰ τὴν τοῦ θεοῦ λατρείαν: Apol. 23C), risked his life for the sake of philosophy because he had a divine command to stay at that post (Apol. 28E, cf. Origen, Contra Cels. 1.3), and he sacrificed his own affairs and any possible profit to play the role of the reproving gadfly because he believed he was the god's gift to the city (οἷος ὑπὸ τοῦ θεοῦ τῇ πόλει δεδόσθαι: Apol. 31:A-C). Plato even has Socrates claiming at one point that he has been commanded by the god "in oracles and dreams and in every way by which any divine power ever commanded a man to do anything"

---

[49]Nock, Conversion, p. 58.

[50]Op. cit., p. 55.

34

(ἐκ μαντείων καὶ ἐξ ἐνυπνίων καὶ παντὶ τρόπῳ, ᾦπερ τίς ποτε
καὶ ἄλλη θεία μοῖρα ἀνθρώπῳ καὶ ὁτιοῦν προσέταξε πράττειν:
Apol. 33C).

Such generous language indicates that the relationship
between Plato's image of Socrates and popular cultic conceptions of the θεῖοι ἄνδρες of the Empedocles type is much
more complex than Windisch or Hadas and Smith have indicated.[51]
In his effort to make Socrates' self-defense credible, even
Plato can thus give the impression that Socrates was a dream
interpreter and diviner. Such tendencies are, of course,
highly qualified in Plato; yet some other Hellenistic writers
heighten Socrates' supernatural qualities, focusing particularly
on his δαιμόνιον, to an extent that greatly exceeds
rhetorical hyperbole.

Xenophon's defense of Socrates as a truly religious
man points up by contrast the cautious rationalism of Plato's
depiction. Xenophon, for example, explicitly compares the
δαιμόνιον of Socrates to a whole range of signs (θεῖον)
used in divination: augury, oracles, coincidences, and
sacrifices (Mem. I.I. 3); and as a result, he ascribes
a strongly directive role to the δαιμόνιον. As Stenzel
observes, Plato, on the other hand, "restricts the δαιμόνιον
to the purely negative function of merely averting an action;
the voice never gave positive commands, it 'asserts nothing'

---

[51]Cf. E.R. Dodds. "Plato, the Irrational Soul, and the
Inherited Conglomerate," The Greeks and the Irrational
(Berkeley, 1956), pp. 207-235.

- only the λόγος can do that."[52]

The δαιμόνιον of Socrates was of particular fascination
to another Hellenistic writer, the author of the pseudo-
Platonic dialogue Theages (c. second century B.C.), who uses
it as an occasion to treat Socrates in a way that is
uncharacteristic of Plato.[53] This writer plays up the
spiritual power (ἡ δύναμις αὕτη τοῦ δαιμονίου τούτου:
129 E) of Socrates to the point that the δαιμόνιον appears
as a miraculous, even magical, function of his personality
which mysteriously affects his companions. It is particularly
noteworthy that the δαιμόνιον is repeatedly described in the
Theages in terms of δύναμις [129 E (two times), 130 C], which
is strongly suggestive of the vocabulary of miracle accounts.
Furthermore, like a magical mana, this power may have
negative effects and is quantitatively increased by Socrates'
presence, particularly by his touch (130 E).

In the hands of a Platonic theologian like Maximus of
Tyre (second century A.D.), the δαιμόνιον of Socrates can be
used as prime evidence of the existence of a great variety
of intermediary beings reaching from man to the divinity
itself, and this spiritual gift of Socrates can thus be
compared with that of Asclepius, Hercules, and Dionysius
(Hobein: IX,7) and can be called "prophetic" (μαντικόν:
Hobein: VIII,3). Yet Maximus is clear that Socrates'

---

[52]Stenzel, "Socrates," PW III, p. 853.

[53]I am indebted to Prof. H.D. Betz for this reference.

intercourse with the gods is due solely to intellectual
processes (τῷ νῷ ταῖς τῶν θεῶν φωναῖς συγγιγνόμενός τε:
Hobein VIII,3), and Socrates is only worthy of such
associations because of his life of virtue and his noble
nature (κατ' ἀρετὴν τρόπου : Hobein VIII,4).

The diverse traditions about Socrates preserved by
Diogenes Laertius (2.18-47) generally fit the rationalistic
Platonic image, although the principle virtues of some of
the later philosophical schools are also introduced. "He
was the first who discoursed on the conduct of life, and
the first philosopher who was tried and put to death"
(2.20). His simple tastes left him without needs and brought
him closest to the gods (2.27). He sent away Theaetetus
"divinely inspired" (ἔνθεος) by discoursing on knowledge
(2.29), not by imparting magical mana from his δαιμόνιον.
Yet Diogenes also includes an unidentified tradition which
ascribes a very positive role to the δαιμόνιον , "He used
to say that his δαιμόνιον indicated the future to him in
advance" (προσημαίνειν τὸ δαιμόνιον τὰ μέλλοντα αὐτῷ:
2.32).

Such a positive appreciation of Socrates' ability in
divination ought not, however, be too quickly identified
with the outlook that Socrates was a divine miracle worker,
such as the author of the Theages apparently represents.
In the philosophical schools of the Hellenistic world,
particularly in the Stoa after Poseidonius, divination
frequently held a special place as an intellectually

respectable art, even among many of those who were skeptical about other popular, beliefs and practices which were regarded as superstitions. Perhaps this appreciation of divination is evidence of the erosion of scientific outlook and the growth of credulity, which R.M. Grant sees as characteristic of the period,[54] but it seems more likely that the belief in divination is a peculiar phenomenon that can be much more specifically identified in the sectarian controversies among the philosophical schools. Because it was so specific, a Hellenistic author like Cicero could stress Socrates' talents of divination without making other material alterations in the Platonic image of Socrates as the divine philosopher, who leads a life of moral virtue, suffers for philosophy, and tranquilly dies at the hands of unjust tyrants, and a writer like Plutarch could struggle to preserve this portrait by resisting the miraculous element in the popular view of Socrates' δαιμόνιον, without completely denying the power of the δαιμόνιον.

Cicero, in fact, treats Socrates as a model for divination because Socrates' purity of soul (animus purus) ensures that he will not be misguided (de divinatione 1.54. 121-124). Cicero follows Plato in ascribing a prohibitive function to the δαιμόνιον of Socrates; and like Plato, he regards the confidence of Socrates facing death, because his

[54]R.M. Grant, Miracle and Natural Law (Amsterdam, 1952), pp. 4ff.

δαιμόνιον has not warned him of evil, as the high point:
"the utterance of the philosopher, which he made after being
wickedly condemned to death, is noble or even divine"
(de divinatione 1.54. 124).

For the purposes of this study, it would perhaps be
sufficient to show that some traditions follow Plato in
emphasizing the rational and moral qualities of the martyred
Socrates while others follow the remarkable example of the
author of the Theages and portray Socrates as a miracle
worker. Lest this appear to be a fortuitous discrimination,
however, it is necessary to refer to an argument recorded in
Plutarch's treatise de genio Socratis (580-582). Here in a
text probably written in the same half-century as the
gospels,[55] there is a significant disagreement as to what
qualifies Socrates as a charismatic figure of divine or semi-
divine stature: supernatural powers or well-trained reason.

In an argument about what is truly divine (τά γε θεῖα)
and what is mere superstition (δεισιδαιμονία) , Theocritus
the diviner (μάντις : 576 D) refuses to let the rationalists
claim Socrates as their saint who philosophically opposed
all humbug and superstition, including the pretences of
dreams and apparitions. Theocritus appeals to the δαιμόνιον
of Socrates as exceeding even Pythagoras' skill in divination

---

[55]The precise date of composition is perhaps impossible
to compute. Cf. the attack on von Arnim's argument for fixing
the date in W. Hamilton, "The Myth in Plutarch's De Genio,"
The Classical Quarterly 28 (1934), pp. 175-182.

(μαντική) in being great and divine (μέγα καὶ θεῖον : 580 C).

The δαιμόνιον is the active guide (προποδηγός) in affairs
which are unclear and irrational according to human wisdom
(ἐν πράγμασιν ἀδήλοις καὶ πρὸς ἀνθρωπίνην ἀσυλλογίστοις
φρόνησιν : 580 C). Theocritus then alludes to more and
greater examples of the potency of Socrates' δαιμόνιον,
telling one story in detail, and marveling (θαυμάζων) that
the divine power (τὸ θεῖον) never deserted or neglected him
(580 F). Although it is brief, this rehearsal of the
miraculous acts, intensified by the acknowledgement that the
δαιμόνιον gives knowledge of the rationally unknowable, and
concluding with the response of awe or wonder may be
regarded as a paradigm of the aretalogy or recitation of
praise of the charismatic miracle worker. In form and
function such a recitation is more similar to the miracle
stories of Asclepius at Epidauros than to Plato's account
of Socrates as the divine wise man. Clearly that which is
truly divine (τά γε θεῖα) and which authenticates Socrates as
divine in Theocritus' mind is Socrates' performance of
miraculous acts which are inscrutable to reason.

In Plutarch's treatise, Galaxidorus and Polymnis
radically oppose this interpretation of Socrates' δαιμόνιον.
Galaxidorus overtly drives a wedge between Socrates as the
philosopher who is concerned about things that are truly
divine (τά γε θεῖα) and Pythagoras and his followers who left
philosophy "full of phantoms, tales, and superstition"
(φαντασμάτων δὲ καὶ μύθων καὶ δεισιδαιμονίας) and Empedocles

who put philosophy into a Bacchic frenzy (βεβακχευμένην).
Socrates then accustomed philosophy to be directed to
reality and to pursue the truth by sober reason (λόγῳ νήφοντι:
580 C). Galaxidorus also denies that Socrates had any
extraordinary power (περιττὴν δύναμιν) which could do more
than tip the balance of a decision when the rational
options were of equal gravity (580 F- 581 A).

Polymnis points out in agreement with Galaxidorus that
Socrates' δαιμόνιον supposedly took the form of a sneeze.
The idea that Socrates would allow himself to be guided by
fortuitous sneezes, however, implies superstition and is
rejected. It must be something truly divine (note the word
play on δαιμόνιον : 580 B). Then Polymnis summarizes the
nature of Socrates guiding force in a short paragraph which
may well be considered as a paradigm of the aretalogy or
recitation of praise of the ideal wise man:

> "Socrates' impulses to action have an undeflectable
> rigor and intensity visible to everyone, because they
> originate from a correct and mighty judgement and
> principle. For he remained voluntarily poor all his
> life, although he could have had money to the joy and
> gratitude of his benefactors. In the face of so many
> obstacles, he did not forsake philosophy; and, at the
> end, in spite of the zeal of his friends and their well-
> devised scheme for his rescue and escape, he neither
> was dissuaded by their pleas nor withdrew at the
> approach of death. But he met this terror with unshaken
> reason, which is not the act of a man whose judgement
> is at an arbitrary moment altered by voices or sneezes
> but whose conduct is directed by superior attention
> and principle for the good" (581 C-D).

What is particularly striking about this text is the
fact that both sides recognize Socrates as a charismatic
figure of high, even divine stature, but they disagree as to

the basis of such regard. What authenticates Socrates' paradigmatic importance and what kind of a "divine man" is being presented? Although abbreviated in this case, the form of the first account is a recitation of miraculous acts with the function of evoking religious awe, based on a conception of divine presence as revealed in powerful acts.[56] The form of the second is a recitation of the trials and moral courage of the philosopher, particularly as he faces death, with the function of inculcating the life of moral reason, based on a conception of divine presence as revealed in superior intellectual resolve.

This discrimination between differing notions of divine presence and their corresponding semi-literary forms is basic to this study. In order to create the complete aggregate portrait of the "divine man", it was necessary for Hellenistic authors like Philostratus and Porphyry to superimpose these contrasting images and to mix the forms in a way similar to the editorial work of the authors of the gospels of Mark and John. Largely because of the continuing vitality of the Platonic image of Socrates,

---

[56]The one account of the miraculous power of Socrates' sign that is given in detail includes many of the novellistic details of a typical miracle story (cf. M. Dibeluis, From Tradition to Gospel, trans by Bertun Lee Woolf (New York, 1935), pp. 70-103.) Details about the situation, the witnesses, the intense concentration at the moment of the "miracle", the presence of the doubters, and the graphic description of their hapless encounter with a herd of foul swine as a result of their skepticism all leads up to the chorus of confession of the true believers who scoff at the doubters and "marvel" at the continued divine support.

authors like Plutarch, Lucian, and Celsus are able to resist
such syncretism.

When the famous warrior against superstition, Lucian of
Samosata, purports to give an autobiographical account of
his great moral decision for, or even conversion to, a life
of study, he correlates that decision to Socrates' career
choice (cf. The Dream or Lucian's Career, 12).[57] Celsus also
seeks to turn Christians away from the deceivers and sorcerers
(οἱ πλάνοι καὶ γοῆτες : Origen C. Cels. 7.36-37) by appealing
to the inspired poets (ἐνθέοι ποιηταί), wise men (σοφοί)
and philosophers (φιλόσοφοι) who relate divine (θεῖα) truths
(7.41). Although he appears to make a chronological
distinction between Plato and those who were divinely
inspired before him (θεῖοι ἄνδρες : c. Cels. VII 28,58),
Celsus clearly sees the continuity between these "inspired
ancients" and Plato in terms of their communication of
divine truths rather than pointing to dynamic or miraculous
acts. Thus Celsus is still trying to argue against quackery
by appealing to the divine philosopher over against popular
prophets or miracle workers who promise to display the
presence of god in unintelligible utterances and miraculous
feats (cf. c. Cels. VII.9).[58]

_____

[57]Note the similarity of this formulation to that of
the traditional choice of Heracles.

[58]Windisch, op. cit., p. 56 saw this point clearly, but
Windisch felt that Celsus had over drawn the distinction
between the ancient poets and the Palestinian prophets. Even
if Windisch is correct, what is crucial is that Celsus thought
the true "divine men" were in continuity with Plato and

D. The Divine Wise Men of the Philosophical Schools

In the development of the idealized portrait of the
paradigm of virtue and wisdom subsequent to Plato, the image
of Socrates, although fundamental, was not the only com-
ponent. Several other philosophers were of sufficient
stature as charismatic personalities to leave their
impression on the visage of the idealization. A brief
survey may suffice to delineate the particular features
associated with each and to demonstrate the common consensus
in the several schools that the ideal wise man is divine,
not because of his miraculous powers, but because of his
moral courage and wisdom.

Diogenes the Cynic is a greater historical enigma than
Socrates. Best known as a master of the chria or anecdote,
Diogenes appears in cynic tradition as playing the role
of the barbed-tongued critic, recasting the coin of
accepted convention (παραχαράττειν τὸ νόμισμα: Diog.
Laert. VI 20, 71) in a host of standardized situations.

-----

discontinuity with popular charlatans. Of course Plato was
subject to the same reinterpretation as any other figure,
and Hans von Leisegang ("Der Gottmensch als Archetypus,"
Eranos-Jahrbuch XVIII, 1950: Sonderband für C.G. Jung, hsg.
v. Olga F. Kapteyn, Zürich, 1950, pp. 22ff.) has shown that
"Plato and his teaching" are considered divine in fairly
flamboyant 'style by the time of Apuleius (de Deo Socratis),
to the point that he is learning from Persian magi, and by
the time of Olympiodorus (VI A.D.), Plato is himself a
magician. This does not mean, however, that when Philo
calls Plato ἱερώτατος (Quod Omnis, 13: note text problem)
there is a full blown image of a θεῖος ἀνήρ at hand. Philo's
Plato is still primarily a philosopher, and apparently the
same can be said of Philostratus, of all people, when he is
speaking of the theological character of Plato's teaching on
the soul and calls him θεσπέσιος καὶ πάνσοφος: Life of Ap.
VI.11.

Because early traditions about Diogenes were largely oral and since he consistently plays the role of the anti-hero in Cynic skits, the historical veracity of these chriae is questionable.[59] A particular series of these skits are stock: Diogenes and the pirates, Diogenes in the slave market, Diogenes and Alexander the Great, and Diogenes in Olympia.[60] The fact that many of these same stories are told once of Diogenes, again of Heracles (the patron saint of the Cynics) and again of Zeno is merely further illustration of the vitality of this idealization.

Within the variety of stories and sayings in which Diogenes is the principle figure, several explicit statements about the nature of the presence of the divine among men indicate the persistence of the moral and rational criteria which we have recognized in Plato's portrait of Socrates. To be sure, Diogenes can be called "Socrates gone mad" (Σωκράτης μαινόμενος : D.L.6.54), and a follower of his like Menedemus could indulge in a host of fantastic actions (τερατείας : D.L. 6.102) in order to dramatize the Cynic's divine mission as a "spy of god" (ἐπίσκοπος: κατάσκοπος) .[61]

---

[59]Cf. Gunnar Rudberg, "Zur Diogenes Tradition," Symbolae Osloenses, Fasc. XIV (ed. S. Eitrem et E. Skard: Oslo, 1935), pp. 22-43. Id., "Zum Diogenes-Typus," Symbolae Osloenses, Fasc. XV (Oslo, 1936), pp. 1-18.

[60]Cf. Paul Wendland, Die hellenistisch-roemische Kultur (Tübingen, 1912²), p. 77. (Handbuch z. NT I,2)

[61]Such features in the early history of cynicism were subject to expansion in the hands of a more "mystical" cynic like Peregrinus. Cf. Donald R. Dudley, A History of Cynicism (London, 1937), pp. 178-180.

Histrionics aside, however, Diogenes, the iconoclast of the
ancient world (cf. D.L. 6.38,63), is traditionally treated as
a divine philosopher.

He is credited with calling good men "images of the
gods" (τοὺς ἀγαθοὺς ἄνδρας θεῶν εἰκόνας εἶναι:
D.L. 6.51), and with basing the classic cynic argument that
all things belong to the wise on the premise that all things
belong to the gods and their friends (φίλοι), the wise (σοφοί:
D.L. 6.72, of Dio of Prusa 69.4). This set of moral and
intellectual qualifications of the divine wise man is
probably the basis upon which the poet Cercidas (third
century B.C.) points out the divine nature of Diogenes by
punning on his name and on the name of his sect, "Diogenes
son of Zeus, and hound of heaven" (Διογένης Ζανὸς γόνος
οὐράνιός τε κύων : D.L. 6.77).[62] Clearly such regard for
Diogenes as a philosophical ideal can be seen in Plutarch's
quotation of Alexander the Great as saying, "If I were not
Alexander, I would be Diogenes" (On the Fortune of Alexander
331 F, cf. D.L. 6.32).

Dio of Prusa regards Diogenes as an ideal, perhaps as
his idol.[63] Von Arnim has argued that the stories told by

---

[62]Cf. O. Weinreich, "Antikes Gottmenschtum," N. Jahrbuch
für Wissenschaft und Jugendbildung 2 (1926), p. 643.

[63]Cf. Henry A. Fischel, "Studies in Cynicism and the
Ancient Near East: The Transformation of a Chria," Religions
in Antiquity (Essays in Memory of Erwin Ramsdell Goodenough,
ed. Jacob Neusner: Leiden, 1968), p. 374.

46

Dio about Diogenes, particularly in discourses 6, 8, 9, and
10, are actually veiled autobiographical statements about
Dio's activity.[64] This is the best kind of evidence for the
power of the image of the ideal divine philosopher at the
end of the first century A.D., particularly since it furnished
Dio with an objective criterion for passing judgement on the
sycophants and phoney rhetoricians whom he ironically calls
θεῖοι ἄνθρωποι (33.4). Dio is not maligning them because
they are divine men, but because they do not measure up to
the standard of the true divine man, i.e. the philosopher
who is god's agent sent to reprove men for their moral
laxity.[65]

Dio, alias Diogenes, clearly sees his own career as a
divine mission in continuity with the agents of god of
previous eras. He reports that Diogenes diligently imitated
the life of the gods (μάλιστα ἐμιμεῖτο τῶν θεῶν τὸν βίον:
6.31). He casts Diogenes in the Cynic role of the spy of
god and divine ambassador (ἐπίσκοπος - κατάσκοπος - διάκονος:

---

[64]H. von Arnim, Leben und Werke des Dio von Prusa
(Berlin, 1898), 260ff.

[65]Cf. Dieter Georgi, Die Gegner des Paulus im 2.
Korinther-Brief (Wissenschaftliche Monographien zum Alten
und Neuen Testament, Band 11; Neukirchen, 1964), p. 193.
Georgi correctly points out that Dio sets himself apart from
these "experts in divine affairs," whom he satirically calls
"divine", Their precise self-understanding is, however, not
immediately apparent. Perhaps Windisch (op. cit., pp. 27-28)
is correct that they were like Euthyphro, since they said
they knew all things (cf. Euth.4 E- 5 A). From Dio's
criticism, however, it seems clear that he considers them
counterfeits of genuine philosophers. There is no evidence
that these "divine men" claimed the power to work miracles.

cf. 9.1),[66] and he repeatedly refers to the role of the
philosopher as the physician to the morally ill:

> "just as the good physician (ἀγαθὸν ἰατρόν) should go
> and offer his services where the sick are most numerous,
> so, said he, the man of wisdom (ὁ φρόνιμος ἀνήρ) should
> take up his abode where fools are thickest in order to
> convict them of their folly and reprove them" (ἐξελέγχων
> καὶ κολάζων : 8.5, cf. also 9.2,4; 10.1; 33.44).

The distance is great between this divine philosophical
emissary and any who look for divine presence to be revealed
in teratological displays. To be sure, prophecy if given
with "complete self-control and sobriety" (πάνυ ἐγκρατῶς καὶ
σωφρόνως : 1.56) deserves serious attention. But reason is in
control: "I am convinced that if you had reason, you would
have no need of divination" (μαντεία: 10.28).

> "Only the word of judicious and wise men, the kind of
> men as were numerous in the past, is an adequate and
> perfect guide and aid for an agreeable and moral nature,
> encouraging and teaching appropriately to all virtue"
> (1.8).

Epicurus is a second example of a philosopher whose
charismatic personality was intimately connected with his
teachings in the memory of his followers and who served as·
a paradigm of the divine philosopher. None of the other
schools are as directly dependent upon their founder to the
extent that the whole tradition bears his name and revolves
around the memory of Epicurus and his philosophy. DeWitt
correctly observes that even "the dead Epicurus (is) a
living criterion of conduct."[67] To refer to the Epicurean

---

[66]Cf. Georgi, op. cit., pp. 32-35.

[67]N.W. DeWitt, Epicurus and his Philosophy (Minneapolis,
1954), p. 283.

fellowship as a "personality cult" may be a false modern-
ization, but Festugière's term, "cult of friendship" is only
more satisfactory if it is clearly borne in mind that the
"friends" are "nestled down together under the protection of
the Sage."[68]

Without engaging in a detailed analysis of the religion
of Epicurus,[69] it can be observed that he was famous in the
ancient world for his radical criticism of religious
practices which tended toward superstition or magic,
especially divination, and as a result, was frequently regarded
as an atheist. At the same time, he introduced a new piety
or religious reform according to which the wise man lives
as a god among men (D.L. 10.135: ὡς θεὸς ἐν ἀνθρώποις) .[70]

Epicurus was himself the recipient of divine honors
during his life and in the memory of his followers.[71] The
conception that Epicurus had of the divine condition as that
which is perfectly serene did, of course, make the trans-
ition from human to divine easier for him than it may have
been for other hellenistic philosophers since a man could
be said to be divine to the degree that his life was tranquil

---

[68]A.J. Festugière, Epicurus and His Gods, trans. by
C.W. Chilton (Oxford, 1955), p. 42.

[69]Cf. Festugière, op. cit.; DeWitt, op. cit., pp.
249-288; R.D. Hicks, Stoic and Epicurean (New York, 1910),
pp. 282-311.

[70]Cf. Philodemus, Epicurea (ed. Hermannus Usener:
Lipsiae, 1887), #386: 16-17, "he also calls wise men the
friends of the gods and the gods the friends of the wise."

[71]Cf. Paul Wendland, "ΣΩΤΗΡ" , ZNW 6 (1904), pp. 346ff,
notes 3 and 4.

and untroubled.[72] His impetuous pupil, Colotes, overcome with emotion, falls on his knees in worship of Epicurus only to receive a mild reproof from the master for assuming a worship pose inconsistent with Epicurean philosophy of nature (ἀφυσιλόγητον).   After reciprocating the gesture, however, Epicurus sends him on his way saying, "Go about as one who is in my opinion imperishable (ἄφθαρτος) and think of us as imperishable too" (Usener Fragment 141: cf. Plutarch, Reply to Colotes, 1117 B-C).

Plutarch scorns Colotes for this action since it was ill-informed and did not elevate him to the status that was truly worthy of reverence, that of the wise man (Reply to Colotes, 1117 C).   Indeed, Epicurus appears to have bestowed the title of wise man (σοφός) on only one of his followers, Metrodorus (Cicero de fin. 2.3.7).[73] If Epicurus and Metrodorus are the only ones that the Epicurean tradition regarded as its "wise men", this would be significant not

---

[72]Cf. Epicurus' letter to his mother, Fragment 65, 29-40 ed. Arrighetti, quoted by Benedict Einarson and Phillip H. DeLacy in Plutarch's Moralia (Loeb Edition XIV; Harvard 1967), p. 250, note b: "for these things that I gain are nothing small or of little force, things of a sort that make my state equal to a god's, and show me as a man who not even by his mortality falls short of the imperishable and beloved nature. For while I am alive, I know joy to the same degree as the gods." Cf. also Lucretius III, 320: "so trivial are the traces of different natures that remain, that nothing hinders our living a life worthy of gods" (ut nil impediat dignam dis degere vitam).

[73]Even with this august rank, Metrodorus was regarded as falling short of Epicurus. Cf. Seneca, Epist. 18.9.

only because Metrodorus could speak of "escaping from the earthbound life into the mysteries of Epicurus which are in truth divinely revealed" (τὰ 'Επικούρου ὡς ἀληθῶς θεόφαντα ὄργια : Plutarch, <u>Reply</u> <u>to</u> <u>Colotes</u> 1117 B), but also because Metrodorus is specifically named in the will of Epicurus as a recipient of commemoration along with Epicurus in prescribed monthly meetings of the school.[74] This endowed banquet in honor of the Epicurean σοφοί continued for centuries,[75] and the possible similarities between such memorial feasts and the Christian practice of the Lord's Supper have been carefully studied.[76]

In his poem <u>De</u> <u>rerum</u> <u>natura</u>, which Robert Grant calls "the high water mark of the tide of scientific skepticism,"[77] Lucretius waxes eloquent on Epicurus as a god who rescues man from superstitions and terrors. As in Cicero (<u>De</u> <u>fin</u>. 1.5.14; <u>Tusc</u>. 1.21.48) where the opinion is recorded that Epicurus is venerated as a god (<u>venerantur</u> <u>ut</u> <u>deum</u>) because his scientific studies liberated the mind, Lucretius

---

[74]At the annual celebration of his birthday, however, only Epicurus appears to have been feted.

[75]Cf. Cicero, <u>De</u> <u>fin</u>. 2.31.101.

[76]Rash statements about the parallels in the memorialization of a "divine man" like Epicurus and the Christian treatment of Jesus are, of course, exactly what this study seeks to curb. For a sober review of this issue, cf. J. Jeremias, <u>The</u> <u>Eucharistic</u> <u>Words</u> <u>of</u> <u>Jesus</u>, trans. by Norman Perrin (New York, 1966), pp. 238-243, and see the literature cited there.

[77]Robert M. Grant, <u>op</u>. <u>cit</u>., p. 56.

elaborates this theme from the point of view of the true
believer: "For as soon as your reason which originates
from divine intelligence (divina mente coorta) begins to
exclaim the nature of things, the terrors of the soul
disappear, the walls of heaven open ..." (3.1-30; cf. 14ff).
It is also worth noting that in contemplating this image and
the world of nature which Epicurus has uncovered, Lucretius
is himself gripped with a divine delight (divina voluptas) and
a shuddering (horror: 3.28-30). Again Lucretius hymns the
praise of Epicurus and his discoveries, claiming that "he
was a god ... a god he was who first discovered that reasoned
plan of life which is now called wisdom" (5.8-10). Furthermore his divine discoveries are unrivaled in value to
mankind, even by the deeds of Hercules (5.20). Because he
purged the mind of the fear of mythical creatures and the
cares generated by lust, he is to be counted among the gods
(5.25-50); and Lucretius "treads his footsteps" and "follows
his reasonings" in his teaching (5.55ff).

As with the rationalistic idealization of Socrates
recorded by Plutarch and Dio's presentation of Diogenes,
the image of Epicurus as the "true divine man" was cultivated
in Epicurean tradition in radical contrast to any image of
divine presence that rested on supernatural displays of
divine power which contravened reason. Once again the
personality of the sage is focal and intimately connected
with his accomplishments, eliciting a response of worship
from the mature scientist as well as the impetuous youth.

Such religious ardour for the divine Epicurus is particularly
significant since it directly involves the denial of any
conception of divinity connected with the teratological,
occult or magical. If Lucretius' account of the personal
career and accomplishments of Epicurus (5.25-50) is to be
broadly described as aretalogical, i.e. a formal recitation
of praise of the accomplishments of a remarkable man, it
must be observed that this idealization stands in direct
antipathy to any positive evaluation of the miracles of Jesus
or the career of Alexander the (false) prophet, which
observation was clearly made by Lucian, the Epicurean
opponents of Alexander, and Celsus. The intent of all of
these diverse "aretalogical" traditions may be generally
propagandistic; they may all focus on the personality of
the hero; and the religious overtones may be clear; but
they arise from different understandings of the nature of
divine presence and of the style of religious life.

Although the Stoa regarded its founder as an exemplary
σοφός, the figure cf Zeno never exerted the kind of singular
personal force on subsequent traditions as has been observed
for Socrates, Diogenes, and Epicurus. It is also notable
that the Stoa was less exclusive with respect to appropriating
traditional religious myths and divination, in particular,
than Epicurus would have ever allowed.[78] Yet in the elaborate

---

[78]Cf. Cleanthes' "Hymn to Zeus"; Cornutus' "Epidrome";
and D.L. 7.151. Cf. also the above discussion on the art of
divination.

development of the concept of the Ideal Stoic Sage,[79] it is clear that the wise man's close bond with the gods, indeed his own divinity, is a function of his rational understanding and not due to any magical short circuit by which he gains power to defy the order of nature.

The descriptions of the ideal sage which are scattered throughout a wide range of literature have been collected and arranged according to specific attributes by von Arnim.[80] Certain features of the Stoic idealization can be briefly highlighted, however, to identify modifications in the general image of the divine wise man in the Hellenistic schools.[81]

The Stoic wise man is a perfect (τέλειος) paradigm of moral virtue as far removed from the fool as virtue is from vice (cf. D.L. 7.127, Stob. Ecl. 2.7.119) or as far as a divine being is separated from the ungodly: θείους τε εἶναι (τοὺς σπουδαίους). ἔχειν γὰρ ἐν ἑαυτοῖς οἱονεῖ θεόν. τὸν δὲ φαῦλον ἄθεον : D.L. 7.119, von Arnim #608. A close connection between "godliness" and wisdom also implies

---

[79]Cf. Kurt Deissner, Das Idealbild des Stoischen Weisen (Greifswald, 1930), reviewed by Karl Groos in Deutsche Literaturzeitung 51 (1930), pp. 1688-1691. For a more general discussion cf. R. Bultmann, "The Stoic Ideal of the Wise Man," Primitive Christianity, trans. by R.H. Fuller (New York, 1956), pp. 135-145.

[80]Johannes von Arnim, Stoicorum Veterum Fragmenta (Leipzig, 1903-1924, 4 vols.: 2nd ed. Stuttgart, 1964), vol. III, #544-684, pp. 146-171.

[81]Cf. R. Hoistad, Cynic Hero and Cynic King (Uppsala, 1948). C.J. DeVogel, Greek Philosophy, vol. III: The Hellenistic-Roman Period (Leiden, 1959), #1038-1050, pp. 158-168.

54

that the wise man is the only one truly qualified to perform
in cultic roles as diviner (μαντικός = σπουδαῖος : Stob.
Ecl. 2.114.16w, von Arnim #605) and priest (σοφός = ἱερεύς:
Stob. Ecl. 2.67.20w, von Arnim #604, D.L. 7.119). Thus the
ideal stoic sage may display traditional piety (D.L. 7.151),
but "he (σοφός) never marvels (θαυμάζειν) at any of the things
which appear 'extraordinary' (παράδοξα) , such as Charon's
mephitic caverns, ebbings of the tide, hot springs or fiery
eruptions" (D.L. 7.123).[82] Rather the wise man discovers
that which is truly "extraordinary" (παράδοξον) in a set of
propositional statements such as "only the sage is free and
every fool is a slave" or "only the sage is rich."[83]

The insistence on the absolute perfection of the true
sage tended to make the wise man into an unattainable ideal;
but in the Roman period the sage becomes a pattern of perfection whose goodness and truth is linked to his ability to
mediate it to others.[84] The great saints of the tradition
such as Socrates, Diogenes, and Antisthenes are already

[82]Poseidonius did study the effect of the moon on tides,
and these studies provided evidence for his view of the unity
of the universe upon which he based his defense of divination.
But his purpose in the study was to gain a rational and
systematic understanding of natural phenomena, in obvious
contrast to a view which merely stands in numinous awe of
perplexing occurrences in nature.

[83]Note that Cicero finds the stoic "paradoxes" to be
Socratic "to the highest degree and far and away the truest
(Paradoxa Stoicorum 4, Acad. 2.136).

[84]Cf. Karl Groos, op. cit., pp. 1688-1691. M. Hengel,
Nachfolge und Charisma (BZNW, Beiheft 34; Berlin, 1968),
pp. 33-34.

regarded by Poseidonius not merely as absolute ideals of perfection, but also as examples of moral progress (προκοπή: D.L. 7.91). Seneca, who thinks that the study of philosophy will yield divine tranquility making a man more like the gods than like other men (Epist. 41, 4-5; 53:11), advises taking a man of high character as a model (Epist. 11.8). The fact that the true sage is something of an unattainable ideal does not diminish his paradigmatic value:

> "Do I say I am a wise man (sapiens). By no means, for if I could make that claim, I should thereby not only deny that I am unhappy but should also declare that I am the most fortunate of all men (fortunatissimum) and had been brought into nearness with God (in vicinium deo). As it is, fleeing to that which is able to lighten all sorrows, I have surrendered myself to wise men" (Seneca to Helvia in Consolation 5.2).

Again Epictetus, who frequently placards Socrates as the true philosopher, regards him as a standard for comparison as well as an ideal: "Epictetus will not be better than Socrates; but if only I am not worse, that is enough for me" (Diss. I.2. 34-36). And in advising a man to live ὡς τέλειον καὶ προκόπτοντα , Epictetus treats Socrates as a pattern of attainment: "and even if you are not yet Socrates, you still ought to live as one wishing to be Socrates" (Encheir. 51).

The religious quality of such high regard for the divine sage ought not be overlooked. Seneca insists that the wise man is not inferior to a god (On Providence 6.6; Epist. 73.14-16) and that every good man (=wise man in Stoic terminology) has a god dwelling in him (Epist. 31.11, 41.1), and he describes the beatific vision of looking into

the face of a truly good man: "No one could call such a
face loveable without also calling it worshipful, be struck
down like with a vision from above and ... bow down and
worship" (Epist. 115.3ff). But the focus of this reverence
for the divine wise man is found in the frequent repetition
of stories of the death of illustrious men with Plato's
account of the death of Socrates serving as the paradigm.[85]

Socrates was not the only saint of the philosophical
tradition to whom the schools looked for forming their ideal
of how a divine sage faces death. Zeno and Anaxarchus are
both reported to have displayed virtuous contempt for their
physical suffering to the point of biting off their tongues
and spitting them in the face of their tormentors (D.L.
9,27, 59; Philo, Quod omnis prob. lib. sit 109; cf Plutarch
Adv. Col. 1126 D, De garrulitate 505 D, De stoicorum repugn.
1051 C). Furthermore this theme of the death of the sage
leaves its distinctive stamp on the retelling of the deaths
of other men of virtue. The story of the heroic death of
Calanus, a specimen of barbarian wisdom, according to Philo,
who burns himself rather than obey Alexander the Great
against his own will, is retold in eight places.[86] Plutarch's

---

[85]Cf. Moses Hadas, Hellenistic Civilization (New York,
1959), p. 177. In note 10, p. 306, Hadas also refers to a
study by A. Ronconi, "Exitus illustrium virorum," Studia
italiani di filologia classica 17 (1940), p. 332. Hadas
states that "Ronconi shows how the tradition established by
the death of Socrates was carried on by the Stoics and then
taken up by the pagan and Christian martyrdoms."

[86]Cf. PW X (1919), pp. 1544-1545. Arrian 7:2-3, Strabo
15.715ff, Diodorus 17.107, Plutarch Alexander 65, 69-70,

account of the heroic death of the Spartan reformer Cleomenes
brings a popular tale up to the level of philosophical
respectability by rationalizing the apparitions of a snake
protecting the corpse (Cleomenes 29).[87] Anticipating the
discussion in the next chapter, it is also worthwhile to
contrast the treatment of Eleazar in II Maccabees and
IV Maccabees. Not only does the author of IV Maccabees
considerably tone down the miraculous motifs,[88] completely
eliminating the references to the resurrection of the flesh
(cf. II Macc 7:11; 14:16), but IV Maccabees is explicitly
a treatise on "whether reason is supreme ruler of the
passions" (1:1; 1:13; 6:31; 7:17). Thus IV Maccabees regards
Eleazar, the seven brothers and the mother as "the best
instance by far that I can give of the noble conduct of those
who died for the sake of virtue" (ὑπὲρ ἀρετῆς : 1:8).
Eleazar's titles indicate his philosophical depiction:
ὁ ἱερὸς ἀνήρ (6:30), ὁ πανάγιος (7:4), σύμφωνος νόμου
καὶ φιλόσοφος θείου βίου (7:7); and the account of his death ends
with the judgement that "only the sage (σοφός) and man of
courage is master of the passions" (7:23). As Hadas and

Athenaeus 10.437a, Aelian 2.41, Lucian's Pereginus 25, Philo
Quod omnis. prob. lib. sit, pp. 94-96.

[87]Note the clear contrast that Plutarch sets up between
the superstitious women who worshipped Cleomenes as a hero
and child of the gods (ἥρωα καὶ θεῶν παῖδα)   and the wiser men
(οἱ σοφώτεροι)   who are able to explain the phenomenon.

[88]Cf. R. Grant, op. cit., pp. 163, 223.

Smith conclude:

> "In itself the story of Eleazar may be only an
> imperfect example of aretalogy, but it is an important
> monument in the history of the genre because, on the
> one hand, it is so palpably influenced by the image
> of Socrates and, on the other, it is so palpably
> the prototype for a long series of subsequent
> martyrdoms."[89]

The evidence for the particular strength of the Platonic

image of Socrates as a martyr in the accounts of the deaths

of illustrious wise men[90] can be supplemented from Seneca

and Epictetus. Epictetus (1.9.22-26) gives a direct

paraphrase of Plato's Apology 29c and 28e where Socrates

refused to abandon the post God assigned him in order to

save his own neck, and Epictetus concludes, "this man is truly

akin to the gods" (συγγενὴς τῶν θεῶν). Furthermore Epictetus

regards the imprisoned Socrates as a model for wise men;

"then we shall be zealous imitators (ζηλωταί) of Socrates,

when we are able to write paeans in prison" (2.6.26).

Socrates is truly a paradigm (παράδειγμα: 4.1.159), and

---

[89]Hadas and Smith, Heroes and Gods (New York, 1965),
p. 90. M. Hadas has argued previously that the specific
background of IV Maccabees is Plato's Gorgias (The Third
and Fourth Books of Maccabees, New York, 1953, pp. 116-117).
The detailed arguments need not be rehearsed here, since
it is sufficient to recognize that IV Maccabees has been
influenced by the conception of the death of the wise man
for which Plato was largely responsible. Apparently Hadas
is directly dependent upon the arguments of J. Gutman,
"Ha-em v'Shivat Baneha b'Aggada u'b'Sifre Hashmonaim II
v'IV," in Commentationes Iudaico-Hellenisticae in Memoriam
Iohannis Lewy, ed. M. Schwabe and I. Gutman (Jerusalem,
1949), pp. 35-36.

[90]Caution is again urged lest the reader confuse such
a propaganda motif as the accounts of the deaths of wise
men with the miracle collections simply because Hadas and
Smith (see previous note) may refer to both phenomena as
aretalogical.

"now that Socrates is dead the memory of him is no less
useful to men, nay, is perhaps even more useful than what
he did or said while he still lived" (4.1.169).

The suffering Socrates is thus one of the most potent
models of the "divine man" of the philosophical tradition,
even influencing the way other sages of other traditions
are depicted. It has been argued here, furthermore, that
this "divine man" stands in marked discontinuity with the
"divine men" who are authenticated by miracles, magic, or
other powerful acts which defy rational explanation. The
divergences between these types is too sharp to be discounted
as mere "shadings" of the image of "the ideal divine man."[91]
Perhaps the dramatic impact of this contrast is seen nowhere
more clearly than in Seneca, De vita beata 26.8-27.1. In
retort to those who declare that someone is divine on the
basis of dramatic cultic displays which defy sensibility,
Seneca portrays Socrates as crying out from his prison to
defend the virtues, good men, and the truly sacred things:

> "Whenever someone, shaking the rattle, pretends to speak
> with authority, whenever someone dexterous in slashing
> his muscles makes bloody his arms and his shoulders
> with light hand, whenever some woman howls as she
> creeps along the street on her knees, and an old man,
> clad in linen and carrying a lamp in broad daylight
> and a branch of laurel, cries out that some one of the
> gods is angry, you gather in a crowd and give ear and,
> fostering each other's dumb amazement, affirm that he
> is divine!
>
> Lo! from that prison, which he purified by entering it
> and made more honourable than any senatehouse, Socrates
> cries out: 'What madness is this, what instinct is

[91]Cf. Bieler, op. cit., p. 143.

this at war with gods and men that leads you to calumniate the virtues and by your wicked talk to profane holy things? If you are able, praise the good, if not, ignore them; but if you take pleasure in indulging in your foul abuse, assail you one another."[92]

In an earlier discussion of the Pythagorean traditions, it was lamented that, although significant divergence appeared recognizable between the paradoxographical writers who treated Empedocles and Pythagoras as supernatural miracle workers, just as the early traditions of Apollonius of Tyana represented him as a wizard, and the more rational assessments of these figures as "true philosophers", it appeared impossible to be certain that this discrimination was not arbitrary. It is still possible that the Pythagoreans synthesized these diverse models at a very early date and that Apollonius of Tyana did claim to be a miracle working philosopher. But this review of the ways in which the saints of the other philosophical traditions came to be regarded as "divine men" has demonstrated that the image of the divine wise man, which can be recognized in diverse forms after Plato, resists the admixture of teratological elements. Socrates' δαιμόνιον may be treated by some as a magical power, but the moral and rational image that Plato drafted of the dying Socrates provides a criterion by which such interpretations are judged incorrect. Epicurus was

---

[92]Trans. by John W. Basore, Seneca's Moral Essays, Loeb edition, vol. II (London, 1932), pp. 174-177. For an additional example of the religious esteem which Seneca has for the man who attains tranquility by virtue of his life of reason and moderation, cf. Epist. 41.

hailed as divine precisely because he denied the reality of
the irrational and terrifying, and the image of the wise man
condemned for the sake of virtue provided the inspiration
for a dramatic denial of the conception of divine presence
as revealed in stupefying displays. These powerful models
at least make it clear why the lives of Apollonius and
Pythagoras, which are finally composed much later by
Philostratus and Porphyry, still appear to be an uneven
mixture of miraculous and philosophical traditions rather
than a unified blend of homogeneous elements.[93]

Lucian's parodies of a variety of popular semi-literary
pieces provide evidence that in the second century market-
place of propagandistic competition, the philosophical
traditions were increasingly more open to incursions of the
missionary techniques of a variety of religious traditions
which were generally of oriental origin and which regarded
miracle and dramatic or ecstatic display as a primary
metaphor. Reitzenstein regarded Lucian's parodies as a
mirror image of an aretalogy,[94] and thus the style of

---

[93]In spite of the fact that these writers included many
tales that reflected magical arts, they continued to insist
that the wise men would not be taken in by magic. Origen
(c. Cels. VI.41) points out this inconsistency to Celsus by
referring to Apollonius of Tyana. Philostratus (Vit. Soph.,
p. 590 Boissonade) insists that "an educated man would not be
led astray into the practices of magicians: (cf. Life of Ap.
7.39). Plotinus (IV.4.43-44) also maintains that the wise
man is "immune from magic, his reasoning part can't be
touched by it."

[94]Hellenistische Wundererzählungen, op. cit., pp. 1-8,
38-39.

propaganda or aretalogy that Lucian's opponents were using could be described as they were reflected in Lucian. This methodological insight clearly had a profound effect on the conception of an aretalogy that has been operative in much subsequent discussion.[95]

It ought to be observed, however, that Lucian is opposing a variety of miraculous, mythical, and hyperbolic religious accounts with the canons of reason and the epistemological categories of earlier philosophical discussion. The consistency lies with Lucian and can be identified in the several contexts perhaps principally by referring to his philosophical heritage.[96] It is an over-simplification to congregate all of Lucian's opponents under the general rubric of "divine men" who are praised by "aretalogists."

Lucian's esthetic theory of how "true history" ought to be written corresponds to the three fold division of narrative prose of the hellenistic world: true history, false history, and history as it may likely have happened.[97] His treatise on "How to Write History" and the stories in

---

[95]Cf. Hadas, Hellenistic Civilization, op. cit., pp. 172-173.

[96]Admittedly Lucian is a complex thinker, and difficult to classify. Cf. Marcel Caster, Lucien et la pensée religieuse de son temps (Paris, 1937), pp. 9-122. H.D. Betz, Lukian, op. cit., p. 5 & p. 23, n. 1. R. Höistad, op. cit., pp. 64-73. J. Bompaire, Lucien écrivain(Bibliothèque des Écoles françaises d' Athènes et de Rome, 190; Paris, 1958).

[97]Cf. Reitzenstein, op. cit., pp. 2ff. M. Hadas, Hellenistic Civilization, op. cit., p. 121.

his "True History" clarify his criteria and make it obvious
that he regards the anecdotes in the Lover of Lies as
completely false and worthless. But in this case, the
collection of incantations (Lover of Lies: 8,12,17,33F),
charms (11,14,17), and exorcisms (16,31) that Lucian is
ridiculing probably corresponded more closely in form and
function to a collection like that of the magical papyri
than to fantastic historical writing.[98]

It is also Lucian's consistency that brings his parody
of the life of Alexander the (false) prophet into comparison
with his burlesque imitations of fantastic historical and
magical writings. Since all of these writings share a
teratological content, Lucian can invoke the criterion of
the true wise man or philosopher in addition to the canons
of historiography in order to launch his attack. In The
Lover of Lies, he explicitly states his amazement that a
devotee of philosophy like Eucrates together with Cleodemus
the Peripatetic, Deinomachus the Stoic and Ion the Platonist,
all extremely learned men (σοφοί) would allow such lies to
be told in their midst (5-6,18).

The account of the life of Alexander of Abonoteichus,
the (false) prophet, is doubtless a parody of a semi-literary

---

[98]Authors like Pliny (cf. Natural History, especially
#30) could include such paradoxographical material with only
mild disclaimers (praef. 12, Nat. Hist. 7.8), and Lucian's
"True History" mocks such historiography. But in "The Lover
of Lies" (1), Lucian claims that he is speaking of liars
for whom he can see no national or even personal cause for
their mendacity.

attempt to glorify the prophet. Unlike the account of the death of Peregrinus, which will be discussed in another context, the "aretalogy" of Alexander that Lucian is mocking appears to have attempted to authenticate the "prophet" primarily on the basis of anti-rational and magical-miraculous acts.

Although Lucian continually insists that Alexander gained his stature at the expense of the simple minded (cf. 6,9,15,20,42,50) or because of devious control of those in power (30,32,48), Alexander appears to have attracted an immense following by carefully cultivating that image of divine presence that has been seen in direct opposition to the image of the divine wise man. His reported success among the Platonists, Pythagoreans, and Stoics (25) probably demonstrates that this conception of divine presence had penetrated certain philosophical circles, just as was previously observed in the Theages, Plutarch's De genio Socratis, and perhaps also in Seneca's De vita beata.[99] The clear focus of his pretence to being divine, however, lies in his dramatic frenzy (θεῖόν τι καὶ φοβερόν : 12) including glossolalia or incantations in a foreign tongue and the promise of a visible manifestation of the god (ἐναργῆ τὸν θεόν:

---

[99]R. Reitzenstein, Die Hellenistischen Mysterienreligionen (Leipzig, 1910), p. 12, observes that the success of Alexander and Apollonius of Tyana is inconceivable unless such conceptions of divine presence were current. Lucian also makes the direct correlation between Alexander and such cultic pretenders (Alex. 9). What has been neglected, however, is the recognition of the direct competition between this conception and that of the holy and divine wise man.

13), assuming the name Glycon as the divine object of cult
worship (18), and claiming to be a latter-day Asclepius
(43, cf. 14 where the title refers to the snake and 15 where
the ruse is completed) on the basis of such activity.
Furthermore he appears to have made direct appeals to magic
to bolster his claims, as is perhaps best evidenced by his
distribution of a doorway amulet against the plague (36),
which Lucian reports in order to discredit, but without
rehearsing his whole attack on Alexander as a magician
(cf. 1,5,6).

Alexander's own tie with the philosophical traditions
is very difficult to determine, but it is obvious that
Lucian felt that any attempt to portray him as a philosopher
was a thin veneer which would be highly inconsistent with
the underlying image. Even if Lucian is unfair in slighting
Alexander's ties with Pythagoreanism, the underlying
"aretalogy" or recitation of Alexander's feats that Lucian
is mocking appears to have made relatively few references
to Alexander as a philosopher. Alexander's propagandists
seem to have portrayed him as a wonder worker first of all;
and as Betz has shown, the real "historical occasion" for
the idealization of anyone as divine lies with the literary
creator or storyteller rather than with the historical
personage himself.[100]

---

[100]Lukian, op. cit., p. 104.

Almost all of the attempts to make Alexander palatable to those of more philosophical tastes are concentrated in the opening paragraphs of Lucian's parody. The account of Alexander's physical appearance, which Lucian admits was divine (θεοπρεπὴς ὡς ἀληθῶς : 3), his claim to be like Pythagoras (4), the brief list of his moral virtues, which Lucian disregards as a mask (4), and the later passing remark that he regarded intercourse with boys as impious (41), all may be read as appeals to philosophical models.[101] This may be evidence of the kind of superimposition of images that characterizes the "divine men" whom Philostratus and Porphyry depict.[102] But the brevity of such details and Lucian's comparatively casual treatment of them suggest that they functioned as something of a gloss on the presentation of Alexander as a divine miracle worker.

Lucian's attack on Alexander is clearly directed at his pretentions to display the presence of the divine in his

---

[101]Alexander's statement that Sacerdus will in later lives be "a camel, then a horse, then a wise man and prophet just as great as Alexander" (εἶτ' ἀνὴρ σοφὸς καὶ προφήτης: 43) is the kind of succinct aphorism that could be defended as historically reliable. Its Pythagorean coloring may also indicate that Alexander himself found in Pythagoreanism a way to synthesize the images of wise man and miracle worker. Even the minimalistic method of this study does not exclude such a possibility. Yet the evidence is too thin to follow Windisch in suggesting that the Pythagoreans were responsible at an early date for the creation of this conglomerate image.

[102]Origen's depiction of Jesus and Moses as "divine men" should probably also be considered as an example of the way diverse kinds of material can be agglomerated in the later idealization.

person by such teratological and magical actions, and he uses
the criterion of the truly divine wise man as his weapon.

Lucian appeals to three different idealizations of
charismatic figures who are regarded as "divine men" in
philosophical tradition in order to ridicule the claims of
Alexander. First of all, Lucian makes a passing and
apparently crude reference to the similarity between his task
of exposing Alexander and Hercules' labor of cleaning the
dung from the Augean stables (Alex 1, cf. Dio of Prusa
8.35).[103] As will be discussed in the next section,
Hercules had become a favorite example of a divine man in
Cynic and Stoic traditions, in particular, and his labors
had been transformed into paradigmatic moral actions. Even
if the text where Hercules is called θεῖος ἀνὴρ καὶ θεός
(Cynic 13) probably originates from pseudo-Lucian, it is
possible to anticipate the discussion of the next section by
saying that Lucian's reference to this crass task of
Hercules is more than a risqué flourish and probably ought
to be read as a humorous yet serious appeal to the model
of one of the true divine men in order to justify Lucian's
"task".

Secondly, Lucian's reference to Pythagoras as σοφὸς ἀνὴρ
καὶ τὴν γνώμην θεσπέσιος   (4) ought not be too strongly

---

[103]I am indebted to Mr. Eugene Jeff Miller for his
idiomatic translation of this passage in Lucian which brought
the text of Dio to mind. The ancients did not shrink from
speaking of dung in the way Loeb translators feel obliged
to do.

disregarded as irony or hyperbole. As has been previously argued, this text is probably a serious attempt on Lucian's part to contrast the activity of Apollonius of Tyana and his followers, including Alexander, to the Pythagoras of the philosophical traditions, the true "divine Pythagoras" by Lucian's standard. Lucian does refer (4) to the existence of a cycle of stories about Pythagoras which he finds incredible, but at least Lucian was able to sort out such tales which were probably teratological so that Pythagoras remains a divine wise man in his eyes.[104]

Yet the strongest example of a truly divine man that Lucian can muster to discredit Alexander is Epicurus. It is possible that Lucian was merely picking up an argument that arose from the historical conflict between the Epicureans and Alexander and his followers and which Lucian felt held special appeal to Celsus for whom Lucian claims to be writing (1,61).[105] No doubt Lucian is aware of actual historical conflicts between Alexander and the Epicureans, including the attempt to have an Epicurean stoned who publicly

_____

[104]This may be evidence that the cycles of stories about Pythagoras the divine philosopher were still circulating apart from the stories about Pythagoras the miracle worker. But even if the case was less clear cut, it is still true that Lucian can regard Pythagoras the divine philosopher to be a striking contrast to Alexander and Apollonius of Tyana.

[105]The inclusion of Christians as opponents of Alexander is curious. Their precise objection to Alexander is hard to determine, but it may be they were merely included with the Epicureans as atheists (cf. 25, 38-39, 46).

exposed Alexander (44-45) and the public burning of the
"Sovereign Maxims" of Epicurus (47). Furthermore Epicurus
was the best image of the divine wise man with which to
oppose Alexander, as the contemporary Epicureans doubtless
knew,[106] since, as this study has shown, Epicurus' divine
status was seen to rest precisely upon his scientific
opposition to everything superstitious and teratological
which terrorizes the mind of man, with particular vengeance
shown against oracles.

But Lucian himself plays up Epicurus as a divine sage
to the point that although Lucian was probably not an
Epicurean he clearly regarded Epicurus as a prime example
of the kind of divine man by which all charlatans were to
be judged. Lucian praises the followers of Epicurus as
among the sensible men (οἱ νοῦν ἔχοντες : 25) who in
contrast to the Platonists, Stoics, and Pythagoreans opposed
Alexander, and he notes that Alexander did have enough
sense to recognize Epicurus as his real foe:

> "upon whom else would a quack (γόης ἄνθρωπος) who loved
> humbug (τερατείᾳ φίλος) and bitterly hated truth more
> fittingly make war than upon Epicurus who discerned the
> nature of things and alone knew the truth in them?"
> (25).

Lucian explicitly recognized Epicurus as the critic of the
teratological and witching ways (μαγγανεία : 43) of persons
like Alexander. Consequently Lucian has fully grasped the

---

[106]Cf. De Witt, op. cit., p. 285. Hicks, op. cit.,
pp. 307-309.

impact of the Epicurean concept of their founder as a divine man, and he uses this criterion in a masterful way as Lucretius did to break the back of teratological traditions of divine presence by characterizing Epicurus as "a man who was truly saintly and divine in his character and disposition, who alone truly recognized and transmitted the ideals and who was the liberator of all who conversed with him" (ἀνδρὶ ὡς ἀληθῶς ἱερῷ καὶ θεσπεσίῳ τὴν φύσιν καὶ μόνῳ μετ' ἀληθείας τὰ καλὰ ἐγνωκότι καὶ παραδεδωκότι καὶ ἐλευθερωτῇ τῶν ὁμιλησάντων αὐτῷ γενομένῳ: 61).[107]

---

[107]This text has been analyzed from quite a different angle by Professor Betz who regards Lucian as attempting to treat Epicurus as a man who is truly holy and divine in his character and disposition. Betz thinks Lucian has failed in this effort and calls the characterization an "empty phrase". Cf. Lukian, op. cit., p. 100.

E. The Divine Hercules

The vitality of the idealization of the wise man is perhaps best seen by the way in which it can affect the Hellenistic portraiture of a hero of great antiquity in Greek tradition, such as Hercules. As the saint of the Cynics and a favorite of the Stoics, Hercules serves both as the paradigm of philosophic virtue and as the ideal of political kingship. Rather than attempt an elaborate defense of this position which has been well-argued by Höistad,[108] among others, a few key features can be observed which show the way the image of Hercules was shaped to conform to that of the ideal wise man in Cynic and Stoic tradition.

It must be observed at the outset that by the time of the fifth century B.C., the figure of Hercules was both very popular and already highly differentiated. Höistad gives a good review of the diverse facets of the depiction of Hercules from that of the "ethically and religiously refined Hercules ... already half way on the road towards becoming the object of a cult" to "the burlesque type of Heracles in the Satyr plays, and finally the suffering god in Sophocles and the suffering man and benefactor in Euripides."[109] Thus it is no surprise to find Plato's

---

[108]Ragnar Höistad, Cynic Hero and Cynic King (Uppsala, 1948).

[109]Ibid., p. 28. Cf. A.R. Anderson, "Heracles and His Successors," Harvard Studies in Classical Philology 39 (Cambridge, 1928), pp. 9ff.

Socrates describing his quest for verification of the Delphic oracle as a "Herculean" labor,[110] but the precise force of such a correlation is still unclear.[111]

By the time the Cynics had adopted Hercules as their patron saint, the mythological accounts of his life had already undergone certain rationalistic adjustments in the direction of individualistic ethics, particularly in the lengthy allegory on the "Choice of Hercules" in which Prodicus incorporated the "two ways" theme (cf. Xenophon Mem. 2.1.21 ff).[112] The force of this motif is that Hercules, by an act of will rather than as a tragic victim of fate subjected to tribulation, chooses the ethically important labors (πονοί) in order to complete his own virtue (ἀρετή). Such a choice was frequently regarded as paradigmatic of the choice that a philosopher or a ruler must make (cf. Lucian, The Dream 7ff where the choice Lucian makes is allegedly patterned after Socrates' choice; Philostratus, Life of Apollonius 6.11; Dio of Prusa 1.66 ff).

---

[110]Cf. Plato's Apology 22a. Only the word πόνος is used and Hercules is not named, but the parallel seems well accepted. Cf. Anderson, op. cit., pp. 10-11.

[111]Bieler, op. cit., II, p. 85, is doubtless correct that Plato is pointing to a divine service that Socrates is laboring to perform. But is this a labor for the benefit of mankind or in service of the cult?

[112]The dating of another allegorical fragment from Herodorus (#14, Jacoby, Fr. Gr. Hist. I, 218) is problematic, but Höistad regards it as coming from the late fifth century, op. cit., pp. 30-31.

One of the most important clues to the specific Cynic
coloring of the portrait of Hercules is the interpretation
of his πόνοι . Höistad has pointed to the equation that
Antisthenes made between πόνος and ἀγαθόν on the basis of the
example of Hercules (Diog. Laert. 6.2). This morally
positive evaluation stands in contrast to the interpretation
of Hercules' suffering in Euripides, where although the labors
are of high value, "from Hercules' point of view πόνος
is an involuntary evil inflicted on him by fate."[113] The
biting edge of the Cynic equation πόνος= ἀγαθόν is found in
the fact that πόνος is not a good in itself, but must be set
in a context of ethical self-improvement. Thus the Cynics
could regard the labors of musicians and athletes as
unprofitable and pointless (ἀνωφελῶς καὶ ἀτελῶς : Diog. Laert.
6.70),[114] and they made every effort to relate their pleasure
in rejecting all conventional pleasures to the well
disciplined life of Hercules (Diog. Laert. 6.71).[115] It is
clear, furthermore, that in the history of Cynicism there
was some disagreement even within the tradition as to
whether the πόνοι of Hercules and particularly his death
had any philanthropic intention or exemplary value for

---

[113]Ibid., p. 27.

[114]Note the Cynic definition of the τέλος : "They
regard life according to virtue (ἀρετή) as the end (τέλος) as
Antisthenes says in his Heracles": Diog. Laert. 6.104).

[115]Höistad argues strenuously for the antiquity of this
Cynic tradition, op. cit., pp. 27 ff.

mankind.[116]

In Dio of Prusa, it is possible to recognize both the
resistance to such spiritualizations and their importance
for Dio's own idea of Hercules. The view of Hercules as
the rugged individualist who does his labors and dies
strictly for his own benefit, i.e. the concept of ἀγαθόν
as complete self-sufficiency, is primary for Dio. In
Discourse 60, Dio relates the story of Hercules' seduction
into a life of softness by Deianeira with the result that
his suicide is a moral act only in the individual sense
that Hercules improves his own condition by dying rather
than being enslaved in a weakened, flabby, self-indulgent
life. In the context of one of the "autobiographical"
Diogenes discourses (8:34-36), Dio also insists that
Hercules was not doing anyone any favors by his labors. He
merely discarded the golden apples with grand Cynic disdain,
since they were useless to a man.

But as Dio elaborates his picture of Hercules in
Discourse 8, he supplements this hard line Cynic image with
additional traditional shadings.[117] On the one hand, Dio

---

[116]Cf. Hoistad, Ibid., passim, who argues that authentic
Cynic tradition resisted such allegorizations and H.M.
Hornsby "The Cynicism of Peregrinus Proteus", Hermathena 48
(Dublin-London, 1933), pp. 65-84, who argues that the suffer-
ing and death "for the sake of continence" is an old Cynic
motif.

[117]Whether such additional features were acceptable to
Cynics of the period is a disputed question (cf. previous
note). But since the Diogenes discourses are generally
considered to be Dio's most radically Cynic expressions,

still insists that Hercules committed suicide merely because of the self-motivated reason that he was afraid he couldn't continue his former style of life (φοβούμενος μὴ οὐ δύνηται ζῆν ὁμοίως : 34) because of the approach of old age; and Dio maintains that Hercules prefaced this final act of self-determination by cleaning the Augean stables, a clear display of Cynic ἀναιδεία "to avoid creating the opinion that he did only impressive and mighty deeds." On the other hand, Dio includes the statement that Hercules was afflicted with some disease (ἔπειτα οἶμαι νόσου τινὸς καταλαβούσης: 34). Dio probably regards this "affliction" as merely the concrete reason why Hercules was unable to continue a self-sufficient life since he has just finished criticizing the inconsistency of those who regard the living Hercules as a miserable figure (ἄθλιον) but later deify him (θεὸν νομίζουσι: 27-28).[118] But such "affliction" is also open to the interpretation that he was a tragic figure driven to his death (cf. Lucian, Peregrinus 25). Dio also includes a second interpretation of Hercules' act of cleaning the stable remarking that Hercules believed "he ought to fight no less diligently and war with opinion as with wild beasts and men" (35). This view is still well within the Cynic

---

even moderate shadings of the image may point to some divergence of opinion in contemporary Cynicism. Without some picture of the differentiation of the image of Hercules, Peregrinus appears as a complete anomaly in Cynic tradition.

[118]Cf. Höistad, op. cit., p. 52.

understanding of ἀναίδεια , but points beyond mere self-
service to a more philanthropic intention. This broader
interpretation of the act increased its exemplary value,
as is best seen from the fact that the memory of this display
of shamelessness prompts Dio's spokesman, Diogenes, to
perform an obscene action himself.

In observing Dio's use of traditional material, it is
also worth noting that when he appropriates traditional
myths and popular religious language about the demi-gods
and heroes of the past, it is explicitly their moral virtue
that authenticates their divine status. In 31.16, for
example, he lists several great benefactors of mankind,
ending up with Hercules, Theseus and other semi-divine
heroes (ἡμίθεοι ποτὲ ἥρωες) of the past, all of whom "worked
great labors for the sake of virtue" (οἱ πόνους μεγάλους πονήσαντες
ὑπὲρ τῆς ἀρετῆς).[119] In Discourse 69.1, Dio allows that
although people tend to spend their lives pursuing the
wrong desires, they do in fact understand that it is the
virtues (ἀρεταί) that are divine and holy (θεῖα καὶ σεμνά)
and they regard those who have been characterized by such
virtues as gods, heroes, or demi-gods,[120] for example,

---

[119]It is unclear in this text whether Hercules' labors
were done strictly for the sake of virtue or for the benefit
of mankind as well. The philanthropic motif is clear with
respect to the others in the list and provides the basis for
their emulation by others. On the demi-gods, cf. also 33.1
and 33.4 (where Dio is opposing the rhetors or counterfeit
"divine men").

[120]This specific definition of the θεῖος ἀνήρ as one who

Hercules, the Dioscuri, Theseus and Achilles. Since kingship
is the topic under consideration in this text, the concept
of virtue is broader than mere Cynic self-determination.
Thus the precise definition of virtue and the corresponding
image of Hercules show some variation, but his divine status
and importance as a paradigm for philosophers and kings rest
consistently on his possession of moral virtue.

Dio's treatment of Hercules clearly documents that this
divine man was too important a figure to be possessed by
the Cynics alone. A study of the facets of his highly
differentiated image would doubtless provide a meaningful
typology of Hellenistic belief systems from the most
parochial shrines competing with each other for the possession
of the real Hercules, to the schools competing for the
verification of their image of the divine wise man. In this
vein, the Stoics, with their great interest in the deaths of
illustrious men, also picked up the Hercules legends,
particularly as transmitted by the tragedians, and molded
the image of Hercules to that of the ideal Stoic sage. Once
the individualistic conception of virtue of hard line Cynics
and the Stoic fascination with death scenes have been
identified, however, the remaining traditions about Hercules

---

has an abundance of virtue is by no means new with Dio (cf.
Aristotle, Nich. Eth. VII.1-3: 1145a, 15-33), but its
vitality in Dio's understanding must be emphasized.
Specifically on Hercules cf. Dio 2.78; 5.23; 4.31. For a
Euhemeristic argument that Hercules' virtue makes him
divine, cf. Cornutus, Theologiae Graecae Compendium 31 (ed.
Teubner, p. 63).

as a benefactor, ruler, and religious hero are so tightly
bound together that it is necessary to deal with the myth of
Hercules, including accounts of his death, as a whole, while
watching for clues to features that are peculiarly Cynic
or Stoic.

.For the purposes of this study, a very crucial piece of
work has been done by Marcel Simon in his analysis of the
relationship of the myth of Hercules, as detailed in
Seneca, Dio of Prusa, and Epictetus, to the early Christian
gospels.[121] Simon's review of the history of scholarship on
this question demonstrates the perplexing complexity and
abundance of parallels between the traditions of Hercules and
the gospel traditions. Toynbee abstracts a series of studies
of such parallels[122] to compile a list of 89 similarities,
falling in clusters around five foci, birth, infancy,
travails of adulthood, death and ascension, death and
assumption of the mother.[123] Without becoming embroiled in
a discussion of those parallels, many of which are facile,
it ought to be noted that Pfister regarded these
similarities to be so striking as to suggest that "the

---

[121]Marcel Simon, Hercule et le Christianisme (Paris, 1955).

[122]E. Ackermann in Philolog. Suppl. X (1907), pp. 410
ff, and Rheinisches Museum LXVII (1912), pp. 456 ff. Th.
Birt, Aus dem Leben der Antike3 (Leipzig, 1922). F. Pfister,
"Herakles und Christus", Archiv für Religionswissenschaft
XXXIV (1937), pp. 42-60. I have depended on Simon and
Toynbee for their summaries of this work.

[123]Arnold J. Toynbee, A Study of History VI (London,
1939), pp. 465-476.

author of the proto-gospel, recognizable in the different
recensions of the three synoptics had a Cynic-Stoic
biography of Hercules under his eyes and has modeled the
life of Jesus in strict dependence upon this document; this
is an affirmation which can be made with complete
certainty."[124] Such confidence was obviously unfounded for
a number of reasons, and was not shared by Simon or Toynbee,
but it rested upon careful observation of the religious
and salvific importance of the figure of Hercules. In his
chapter on "Herculean Theology and Christology", Simon
summarizes Hercules' significance:

> "Hercules is not only an example and a model. He is
> also the divine man, the son of god who purifies the
> world of sin, disturbs and destroys the empire of evil
> and reigns as savior of the human race before he is
> finally elevated to heaven as a just reward for his
> labors."[125]

Small wonder that Justin thought that the devil was at work
creating fictitious parallels to the life and saving work
of Christ (Dial. 69; First Apology 21).

The climax of the myth of Hercules is seen, moreover,
in the accounts of his death. One of the most important
examples of the religious quality of the Hercules myth is
Seneca's Hercules Oetaeus where the fascination that the
Greek tragedians felt for his death is once again focal,

---

[124]Pfister, op. cit., pp. 58-59. For a direct rebuttal,
cf. H.J. Rose, "Herakles and the Gospels," HTR 31 (1938),
pp. 113-142.

[125]Op. cit., p. 80.

i.e. in contrast to Cynic minimalist interpretations which could still be described as religious in tone.[126] Seneca clearly regards the death of Hercules as having sacrificial significance, furthering the work of benefactions that Hercules has done (794-796). Indeed his death is the crowning labor of his life; all his other virtuous acts are inconsequential (leve); only this act will make him divine (1700-1725). The cosmic significance of this death is magnified, chaos is overcome (1946) and Hercules now reigns in power (1996-1997; cf. Hercules Furens 47-49, 55-56, 423, 566-568 where the victory of Hercules over the powers of Hades is celebrated).

Even when allowances are made for poetic license, the power of the image of the dying and conquering Hercules, the paradigm of moral virtue, is compelling. The myth rounds out the portrait of this θεῖος ἀνὴρ καὶ θεός (Ps. Lucian Cynicus 13) to the point that he is a clear rival to the Christ of the gospels, as the early Church recognized him to be. Such wealth of mythical metaphor, however, must not be allowed to obscure the specific conception of divine presence from which this myth springs. In spite of an abundance of pathetic fallacies used by

---

[126]Höistad, op. cit., pp. 61-63, discusses Epictetus' use of the Hercules myth and argues for its Cynic character. He remarks that "nowhere in cynicizing literature, so far as I am aware, is such a purely personal-religious use made of the figure of Heracles and the Heracles Epic." Perhaps he is unfair to Peregrinus.

Seneca in his description of the apotheosis of Hercules, it is Hercules, the paradigm of virtue, who is elevated to divinity.

The specificity of this understanding of Hercules is still recognizable. One of the most important clues has been found by Simon in his comparison of the tradition with the gospel accounts of Christ: "No precise detail connects the preaching and the miracles of Jesus to the feats of Hercules: the correspondences are limited here to a general identity based on the vocation of salvation."[127] The absence of the attribution of miracles to Hercules in this context as a means of authenticating him as divine man or benefactor or σωτήρ is not accidental or merely due to the fact that Hercules was not traditionally regarded as a miracle worker,[128] but the Hercules myth has been molded under the influence of the philosophical traditions where it is the life of moral virtue, particularly as evidenced in courage in the face of death, that authenticates the true divine man.[129]

---

[127]Op. cit., p. 64, my underlining.

[128]A writer like Philostratus, who is seeking to authenticate a miracle worker as a philosopher, does not hesitate to call on Hercules as a model for Apollonius' miracle working: Life of Ap. 4.45; 8.7 - here Hercules is cited precisely because he is a pure (καθαρός) deity and kindly to man who could never be accused of being a wizard (γόης).

[129]Although a writer like Justin who is defending a whole gospel tradition, including Jesus saving death, his sayings, and his miracles lines up Hercules right next to

This analysis of the vitality of the Hercules traditions in the Cynic and Stoic presentations and of the range of interpretations of this figure, from a hard-line Cynic ideal of self-sufficiency to a mythological image of a champion over the powers of Hades, provides a starting point for approaching Lucian's treatment of Peregrinus Proteus. First of all, it must be observed that Lucian is not indiscriminately opposed to the Hercules myth, particularly as interpreted in some Cynic traditions. Lucian can take broadsides at a Cynic like Alcidamas whom he considers to be a crass imitation of Hercules (cf. The Carousal 13,14,16). But he can also use the image of Hercules as a means for finding inspiration for facing his own old age with courage. The Hercules he looks to is Hercules the σοφός (Heracles 6) who accomplished everything with eloquence and used persuasion as his greatest force.[130] As the complete satirist, he can also mock Hercules as being among the dead while people are sacrificing to him as a god (Dialogi Mortuorum 16), but this may represent a stock Cynic attack on popular understandings of Hercules.[131]

Furthermore Lucian was clearly impressed by the Cynic

Asclepius (Dial. 69, I Apol 21), his criterion for deification is still the life of "holiness and virtue" (βιοῦν ὁσίως καὶ ἐναρέτως : I Apol. 21).

[130]For passages which show Hercules as the true philosopher, cf. Gruppe, PW Suppl III, p. 1011.

[131]Cf. Höistad, op. cit., pp. 64-65.

view of the true wise man and can use the great heroes of
Cynicism such as Antisthenes, Diogenes, and Crates to speak
for his own convictions.[132] In addition to the lost work
praising the Boeotian Sostratus "whom the Greeks called
Heracles" (Demonax 1), Lucian's praise for the Cynic Demonax
is a recitation of the virtues of the true philosopher, or,
if you will, an aretalogy, that explicitly intends both to
preserve Demonax in the memory of cultivated men and to
provide a paradigm (κανών/παράδειγμα) for young men to
emulate (ζηλοῦν : Dem. 2). The account of his youth (1-11)
does not display any supernatural origin but a disciplined
training in philosophy. Lucian insists that Demonax
belonged to no single philosophical school, but his life
style and his mode of aphoristic speech clearly follows
Diogenes (cf. 5, plus chriae in 12-62, 66). Moreover,
Socrates once again serves as a primary model for a true
philosopher, particularly when Demonax is being threatened
with death (cf. 5-6, 11, 58, 62). Lucian also portrays this
true philosopher as opposing magic (cf. 23, 25 (?)) and
divination (37), as being very cautious about any relationship with the cults (11, 27, 34), and critical of false
Cynicism (21,48).

As one well trained in philosophic virtue, Demonax also
knows how to die. Like a second Socrates, he clearly feels
his accusers who face him with stones in both hands can

---

[132]Cf. Marcel Caster, Lucien et la Pensée Religieuse de
son Temps (Paris, 1937), pp. 64-65.

really do him no harm (11), and like Hercules in the hard
line Cynic interpretation (cf. Dio of Prusa 8.34) and a host
of Cynic predecessors (cf. Diog. Laert. 6.18, 76, 95, 100),
Demonax voluntarily (ἑκών: 4) departed from life (ἀπῆλθεν
τοῦ βίου: 4, 65) without any grand vision that his death
would benefit anyone but himself (66).

This is the figure whom Lucian is willing to regard as
a divine man. Without his usual disclaimers, Lucian reports
that Demonax was a true healer of the soul, capable of
forgiveness which is the province of a god or of a man
equal to a god (θεὸς ἢ ἀνὴρ ἰσόθεος) , while it is man's
lot to sin (7). His gentle forgiveness also led people of
high and low station to regard him as a superior being (τὶς
τῶν κρειττων: 11). He was welcomed into the homes of all as
a divine visitation (τὶς θεοῦ) and bearer of good fortune
(τινὰ ἀγαθὸν δαίμονα : 63). And in spite of his own lack of
concern about his dead body, the Athenians gave him a big
funeral, mourned him long and worshipped (προσκυνεῖν) the
stone bench where he used to rest, decking it with garlands
and regarding it as sacred (ἱερόν: 67).

In marked contrast with his regard for the divine
Demonax, Lucian assails Peregrinus Proteus as a pseudo-
Cynic and a phoney imitator of Hercules. Although Lucian
scoffs at both Alexander the (false) prophet and Peregrinus
for their alleged divinity, it must be observed that the
primary bases for their claims were different. The
evidence for this discrimination must not be overstated.

Certainly the presentations overlap, and the traditions concerning these two figures quickly ran together in the second century.[133] But even in this period when the frequency of mixing propagandistic forms is increasing, it is possible to recognize that the foci of the two "aretalogies" that Lucian is mocking are distinct. The propagandistic presentation of Alexander has already been analyzed as concentrating on his miraculous acts, with less effort spent on making him philosophically respectable. Peregrinus, however, is primarily advertised as a Cynic philosopher who imitates Hercules to the point of death, and the accounts of miracles are merely secondary verification.

Clearly the true believers in Peregrinus wanted to present him in much the same light as Lucian presented Demonax. If the report that the Christians revered him as a god (ὡς θεός) can be set to one side as perplexing, even Lucian's report demonstrates that the followers of Peregrinus saw themselves as Cynic philosophers (2-4,24, 26,29,36,37,43), and the specific dispute between Demonax and Peregrinus appears to have been over who was truly Cynic (Demonax 21). Thus it is no surprise that Theagenes climaxes his oration on virtue (ἀρετή) by appealing to the

_____

[133]Cf. Athenagoras, Leg. de Christ., 26: the statues of Alexander and Proteus are said to have divine powers. The arguments that Hornsby, op. cit., pp. 73-77 puts forward to link these two figures on the basis of a neo-Pythagorean influence on Peregrinus are not particularly impressive.

example of Peregrinus (<u>Per</u>. 3-4). Peregrinus is credited
with the kind of histrionic display of the Cynic virtue of
indifference that Dio reports of Diogenes (<u>Per</u>. 17; <u>Dio</u>
6.16-20, 8.36; cf. <u>Diog</u>. <u>Laert</u>. 6.46). Such virtues may
have been distasteful to Demonax, but it is still clear
that Peregrinus is feted by the Cynics first of all as a
holy image (ἱερὸν ἄγαλμα : 6, 8) of virtue, comparable with
Diogenes, Antisthenes, Socrates, and even Zeus (6).[134]

The figure of Socrates, furthermore, has specific
exemplary value for interpreting the imprisonment and death
of Peregrinus. The references to this motif, however, are
so overlaid with polemic in Lucian that it is risky to attempt
to describe too precisely how Peregrinus' followers used
it. Yet in the light of the appeal to Socrates as a model
of virtue (6), the reference to the imprisoned Peregrinus
as the "new Socrates" (καινὸς Σωκράτης : 12)[135] and the taunt
about those who attended him at his death expecting to be
memorialized in a painting like the companions of the dying
Socrates (37) probably betray an appeal to the image of
Socrates to authenticate Peregrinus' own stature as an
imprisoned and dying model of virtue.

Hercules is the primary model for the passion of

---

[134]That the issue is moral virtue is clear both from the
fact that the oration was dealing with virtue (3) and also
from the rebuttal which seeks to discredit Peregrinus as a
model of moral virtue (8ff).

[135]It is also difficult to decide if it is significant
that this imprisonment took place while Peregrinus was a
Christian.

Peregrinus, but it is the Hercules who dies to prove a point
and not merely because it is in his self-interest to do so.
Here the presentation of Peregrinus parts company with
hard-line Cynicism, and Lucian catches him at it by insisting
that Hercules only committed suicide because he was ailing
(25). Peregrinus' aggressive imitation of Hercules has been
variously analyzed as "an isolated phenomenon" as proven
by "Lucian's own indignation,"[136] and as proof of the
existence of a "mystical Cynicism alongside of the skeptical
Cynicism of the second century".[137] Such an active pursuit
of apotheosis (29) is clearly singular.

Whatever the inspiration was for such an assertive
imitation of the death of Hercules,[138] Lucian clearly
opposed it as an attempt to allegorize such suicides as
philanthropic acts crowning a life of virtue. In addition
to the appeals to Hercules for the mode of suicide by fire
(4,21,33), the account of the death of Hercules/Peregrinus
clearly saw it as having a philanthropic value of teaching
men to despise death and bear with what is fearsome

---

[136]Höistad, op. cit., p. 68.

[137]Donald R. Dudley, A History of Cynicism (London, 1937),
cf. pp. 144, 178. Hornsby, op. cit., correctly insists,
however, that this exceptional feature must not be allowed
to obscure the clear Cynic features: "in its theatricality,
in its adherence to the Heracles myth and to the example of
the Brahmans, the death of Peregrinus is not un-Cynic."

[138]The verbal correlation with Ignatius Epistle to
Polycarp 7, which J.B. Lightfoot, The Apostolic Fathers,2 II,
(New York, 1889), p. 356, pointed out, may still bear scrutiny
since the Christian phase of the career of Peregrinus is well
documented by Lucian.

(ἐγκαρτερεῖν τοῖς δεινοῖς : 23). The last speech of Proteus
is reported to have been an account of his life and the
dangers he had faced and all the things he had endured for
the sake of philosophy (φιλοσοφίας ἕνεκα : 32). Thus the
climax to the account is clear, "one who has lived like
Hercules, should die like Hercules" in a display of disdain
for death (33).

Certainly the true believers of Peregrinus were not
hard-line Cynics; but apart from the feature of assertive
imitation, most of the details of the scenario of the death
of Hercules/Peregrinus could have been written by an admirer
of Hercules like Seneca. Even the pathetic and mythological
embellishments of the myth which Lucian mocks (39,41) might
have figured in a rehearsal of the event of Hercules' death
as narrated by a Stoic. But when Lucian implies that
Peregrinus was gaining a post-mortem reputation as a healer
(28)[139] and that an institutional cultus was growing around
his memory (27-28, 41, cf. also 11,13), and when Athenagoras
reports that the statue of Peregrinus is credited with
uttering oracles (Leg. ad. Christ 26), the philosophical
focus of the propaganda for Peregrinus has been obscured.

The charges from Lucian about what will probably result
(and did!) from the glorification of Peregrinus and the

---

[139]The concentration of miraculous material in paragraph
28 is unique. Did Lucian's source attempt to authenticate
him as divine on the basis of his ability as a healer or is
this Lucian's addition from growing cultic traditions about
Peregrinus and his shrine?

citation in Athenagoras demonstrate that the distinction
between the glorification of a hero of philosophical virtue
and the praise of a mighty miracle worker was becoming
increasingly blurred. In the case of Peregrinus, Lucian
deals with the formulation of his praises in a way which
shows that the positive presentation of him was still
recognizable as an attempt to authenticate him primarily
as a divine philosopher in much the same way as Lucian
praised Demonax. Thus the promoters of Peregrinus and
Lucian as the spokesman for Demonax attempted to treat their
respective subjects as models of divine virtue by using a
conventional form of appealing to the similarity of the
subject to the great models of philosophical virtue and
moral courage, as seen particularly in their disdain for
death.

A further illustration of the prevalence of the conception
of divine presence as revealed in moral excellence and the
specific strength of the image of Hercules as a paradigm
of divine virtue can be seen in the impact that his idealization had on the way Hellenistic rulers were glorified and
worshipped. Certainly this development is far too complex
to be explained simply by appealing to the Hercules motif,[140]
but as Anderson states it:

---

[140]Cf. Erwin R. Goodenough, "The Political Philosophy of
Hellenistic Kingship," Yale Classical Studies I (1928),
pp. 55-102. Note the discussion of the equation of being
godlike and knowing the virtues which Goodenough finds in
Musonius and Plutarch, pp. 94-98.

"Heracles will inaugurate an era of idyllic peace - a kind of golden age. Thus Heracles became the symbol of service, an outstanding σωτήρ in Greek religion, and to the subsequent pagan world he became the type of hero who chose to do the right irrespective of rewards or consequences."[141]

The force of this idealization was great on the growing impulse to deify the Hellenistic ruler. In the light of the previous assessment of Hercules as a paradigm of divine virtue, Taeger's discussion of Hercules as royal bearer of salvation further supports the observation that miracle working was not a primary means of authenticating the stature of such figures:

"Omen und Wunder waren hier noch weitverbreitete Vorstellungen, die der Rationalismus des 5. Jahrhunderts nur in ganz wenigen Menschen radikal ausgerottet hatte. Daran änderte die Tatsache nichts, dass sich hier das griechische Denken weit von dem orientalischen entfernt und den Raum des Wunders als Beglaubigung der Berufung auf ein Minimum reduziert hatte."[142]

The successors of Hercules are not miracle workers.

This does not mean that Hellenistic kings were never credited with miraculous acts. In the East, particularly in Egypt, traditions about kings as magicians and miracle workers demanded that the successors of a Pharaoh like Nectanebus, for example, be portrayed as a miracle worker or magician.[143] But Plutarch's Life of Pyrrhus provides a good illustration of the way attempts to authenticate a king on

---

[141]A.R. Anderson, "Heracles and His Successors," Harvard Studies in Classical Philology 39 (1928), p. 10.

[142]Fritz Taeger, Charisma (Stuttgart, 1957), I, p. 187.

[143]Cf. Martin Braun, History and Romance in Graeco-Roman Literature (Oxford, 1938), pp. 22-25.

the basis of miraculous actions were handled in the
philosophical tradition. In 3.4-5, Plutarch reports Pyrrhus'
reputation of miraculous power (δύναμιν θείαν) in a paragraph
which describes his bearing as being more terrible or
awesome (φοβερώτερον) than kingly. Plutarch includes the
kind of details which are prized in traditions about
magicians, such as the residence of this divine healing power
in Pyrrhus' big toe, which was imperishable, and the
honorarium of a white cock which indicates that the true
believers put him on a level with Asclepius on the basis of
this power. But such awesome tales have no authenticating
force in Plutarch's mind for describing Pyrrhus as a king.
As Mackay has pointed out, Pyrrhus is "the only subject of
the 'Lives' with a charismatic gift of healing" and "plainly
there is no expectation whatever in Plutarch's mind that a
hero ought to display supernatural gifts of healing."[144]

The healings attributed to Vespasian in Tacitus (Hist.
4.81 - Cass. Dio. 65.8) and Suetonius (Vespasian 7) are also
singular examples of an attempt to authenticate a ruler by
his possession of divine miraculous power. To be sure, a
writer like Suetonius can treat such performances as one of
the portents which authenticate the emperor,[145] but the

---

[144]B.S. Mackay, "Plutarch and the Miraculous," Miracles:
Cambridge Studies in their Philosophy and History, ed.
Charles F.D. Moule (London, 1965), pp. 106-107.

[145]Cf. R. Lattimore, "Portents and Prophecies in
Connection with the Emperor Vespasian," The Classical Journal
29 (1933), pp. 441 ff. R. Grant, Miracle and Natural Law,
op. cit., pp. 58, 176-177.

instance is unique because it is not merely another proof of
divine favor since, as Suetonius himself shows, the act
supplied Vespasian with dignity and a certain (divine?)
majesty (auctoritas et quasi maiestas quaedam) which he lacked
to that point.[146]

The importance of the fact that this event occurred in
Egypt was not wasted on Tacitus.[147] Clearly this kind of
authentication was possible and meaningful in that setting,
and the priests of Sarapis doubtless used it to fortify their
cause.[148] But meteorological and zoological prodigies aside,
such stories of a miracle working ruler are highly exceptional
in first century Rome.[149] Even in the hands of a hostile
witness like Tacitus who berates Egypt as the "most
superstitious of nations," the story points to a positive yet
completely different framework of understanding of the
"divine king" from any pattern affected by the image of
Hercules. Thus Morenz is probably correct that this event
relies on a peculiar local understanding of the miracle-
working pharaoh as θεὸς ἐπιφανής , but Morenz' attempt to

[146]Cf. Cassius Dio LXV 8.2: τὸ μὲν θεῖον τούτοις
αὐτὸν ἐσέμνυνεν.

[147]Cf. Siegfried Morenz, "Vespasian, Heiland der Kranken,"
Würzburger Jahrbuch für die Altertumswissenschaft IV/2 (1949/
1952), pp. 370-378. I am indebted to Professor Howard Kee
for this reference. Note that Taeger, op. cit., vol. I, p. 34
also emphasizes the geographical localization of the idea
that a ruler would be a wonderworker.

[148]Cf. Morenz, op. cit., p. 374.

[149]Cf. R. Lembert, Der Wunderglaube bei Römern und
Griechen (Augsburg, 1905), p. 40.

link this with "the general hellenistic image of the θεῖος ἀνήρ" is less helpful.[150]

Taeger has given a penetrating analysis of another first century writing, the Garland of Philiphus of Thessalonica, where the writer uses a miraculous growth of laurel on an altar of Caesar to authenticate Augustus as a god comparable to Zeus. This text (Anth. Pal. 9.307) is another exception which proves the rule. It is clearly intended to authenticate Augustus as divine and shows how a prodigy can be re-interpreted to fit another framework of understanding where the ruler was expected to work miracles:

> "Gleichzeitig benutzt der Dichter dieses Ereignis aber auch dazu, die Wunderkraft des Herrschers zu feiern und das römische Omen dadurch in die östliche Vorstellung von dem Wunder als der Bezeugung des charismatischen Auftrages umzubiegen."[151]

Traditions concerning Alexander the Great can be effectively classified according to this same distinction. The first fabulous history of Alexander's career which includes a spate of miraculous material has been precisely located by the studies of Budge. It was "composed and written in Egypt soon after his (Alexander's) death by an Egyptian, or by one whose interests were wholly Egyptian; if it was written by a Greek, he made use of materials which have been invented by the Egyptians."[152] One of the most

---

[150]Op. cit., pp. 374, 377.

[151]Taeger, op. cit., II, p. 202.

[152]E.A. Wallis Budge, Alexander the Great (London, 1896), p. ix.

important clues that has been discovered for unravelling the knot of this romance which is attributed to (pseudo) Callisthenes is the concentration of magical stories surrounding the "father" of Alexander, Nectanebus. This kernel of a "Nectanebus romance" is both the strongest evidence for the Egyptian origin of the Alexander romance and the necessary link to authenticate Alexander in the eyes of the Egyptians as the true successor to the divine Egyptian king.[153]

The contrast is marked between such attempts to document Alexander's divine character and the viewpoint that regarded him as a successor of Hercules, a true paradigm of divine virtue. Plutarch, for example, writes two treatises on Alexander, The Life of Alexander and On the Fortune of Alexander, with frequent explicit references to Hercules, in the attempt to display Alexander as a divine philosopher. Obviously he knows traditions which seek to authenticate Alexander's divine stature simply on the basis of miraculous displays, and he can briefly report the stories of the omens that accompanied Alexander's birth (Life: 2.2-3.3). Particularly in the Life, Plutarch records a great host of prodigies and portents and he displays Alexander as increasingly more influenced by such events. But such reports only intend to show Alexander's gradual dissipation as a leader, accompanied by his departure from the life of

---

[153]Cf. Budge, op. cit., pp. ix-xviii. Martin Braun, op. cit., pp. 22-25, & 42. R. Grant, op. cit., p. 176.

philosophy. In his decline and fall, the philosopher
Anaxarchus berates him for losing his royal stature by being
so susceptible (Life 52.3), and Plutarch describes
Alexander's sinking state in terms of superstition (δεισιδαιμονία),
"which, after the manner of water ever seeking the lower
levels, filled with folly the Alexander who was now become a
prey to his fears" (Life 75.2).

The divine Alexander, on the other hand, is a true
philosopher in complete self-control, a genuine successor of
Hercules. The whole point of the treatise On the Fortune of
Alexander is to show that his training as a philosopher and
cultivation of the virtues led to his success, rather than
crediting his accomplishments to any stroke of good fortune
or divine intervention. His beginnings in poverty (On Fort.
327 D-e), his equipment of greatness of soul (μεγαλοψυχία)
keen intelligence, self-restraint and manly courage (328 B)
are all due to philosophy. He was a philosopher comparable
to Plato, Socrates, Aristotle, and Zeno (329 A-C). Even the
account of his skill as a healer shows him not as a miracle
worker, but as an apt pupil of Aristotle (Life 8).[154]

Plutarch is not adverse to the mythological story of
Alexander's divine origin, but the account is allegorized,
and the proof of his divine nature is seen in his acts of
virtue. Alexander is still human, and Plutarch observes
that the wounded Alexander bled real blood, not the ichor

[154]Cf. Mackay, op. cit., p. 106.

that flows from immortals (On Fort. 341 B; Life 28.2).
Alexander was not foolishly affected by those who regarded
him as divine (Fort. 331 A, Life 28.3); rather he displayed
the scars on his body as symbols of virtue (ἀρετή)   and
courage (Fort. 331 C). That which truly displayed his
divine origin was that the god who bore him bestowed upon him
a harmonious combination of many virtues (ἐκ πολλῶν συνήρμοσε
καὶ συνέθηκεν ἀρετῶν ὁ γεννήσας θεός)   so that he possessed
the moral virtues of all the greats (Fort. 343 A-E). Even
the vanquished recognized him as one who was superior to
human nature (τὸ δοκεῖν ὑπ' ἀνδρὸς ἡττῆσθαι
κρείττονος ἢ κατὰ τὴν ἀνθρωπίνην φύσιν)
in his displays of virtue (Life 30.5). Plutarch's Alexander
can recognize all men as offspring of god, but those who are
most noble (ἄριστος) belong peculiarly to the god (Life
27.6); and when he makes a great display of virtue, his men
could look upon that example and even regard themselves as
more than mortal (οὔθ' ὅλως θνητός: Life 42.6).

This divergence between the traditions of Alexander
which show him, in one instance, as the son of an Egyptian
pharaoh whose divinity is displayed in magical feats, and,
in the other case, as the true descendent of Hercules, the
paradigm of divine virtue, further illustrates the
distinction that existed in the Hellenistic world between
conceptions of divine presence in men. Plutarch's Alexander
not only is cast in a different mold, but is authenticated
as divine by reason of his virtue, with explicit cautions
of the attempts to authenticate his divinity on the basis of

a miraculous birth or the possession of power to work miracles.
Plutarch is a great deal less critical in his historical
judgment and inclusion of mythological details than a biog-
rapher like Arrian,[155] but Plutarch's criterion is still
clear: the true successor of Hercules shows his divinity
in his display of philosophical or moral virtue; once he
begins to lose that quality, he sinks to the low level of
superstition.

The cultivation of the image of Hercules as the model
for the ideal king has a complex history of its own in
Cynic and Stoic tradition. It is worth noting that Alexander
was not always credited with measuring up to the pattern
of Hercules (cf. Dio of Prusa 4; Seneca de Ben. 1.13.1-2;
7.3.1). But rather than get too deeply involved in a
discussion of Hellenistic theories of kingship, suffice it
to observe that the figure of Hercules, the divine king,
served as a standard by which rulers were measured. He was
the paradigm of a world ruler, a σωτήρ of the whole earth
and all mankind" (Dio of Prusa 1.84). His reign, however,
was not marked by miraculous displays or tyranical actions,
but by humility, poverty, compassion, homelessness, and
suffering (cf. Dio of Prusa 1.59-65, 9.8-9; Epictetus

---

[155]It is not an accident that Arrian, the student of
Epictetus, was able to sort out the romantic legends and
myths and provide the most historically reliable picture of
Alexander. He, too, can include a variety of legendary
accounts, particularly of the death of Alexander (cf. Anabasis
7.27; 7.30.2), but a catalog of virtues (7.28-30) appeals to
Arrian as the proper summation of Alexander's life.

2.16.44; 3.22.57-59; 3.26.31-32).[156] By this criterion, Dio
of Prusa could evaluate the rule of Domitian and Trajan, and
Philo of Alexandria could describe Gaius as a phoney successor
of Hercules because he did not imitate the virtues (Leg. ad
Gaium 81-91) and could praise Augustus who "surpassed human
nature by all the virtues" (Leg. ad Gaium 143-150).[157]

Thus in the Hellenistic world, diverse attempts to
authenticate the divine stature or power of a charismatic
figure can be identified, and the criteria which were used
to evaluate such claims can still be distinguished. It
should be carefully observed, however, that the witnesses to
this discrimination that have been cited above belong to
the educated and literary stratum of Greco-Roman culture and
can be dated, for the most part, prior to the mid-second
century A.D. Both of these qualifications are important
since it is in those circles that the image of the sage as
the true divine man who authenticates his stature by displaying the virtues was still a lively criterion and because
the vitality of this discrimination was rapidly breaking
down.

It is perhaps possible to take a barometric reading of
the changing cultural climate of this phase of the

---

[156]Cf. Wilfred L. Knox, "The 'Divine Hero' Christology
in the New Testament," HTR 41 (1948), pp. 229-249.

[157]Cf. Josephus' attack on Athronges (Antiq. 17.278)
where he berates a man with no virtue for having the audacity
to aspire to kingship.

Hellenistic period by comparing the perspectives on this point represented by Plutarch and Seneca in the first century, Lucian in the second, and Philostratus and Porphyry in the third. In the texts discussed above, Plutarch and Seneca confidently display the divine sage Socrates and his moral courage in the face of death in order to dismiss attempts to authenticate figures as divine on the basis of miraculous displays. Lucian is fighting on several fronts in an attempt to maintain this criterion, but the growth and convergence of the cults of such figures as Peregrinus and Alexander show he is fighting a bitter and losing battle against popular response. Philostratus and Porphyry, by contrast, appear to have made peace with Lucian's opposition; and although they are still aware of the philosophical standard, they maintain that Apollonius and Pythagoras were divine by describing their heroes as both sages and miracle workers.

The cultural complexity of this period obviously demands that no single factor be isolated and treated as the key to understanding the whole process. The erosion of the resistance to teratological accounts is also to be seen against the background of the futile efforts to preserve traditional Roman religion[158] and the struggle to maintain the political order against the insidious influences of the magicians, astrologers, and soothsayers.[159] Furthermore the

---

[158]Cf. A.D. Nock, Conversion (London, 1933), pp. 66-137.

[159]Cf. Ramsay MacMullen, Enemies of the Roman Order (Cambridge, 1966), pp. 95-162.

direct competition between the attempts to authenticate charismatic heroes as divine and the eventual efforts to use both sets of standards simultaneously suggest a conceptual commonality. From differing perspectives, these praise formulations give evidence of a shared expectation of the documentation of the presence of divinity in particular figures.

Nevertheless, the texts which have been discussed demonstrate that the basis upon which a figure was authenticated as divine was not an indifferent matter to Hellenistic literary authors. The carefully cultivated image of the ideal wise man whose life and death display his divine moral excellence provided a control by which the admixture of teratological elements, which held great fascination for increasingly wider cultural circles, could be resisted.

Chapter Two: IMAGES OF MOSES IN HELLENISTIC JUDAISM
A.   Philo of Alexandria *53373*

The figure of Moses was one of the most important
propaganda instruments that Jews of the Hellenistic period
appropriated for their competition with non-Jewish schools
and cults as well as inter-Jewish sectarian disputes. In
this regard, Judaism is not an exception in the Hellenistic
world. Just as the philosophers, demi-gods, and heroes of
the Greek tradition were variously depicted and imitated in
the attempts to propagate diverse ideologies and life
styles, so charismatic figures of Jewish tradition were
variously idealized and imitated by those who sought to make
a case for Judaism, as they perceived it. And like the
images of Socrates and Hercules which have been discussed
in the previous chapter, the image of Moses was highly
differentiated in the Hellenistic period, which facilitated
diverse presentations of this charismatic figure as
occasioned by particular contexts and divergent religious
understandings.

The abundance and rich variety of Old Testament
traditions about Moses clearly allows for a multiplicity of
portrayals. In contrast to the more fluid divine hierarchy
in the Greek world, no human figure in the Old Testament
is thought to attain actual divine status, although men can
be divinely chosen to speak for God, are occasionally
endowed with divine power, or even may play the role of God
before other men. Moses is a striking example of such an

101

Old Testament charismatic figure who stands particularly
close to God, and clues to his elevated status can be found
in several Old Testament texts.

An indication of the special relationship between Moses
and God which was of interest to subsequent Hellenistic
authors is Moses' title "man of God" (ἄνθρωπος θεοῦ/ הֱאלֹהִים איש)
Deut. 33: 1, Josh. 14:6, Ezra 3:2, Ps. 90:1). It is worth
noting, in passing, that the application of this title to
Moses in the Old Testament is not associated with his role
as miracle worker,[1] but in Joshua and Ezra it is connected
with his continuing authority as legislator.

Several descriptive allusions to Moses' direct
communication with God provide another illustration of the
privileged status that Moses enjoyed in God's presence.
Exodus 33:11 reports that God "used to speak to Moses face
to face (ἐνώπιος ἐνωπίῳ/ פנים אל פנים) as a man speaks to his
friend" (φίλος/רעה). In Numbers 12:6-8, Moses' superiority
to the visionary prophets (προφήτης/נביא) lies clearly in
his direct "mouth to mouth" (στόμα κατὰ στόμα/ פה אל פה)
communication with God. And in the closing verses of
Deuteronomy (34:10-12) after Moses' death has been recounted,
the qualifications for a prophet (προφήτης/נביא) like Moses
are mentioned in terms of knowing God face to face (πρόσωπον
κατὰ πρόσωπον/פנים אל פנים) and signs and wonders (σημεῖα καὶ τέρατα/

---

[1] Note that this title is applied to Elijah and Elisha
in the books of Kings in miracle accounts (I Kings 17:18, II
Kings 4:7), cf. also I Kings 13:1-4.

וְהַמֹּפְתִים (הַאֹתֹת) and mighty powers and great and terrible
deeds (τὰ θαυμάσια τὰ μεγάλα καὶ τὴν χεῖρα τὴν κραταιάν/הֶחָזָקָה דִּיד
(וְכָל) הַמּוֹרָא הַגָּדוֹל). Thus although the Deuteronomist
refuses to let miraculous performances be the sole criterion
for authenticating a prophet like Moses (cf. Deut. 13:1-5,
18:9-22), it is clear that the signs and wonders are essential
for authenticating the special presence of God with the
prophet like Moses.

A third illustration of Moses' special status before God
is his assigned role as "God" (θεός/אֱלֹהִים) before Aaron
(Exodus 4:16) and Pharaoh (Exodus 7:1). In both cases,
playing the part of God means primarily to speak the
message of God, but the presence of the divine in Moses'
speech is verified in both instances by his performance of
miraculous acts.

This correlation between Moses' divine or semi-divine
role as a messenger and his power to work miracles, many of
which involve magic, points up a methodological problem of
handling Hellenistic traditions about Moses. Assuming that
the Old Testament traditions would have been well known by
any group that sought to glorify Moses, Hellenistic
portrayals of him must be distinguished according to the
aspect(s) of the tradition they stress. Of course scholars
have long been aware of differentiation in the image of
Moses and have pointed out Hellenistic adaptations, but the
Moses of the Old Testament tradition has been treated as a
prefiguration of the θεῖος ἀνήρ since all of the necessary

aspects of such an idealization and life history are to be
found there in nuce.[2] This approach has had the effect of
unifying several Hellenistic treatments of Moses, but it is
probably not unfair to maintain that the unity that has
been perceived in those depictions arises as much from the
Old Testament as from the consistency of the Hellenistic
concept of the θεῖος ἀνήρ. If, however, Hellenistic
portrayals of Moses can be seen to diverge on the
importance of a particular feature of the Old Testament
portrait, such as his ability to work miracles, at least
it ought to be possible to recognize differing ways in
which Moses served as a paradigm of divine presence in
various streams of Jewish propaganda.

In a recent Harvard dissertation, John Gager makes an
observation on the images of Moses in pagan literature
which appears to be highly supportive of the kind of
discrimination this study seeks to describe. In contrast to
the treatment of Moses as the lawgiver of the Jews by Greek
and Roman literary authors, Gager discovers that:

> "On the whole, however, the Moses of the magical
> documents is a figure unto himself. Here he emerges as
> an inspired prophet, endowed with divine wisdom and
> power, whose very name guaranteed the efficacy of
> magical charms and provided protection against the
> hostile forces of the cosmos."[3]

---

[2]Cf. Hans Windisch, Paulus und Christus (Untersuchungen
zum Neuen Testament, Heft 24; Leipzig, 1934), pp. 89-114.
Ludwig Bieler, ΘΕΙΟΣ ΑΝΗΡ (Wien, 1934-1935), vol. II, pp. 5-8.

[3]John G. Gager, The Figure of Moses in Greek and Roman
Pagan Literature, (unpublished Dissertation: Harvard
University, 1968), p. 312.

The study of pagan understandings of Moses lies beyond the sphere of this study, but the point is intriguing for two reasons. First of all, the lines between what is Jewish or Jewish syncretistic and pagan are not easily drawn, particularly on the cultural level where magical displays are regarded as a primary means for demonstrating divine presence.[4] Secondly, it appears self-evident that pagan conceptions of Moses would be heavily dependent upon propagandistic presentations of him by Jews. Thus such a differentiation in pagan views of Moses probably points to a divergence between the ways the Jews depicted him and recited his praises.

Within the spectrum of Jewish attempts to rehearse the praises of Moses in the Hellenistic period, Philo of Alexandria provides the most complete picture of how traditions about Moses could be appropriated in a particular setting. Philo's thorough acquaintance with the broad range of Old Testament traditions about Moses is unquestionable, and his interpretation of those materials in order to show Moses to his audience as a "divine man" of great stature has been well established.[5] Yet the questions of the identity of Philo's audience and exactly what kind of

---

[4]Ibid., pp. 312-314. W.L. Knox, "Jewish Liturgical Exorcism," HTR 31 (1938), pp. 191-203.

[5]This insight which provides a point of departure for this study has so permeated the secondary literature that it would be pointless to credit all those who have discussed the point. Certainly the works of Reitzenstein, Bieler, and Windisch which are frequently mentioned in the notes have been fundamental.

divine man he had in view deserve further scrutiny.

As knowledge of the complexity and diversity of Hellenistic Judaism increases, it is less certain whether particular crucial pieces such as De vita Mosis were written for a pagan or a Jewish audience. For a time, a scholarly consensus appeared to be emerging on the point that De vita Mosis was "another apology for the Jews, this one addressed to friendly rather than hostile pagans, who would like to know who the great Moses was of whom Jews were so proud, and what he did."[6] The remaining question was merely whether other pieces such as those in Philo's Exposition of the Law also belonged to the apologetic missionary literature directed to pagans.[7] Recent studies of the diversity of Jewish groups in Alexandria and their varying degrees of Hellenization[8] have, however, made such classifications more tenuous, except in the cases of the explicitly apologetic works such as In Flaccum and De legatione ad Gaium.[9] Indeed, precise determinations as to

---

[6]Erwin R. Goodenough, An Introduction to Philo Judaeus (New Haven, 1940), pp. 37-38. Cf. Dieter Georgi, Die Gegner des Paulus im 2. Korintherbrief (Wissenschaftliche Monographien z.A. & N.T.; Neukirchen, 1964), p. 55, n.5; p. 94, n.5. For a contrary view cf. M.A. Halevy, Moise (Judaisme VI, Études Publiées sous la direction de P.L. Couchard; Paris, 1927), p. 72.

[7]Erwin R. Goodenough, "Philo's Exposition of the Law and His De Vita Mosis," HTR 26 (1933), pp. 109-125.

[8]Cf. V. Tcherikover and Fuks, Corpus Papyrorum Judaicarum, Vol. I (Cambridge, 1957), pp. 1-111. V. Tcherikover, Hellenistic Civilization and the Jews, trans. S. Applebaum (Philadelphia, 1959).

[9]Cf. V. Tcherikover, "Jewish Apologetic Literature Reconsidered," Eos 48,3 (1956), pp. 169-193.

who was a Jew in the era of Philo have become much more elusive.[10]

The recognition that the lines of distinction between paganism and first century Judaism were blurred at many points affects this study directly. First of all, it cautions against hasty attempts to isolate "apologetic" works which are directed at heathens from the general religious propaganda of Judaism which may be aimed at Greeks, Alexandrians, or Hellenistic Jews.[11] Moses may be praised by Philo as much to encourage the cultured Jew who tends to be embarrassed of his tradition as to win respect from the non-Jew. The general rubric of religious propaganda does not limit the missionary effort to the non-Jew.[12] Secondly, this recognition highlights the diversity of interpretations of a figure like Moses who was doubtless claimed as the spokesman for every kind of sectarian viewpoint. There is no one image of Moses which is modified to be made palatable

---

[10]Cf. Comments by H. Koester recorded in the "Minutes" for the New Testament Seminar 201 at Harvard Divinity School, April 6, 1970. Erwin R. Goodenough, Jewish Symbols in the Greco-Roman Period. Vols. 1-12, New York: Pantheon Books, 1953-1965. (Bollingen Series, 37.) Alf Thomas Kraabel, Judaism in Western Asia Minor under the Roman Empire. Unpublished doctoral dissertation: Harvard University, 1968.

[11]I take this point to be one of the implications of H. Koester's clarification that "aretalogies are not used only to defend certain religious tenets; they are not simply apologetic," "One Jesus and Four Gospels," HTR 61 (1968), p. 232, cf. note 101.

[12]Such a clarification is necessary to maximize the usefulness of studies like that of P. Dalbert, Die Theologie der Hellenistisch-Jüdischen Missionsliteratur unter Ausschluss von Philo und Josephus (Theologische Forschung: Wissenschaftliche Beiträge zur Kirchlich-Evangelischen Lehre: Hamburg, 1954).

to pagans, but several groups are each proclaiming "another Moses."

Philo's Moses is a "divine man." Even the specific term θεῖος ἀνήρ is used once by Philo in an apparent reference to Moses (Virt. 177). But the term is by no means focal for Philo, and the precise value that the concept had for him can only be assessed by looking at the way in which he used other figures of Old Testament traditions who approach Moses' peculiar divine or semi-divine stature.

Whether he was speaking to pagans or Hellenistic Jews, Philo clearly elevated the patriarchs to a lofty status by treating them first of all as paradigms of virtue.[13] Beginning at the lower end of the scale of virtue with Enos the hoper, Enoch who migrated from vice to virtue, and Noah who was "perfect in his generation" (Genesis 6:9) but not absolutely perfect, Philo sees these three as mere babes, yearning for virtue, in comparison with the athletes[14] of

---

[13]Georgi, op. cit., pp. 51 ff, has demonstrated the strong element of national pride that was involved in such presentations. This was probably necessary both to bolster Jewish self-consciousness and to defend against anti-Jewish polemics.

[14]The use of the image of "athletes" is striking in the light of Cynic-Stoic use of the term to describe the virtuous Hercules (cf. previous chapter). Donald R. Dudley, A History of Cynicism (London, 1937), p. 186, observes that for Philo "unremitting πόνος is essential if virtue is to be attained: to God alone belongs the faculty of possessing the Good without πόνος." Jacob the wrestler is a particularly fitting example of the athlete who struggles for virtue; cf. Sob. 65, Mut. 84-85, Mig. 26-27, 199-200, Con. 70, Fug. 43, Som. I 126, 129, 131, 168, 179, 251, Abr. 48, Jos. 26, 223, 230, Virt. 210 (contrasted with Esau).

virtue who follow them (<u>Abr</u>. 7-48; <u>Praem</u>. 13-24).

Without repeating the discussion of the ideal Stoic σοφός , whose possession of ἀρετή , moral virtue, qualifies him as divine, it is quickly apparent that Philo's treatment of the patriarchs as models of virtue and "divine men" is directly dependent upon that conceptual framework.[15] The previous chapter on the figure of Hercules has already demonstrated that in an explicitly apologetic framework such as that in <u>De legatione ad Gaium</u>, Philo could appeal to the paradigm of the Cynic-Stoic tradition as a criterion of the true divine man. But Philo's treatment of the ascending scale of patriarchal patterns of perfection from Enos, Enoch, and Noah, to Abraham, Isaac, and Jacob, and ending in Moses, demonstrates that the principle that the σοφός is the possessor of ἀρετή is also determinative of his evaluation of these figures, whether he is dealing with them in treatises that have been regarded as "apologetic" or those which scholars have thought were directed to Jewish audiences. It is because they are σοφοί and to the degree that they are thus possessors of ἀρετή that the patriarchs are the true prophets, priests, and rulers who can exercise these offices in unique partnership with God. Philo may be less critical of miraculous displays of

---

[15]Cf. E. Turowski, <u>Die Widerspiegelung des Stoischen Systems bei Philon von Alexandria</u> (Leipzig, 1927), pp. 41-42. E. Bréhier, <u>Les idées philosophiques et religieuses de Philon d'Alexandrie</u> (Études de philosophie médiévale, dir. É. Gilson, VIII, Paris, 1925), pp. 252-259.

divine presence than Cicero or Seneca, but that which
authenticates his charismatic figures as "divine"[16] is not
their possession of magical or miraculous powers but their
displays of virtue.

Abraham, Isaac, and Jacob who stand on the second level
of perfection as   σοφοί, superior to Enos, Enoch, and
Noah, are all God lovers and beloved of God (φιλοθέοι
καὶ θεοφιλεῖς: Abr. 50) who come to share God's name because
of their "high and life long virtue" (Abr. 50). Philo
emphasizes the view that these three are primarily exemplars
of virtue: "the first called Abraham, the second Isaac and
the third Jacob are symbols (σύμβολον) of virtue acquired
respectively by teaching, nature and practice" (Abr. 52).[17]
Since it is axiomatic for the Stoics and for Philo that none
of the virtues is truly possessed without possessing all,[18]
"Moses thus associated these three together, nominally men,
but really, as I have said, virtues - teaching, nature, and

---

[16]Windisch, op. cit., pp. 108-112, discusses the
observation that Philo may have had some hesitation at using
the adjective θεῖος to describe the patriarchs, but
Windisch shows a synonymous usage of a variety of terms.

[17]Philo appears to be undecided about how to treat
Joseph. While in Leg. All., Joseph appears as a man wise in
his own conceits, in Jos. his administrative skill is praised.
Although the political life is secondary to the contemplative
for Philo, it is necessary. Thus Joseph, whose name is
interpreted to mean "addition" (positively in Jos. 28,
negetively in Mut. 89-90, Som. II 47, 63), is not a primary
example of virtue but secondary.

[18]Cf. S.V.F. vol. III, #295,304, pp. 72-74, especially
Diog. Laert. 7.125, Philo Mos. II, 7.

practice" (λόγῳ μὲν ἀνδρῶν ἔργῳ δ' ὡς εἶπον ἀρετῶν: <u>Abr</u>. 54).[19]
This idealization of the exemplars further extends to the
point where they are said to have married not women but
virtues: "for the helpmeets of these men are called women,
but are in reality virtues (λόγῳ μέν εἰσι γυναῖκες, ἔργῳ
δὲ ἀρεταί), Sarah 'sovereign and leader,' Rebecca 'stead-
fastness in excellence,' Leah 'rejected and faint' through
the unbroken discipline which every fool rejects and turns
from with words of denial" (<u>Cher</u>. 41).[20] Consequently it is
because they are σοφοί and possessors of virtue that these
patriarchs are the bearers of the divine name, "the God of
Abraham, the God of Isaac and the God of Jacob" (<u>Abr</u>. 51,
cf. <u>Mos</u>. I 76, <u>Mut</u>. 11 ff). Furthermore these figures have
a share in immortality because the virtues they possess and
represent are eternal:

> "... thus the eternal name revealed in the oracular
> utterances refers to the stated faculties rather than
> to mere men. For the nature of man is corruptible
> (φθαρτὴ φύσις) but that of virtue is imperishable.
> And it is more reasonable that what is eternal (τὸ
> ἀίδιον) refer to incorruptible things rather than
> mortal (ἀφθάρτοις πρὸ θνητῶν), since imperishability
> is related to incorruption, while death is at enmity
> with it" (<u>Abr</u>. 54f, cf. <u>Sac</u>. 5-7, <u>Som</u>. II 229-231).

---

[19]This passage is explicitly an anticipation of a much
more developed conceptualization of these patriarchs.
Although the treatises on Isaac and Jacob are not extant,
these basic qualifications are heavily elaborated for each
figure in the Philonic corpus we possess. The threefold
division is itself frequently repeated: cf. <u>Cong</u>. 35-36,
<u>Mut</u>. 12, <u>Som</u>. I 168-172, <u>Mos</u>. I 76, <u>Praem</u>. 27, 49-51, <u>Sac</u>. 5-7.

[20]Each of the wives as a representative of virtue is
praised separately in numerous texts. In <u>Post</u>. 62, all six
figures are mentioned as pairs of virtues and their possessors.

Philo is elevating Abraham, Isaac and Jacob to the status of "divine men" by direct appeal to the criterion of virtue. Indeed, the standard of evaluation is so explicitly focal that the historical patriarchs appear at times to have been reduced to abstractions. Further study might determine why Philo appears to outdo his Stoic contemporaries in idealizing his heroes of virtue. For the present purpose, however, it will suffice to point out how Philo follows the Stoic mode of depicting the divine wise man in his discussion of the possession of virtue as the indispensable condition for the fulfillment of the roles of prophet, priest and king.

Philo's conception of prophecy and of the ecstatic state of the prophet is singular. Like the Middle Platonists, he conceived of a gap between the intellectual ascent to knowledge of God and the ultimate grasping of the Divine which required non-cognitive means, but Philo turned to revelation which is imparted to the prophet by the θεῖος λόγος as the divinely initiated effort to bridge that gap (cf. Fug. passim & 101).[21] Consequently his description of prophecy as a special member of the four types of ecstasy (Quis Her. 249-258) allows all those whom he calls prophets to engage in a wider range of religious and cultic activities than many of Philo's contemporaries

---

[21]Cf. H.A. Wolfson, "Albinus and Plotinus on Divine Attributes," HTR 45 (1952), pp. 115-130.

in the schools would have permitted in their idealizations of charismatic figures. But stopping short of a discussion of Philo's "mystic gospel",[22] it is germane to this study to point out the basis on which Philo's charismatic figures are qualified to be prophets. The crucial text follows directly after the description of prophecy as divinely initiated ecstasy, Quis Her. 259-260:

παντὶ δὲ ἀστείῳ προφητείαν ὁ ἱερὸς λόγος μαρτυρεῖ·
προφήτης γὰρ ἴδιον μὲν οὐδὲν ἀποφθέγγεται, ἀλλότρια
δὲ πάντα ὑπηχοῦντος ἑτέρου· φαύλῳ δ᾽ οὐ θέμις ἑρμηνεῖ
γενέσθαι θεοῦ, ὥστε κυρίως μοχθηρὸς οὐδεὶς ἐνθουσιᾷ,
μόνῳ δὲ σοφῷ ταῦτ᾽ ἐφαρμόττει, ἐπεὶ καὶ μόνος ὄργανον
θεοῦ ἐστιν ἠχεῖον, κρουόμενον καὶ πληττόμενον ἀοράτως
ὑπ᾽ αὐτοῦ. πάντος γοῦν ὁπόσους ἀνέγραψε δικαίους
κατεχομένους καὶ προφητεύοντας εἰσήγαγεν.

"The holy word assures the gift of prophecy to every
good man. For a prophet utters no message of his own
but only words foreign to him since another is sounding
through him. And it is not the privilege of a bad
man to be god's interpreter, so that no villain is
divinely inspired. This is fitting only for the wise
man since he alone is god's vocal instrument as he is
invisibly struck and played by God. Hence all those
he (Moses) describes as righteous, he brings forward as
possessed and prophesying."

Among the notable features of this statement is the Stoic flavor of the absolute distinction between the good and evil men. No intermediate moral conditions are considered.

---

[22]Cf. Erwin R. Goodenough, By Light, Light (New Haven, 1935), W. Bousset and H. Gressmann, Die Religion des Judentums im Spathellenistischen Zeitalter (Handbuch zum Neuen Testament, 21, Tübingen, 1966⁴), pp. 249-254, where correlations with Orphism are drawn to account for the peculiar description of prophecy. R. Meyer, "προφήτης," TDNT VI (ed. G. Kittel, trans. by G. Bromiley; Grand Rapids, 1968), pp. 821-823.

On the positive side stands the man who is ἀστεῖος ,[23]
προφήτης, σοφός, δίκαιος, κατεχόμενος.   The antithesis is
represented by ὁ φαῦλος and μοχθηρός . This strict
distinction between ὁ σοφός/σπουδαῖος and ὁ φαῦλος
is not an isolated instance in Philo. Indeed it extends to
his view that the σοφός as possessor of virtue has a share
in the incorruptible life.[24]

Furthermore, the propositional logic of this passage
establishes the qualification of the prophet without
allowing for any exclusions. The statement that only the
sage can bear the name "prophet" eliminates all other
pretenders. No doubt this conception of the wise man as the
only one who can be gripped by the divine word is also
fundamental to Philo's polemic against every other kind of
divination (μαντική)   indulged in by those who are not
perfect (τέλειοι: Spec. Leg. I 59-65) and indicates that

---

[23] ἀστεῖος is a term used by Philo in reference to the
child Moses (Mos. I 9, 18), but since the LXX (Exodus 2.2)
also uses this term for the infant (cf. Acts 7:2 and Hebrews
11:23), the specific value that the term had for Philo is
less obvious in that context. The Stoic coloring of the
word is much clearer in Conf. 106 (109) where the emphasis
on virtue is also connected with Moses' world citizenship
(cf. Op. 3, Mos. I 157, Cong. 132, Quis Her. 19, Som. II 227,
230). The Stoic opposition between ὁ ἀστεῖος and ὁ
φαῦλος is also found in Abr. 103, Fug. 55, Plant. 172,
Conf. 109, cf. Fug. 18 ἀστεῖος opposed to μοχθηρός.

[24]Cf. Det. 49: "The wise man, when seeming to die to
the corruptible life, is alive to the incorruptible; but
the worthless man (ὁ φαῦλος) , while alive to the life of
wickedness, is dead to the life happy." The Stoic theme
that the φαῦλος has no portion of the life of virtue is
also sounded frequently. Cf. Som. II 256, Leg. All. I 34,
54, III 1, 48, 54, Sac. 18.

the imposter (γόης) who appears in the guise of the prophet
could never be divinely inspired like the true θεσπέσιοι
ἄνδρες who assist the law in training others for virtue
(Spec. Leg. I 314-315).[25] But Philo also gives the converse
of the proposition by insisting that "the divine word
assures every ἀστεῖος of the gift of prophecy" and "all
those Moses describes as righteous (δίκαιος) he also brings
forward as possessed and prophesying" (cf. Wisdom 7:27).

It is in this light that Noah, Isaac, Jacob, Moses and
Abraham[26] are authenticated as prophets (Quis Her. 260-266).
There is no appeal made to the possession of miraculous
powers as a means of verification. Although any argument
from silence is questionable, the absence of this criterion
must be noted since the text of Genesis 20:7 to which Philo
is referring in Quis Her. 258 reads: "restore the man's
wife; for he is a prophet, and he will pray for you, and
you shall live" and Genesis 20:17 indicates that Abraham's

---

[25]The ethical criterion for evaluating the προφήτης
and the γόης is clear. The issue of whether such person
had miraculous or magical powers is not even in view. This
observation works against Windisch's comment on Spec. Leg. I
315: "Der Thaumaturg ist entweder ein θεῖος oder ein
'Magier.'" Note that Abraham's experience of ecstasy is
not sufficient to prove him to be a prophet either (Quis Her.
258). Furthermore, when Philo defends Moses against the
charge that he was a γόης, he praises his eloquence and
administrative skills but makes no mention of performance of
miracles (Hyp. 6. 1-4).

[26]Abraham's stature as a prophet also receives comment
in Virt. 219. Here the connection is even more explicit
between his possession of the virtues to the point of a
perfection that exceeds human nature (217) and his receipt
from God, the friend of virtue (φιλάρετος: 218) of the ranks
of prophet and king.

prayer was instrumental in the healing of Abimelech, his
wife, and female slaves. This is the very connection
between the office of prophet and the performance of a
miraculous healing that modern studies of the θεῖος ἀνήρ
have watched for in Hellenistic texts.[27] But Philo appears
to ignore the interpretation of the prophet as miracle
worker which the Genesis text suggests. Philo's silence
on this point may have been shared by (pseudo?) Eupolemus,[28]
and Josephus appears to have taken pains to remove the blame
for Abimelech's illness and the credit for his recovery from
Abraham.[29]

---

[27]Cf. note 25 above.

[28]Eusebius, The Preparation for the Gospel 9.17, 6-7:
"And when there was a famine, Abraham departed for Egypt with
his whole household and dwelt there and the king of Egypt
married his wife because he said she was his sister. And he
further tells that he was unable to consort with her and it
happened that his people and his house were perishing and he
called diviners (μάντις) who revealed that the woman was
not a widow. And the king of the Egyptians thus recognized
that she was Abraham's wife and gave her back to her husband."
The mention of the diviners indicates that Eupolemus has
probably conflated the accounts in Genesis 12 and 20, since
the supernatural communication with the king is only found in
one version of the deception legend. Perhaps this device is
merely Eupolemus' effort to account for how the pharaoh
discovered the deception, as Josephus credits the priests
with the discovery, Antiq. 1:164. On the identity of the
author of this fragment, cf. note #60 below.

[29]Like Philo (cf. Abr. 93-106), Josephus follows the
biblical text in separating the deception of Genesis 12
(Antiq. 1:162-165) from that in Genesis 20 (Antiq. 1:207-
212). In his retelling of the Genesis 20 account, Josephus
has the king request Abraham's intercession with God. But
Abraham denies that he was in any way the cause of the king's
illness and merely agrees to stay with the king to demonstrate
his concern for the monarch's recovery.

Philo's silence appears noteworthy, moreover, because, by contrast, the author of the Genesis Apocryphon makes use of a conflation of the two legends of Abraham's deception in order to elaborate Abraham's role as a healer and exorcist.[30] Thus Philo's criterion of the possession of ἀρετή by the σοφός as the sine qua non of his being a prophet can be recognized both in what he explicitly states as well as in his apparent neglect of the role of the prophet as miracle worker suggested by the biblical text.

Philo again follows the Stoic line closely when he speaks of the qualification of the patriarchs to be priests [cf. S.V.F. vol. III, p. 157 #604-610, especially Diog. Laert.

---

[30]Cf. Gen. Apoc. 20:2-31, especially 28-29: "I prayed ... and the plague departed from him and the evil spirit was rebuked (זער) from him and he lived" [trans. by W.H. Brownlee, The Meaning of the Qumran Scrolls for the Bible (New York and Oxford, 1964), p. 120, n. 41.] Cf. A. Dupont-Sommer, "Exorcismes et guérisons dans les écrits de Qumrân," Suppl. to Vetus Testamentum VII (Leiden: Brill, 1960), pp. 251-253. Howard C. Kee, "The Terminology of Mark's Exorcism Stories," NTS 14 (1967-1968), pp. 233-235, who argues for a strong translation of זער such as "brought into submission." The inability of Pharaoh's wizards, sages, and physicians to heal him is detailed in 19-21 which naturally highlights Abraham's proficiency. It is puzzling to observe that in the book of Jubilees where Abraham is credited with such miraculous power as authority over flocks of ravens (11:18-21), the story of Abraham and Pharaoh (Gen. 12) is briefly recounted with no mention of Pharaoh's recovery. Perhaps the deletion of any mention of Abraham's deception and of any conversation between Pharaoh and Abraham (Gen. 12:18) indicates that the author did not want to discuss the story in detail. Thus the omission of the whole of the deception story of Genesis 20 may result from the author's opinion that in spite of the healing it did not glorify Abraham.

7.119:

> "The good (οἱ σπουδαῖοι) it is added, are also worshippers
> of God; for they have acquaintance with the rites of the
> gods, and piety (εὐσέβεια) is the knowledge of how to
> serve the gods. Further, they will sacrifice to the
> gods and they keep themselves pure; for they avoid all
> acts that are offences against the gods, and the gods
> think highly of them: for they are holy and just in what
> concerns the gods. The wise too are the only priests
> (μόνους θ' ἱερέας τοὺς σοφούς) ; for they have made
> sacrifices their study as also the building of temples,
> purifications, and all the other matters appertaining to
> the gods."][31]

Not only did he see the pious Abraham as fathering a whole

nation of priests and prophets (Abr. 98); but the sacrifice

of Isaac was the most perfect sacrifice which only the σοφός

could perform. In Abr. 202 in a word play on the name Isaac

as meaning laughter, Philo states, "This (joy) the σοφός

is said to sacrifice as his duty to God." In Sac. 111,

Philo elaborates on the sacrifice of Isaac by Abraham as

demonstrating the highest form of sacrifice, the undivided

offering:

> ἑορτὴ γὰρ ψυχῆς ἡ ἐν ἀρεταῖς εὐφροσύνη τελείαις,
> τέλειαι δὲ αἱ κηρῶν ἀμέτοχοι, ὅσας τὸ ἀνθρώπειον
> γένος χωρεῖ. μόνος δὲ ἑορτάζει τὴν τοιαύτην ἑορτὴν
> ὁ σοφός, τῶν δὲ ἄλλων οὐδὲ εἷς· ἄγευστον γὰρ παθῶν
> ἢ κακιῶν ψυχὴν εὑρεῖν σπανιώτατον.

> "For the soul's feast is the joy and gladness which the
> perfect virtues bring, and by perfect is meant virtues

---

[31]Trans. by R.D. Hicks, Diogenes Laertius II (Loeb
edition: Cambridge and London, 1925), p. 225.

unspotted by all the tainting evil to which the human race is liable. Such a feast the wise man only can keep and save him none other. For hardly ever shall you find a soul which has never tasted of passions or vices."[32]

The qualification of the patriarch Abraham to be king is once more his status as a sage who possesses the virtues. This criterion is also one of the basic Stoic paradoxes [cf. Diog. Laert. VII 122: "Not only are the wise (σοφοί) free, they are also kings (βασιλεῖς) ; kingship being unaudited rule, which none but the wise can sustain"].[33] This maxim that "only the wise man is king" is specifically applied to Abraham in Mut. 152-153 as representing Moses' judgment of Abraham's qualification to be king. It is further supplemented in Som. II 244 with the observation that "virtue is a rule and dominion with final authority." The qualification is also explicit in Abr. 261: "Then as the greatness and glory of his virtue in all its pre-eminence were more than they could keep to themselves, they approached him and exclaimed: "Thou art a king from God among us.'" Finally in Virt. 216, the royal status of Abraham is once

---

[32]Trans. by F.H. Colson and G.H. Whitaker Philo II (Loeb edition: Cambridge and London, 1928), pp. 175-177. My italics point to a translation problem since ὁ μόνος σοφός can mean God for Philo (cf. Conf. 39, Mig. 134). The translation "wise man" is favored, however, both because of the predicative position of μόνος and the following sentence which is a reflection of Stoic lamentation on the scarcity of true sages. Note that the sacrifice of Isaac is defended by Philo as complete and perfect (Abr. 177) although Isaac did not die, because Abraham's intention was perfect (cf. also Sac. 121).

[33]The general doctrine is stated by Philo in Mut. 152, Sob. 57, Mig. 197, Som. II 244.

more grounded in his possession of virtue:

> "And having gained faith, the most sure and certain of
> the virtues, so that by those among whom he settled he
> was regarded as a king, not because of the outward
> state, mere commoner (ἰδιώτης) that he was, but because
> of his greatness of soul, for his spirit was the spirit
> of a king."[34]

When Philo's view of Moses as a "divine man" is assessed
against the backdrop of the patriarchs who approach him in
stature, it is clear that his divine or semi-divine status
is only different from theirs in degree, not in kind. Like
them, he is authenticated as standing in a special
relationship with God solely on the basis of his being a
σοφός who possesses and represents the virtues.

Moses stands at the top of the ascending order of the
sages of Israel. Like Abraham, Isaac, and Jacob, he married
a virtue rather than a woman, since "woman" represents sense
perception (Cher. 40-42). Zipporah is depicted as a bird
"hastening upward from earth to heaven and contemplating
there the divine and blessed natures" (Cher. 41: Mut 120).

But Moses excels the earlier paradigms of virtue because
he is called to stand beside God himself: "There are still
others, whom God has advanced still higher and has trained
them to fly above species and genus and established them
beside himself. Such is Moses to whom he says, 'Stand here
with me'" (Sac. 8, cf. Deut. 5:31). The progression is
clear and continuous:

---

[34]Trans. by F.H. Colson, Philo VIII (Loeb edition:
Cambridge and London, 1939), pp. 295-297.

"For the limit of the knowledge attained by Seth became the starting point of righteous Noah; while Abraham begins his education with the consummation of Noah's; and the highest point of wisdom reached by Abraham is the initial course in Moses' training" (Post. 174)

"Seth, inasmuch as he is sprung from human virtue, will never relinquish the race of men, but will obtain enlargement. The first enlargement extends to the perfect number 10, when righteous Noah arises; a second and yet better one from Shem, the son of Noah, up to a second '10,' to which faithful Abraham gives his name; then a third, a '7' now more perfect than '10,' reaching from Abraham to Moses, the man wise in all things (ὁ πάντα σοφός: Post. 173).³⁵

Philo's Moses displays the possession of virtue in his whole life. He is ἀστεῖος in his youth.³⁶ "He displayed the doctrines of philosophy in his daily actions" (Mos. I 29), while disdaining his good fortune of being placed in the Pharaoh's court, since such chance luck is unstable (Mos. I 31).³⁷ He plays the role of the good physician to relieve the plight of his people with sage advice (Mos. I 42).³⁸ In exile, he continued to be exercised in virtue under the training of his excellent reason (λογισμὸς ἀστεῖος:

---

³⁵Trans. by F.H. Colson and G.H. Whitaker, PHILO II (Loeb edition: Cambridge and London, 1928), pp. 431-433. The numerology of the Post. 173 passage deserves further study. If it can be identified as Pythagorean, it is worth noting that the figures on this ascending scale are still all sages who represent the virtues. The ability to work miracles is not a criterion.

³⁶Cf. note 23 above.

³⁷This is precisely the prudence that Plutarch praises in Alexander in his treatise On the Fortune of Alexander.

³⁸The role of the wise man as physician has been discussed in the previous section. Cf. the development of the theme with reference to Moses in Quod Deus 66-67. Cf. also Sac. 121.

<u>Mos</u>. I 48). This process brings him to the level of the possession of virtue where he is uniquely ὁ σοφός/πάνσοφος, τέλειος, ἱερώτατος, θεόφιλος, θεοφιλής, φίλος θεοῦ, μέγας φιλόθεος, φιλάρετος, φιλάνθρωπος, and σπουδαῖος .[39] The account of his death is the fitting climax to the life of a hero of virtue. Complete with a mythological overlay[40] which is heavily dependent upon <u>Deut</u>. 34, his apotheosis is described in terms of a resolution of "his twofold nature of soul and body into a single unity, transforming his whole being into mind, pure as the sunlight" (<u>Mos</u>. II 288). The nation mourns him for a month (<u>Deut</u>. 34:8) "in memory of his vast beneficence and watchful care for each one of them and for all" (<u>Mos</u>. II 291).[41] Thus even in the death scene, the criterion which validates the account is clear. This is the Moses whom God has advanced beyond human nature and stationed beside himself because of his unique possession of virtue: "Thus you may learn that God prizes the wise man

---

[39]The long list of epithets which Philo uses for Moses indicates the grandeur of the portrayal. The philosophical tone of each of the terms would bear discussion, but this might involve belaboring the obvious. A good index to the use of these names for Moses can be found in F.H. Colson and J.W. Earp. <u>Philo</u> X (Loeb edition: Cambridge and London, 1962), pp. 386-389. Cf. Halévy, <u>op</u>. <u>cit</u>., p. 71. J. Jeremias, "Μωυσῆς," <u>TDNT</u> IV (ed. G. Kittel, trans. G.W. Bromiley: Grand Rapids, 1967), pp. 849-853.

[40]Cf. the discussion in the previous section of Seneca's account of the death of Hercules.

[41]This brief eulogy would have been fully appropriate for any "divine man" of the philosophical tradition. Cf. Lucian, <u>Demonax</u> 66-67.

(σοφός) as the world, for that same word by which he made the universe, is that by which he draws the perfect man (τέλειος) from things earthly to himself" (Sac. 8, cf. Virt. 77-79.

Philo's treatment of Moses as a "divine man" is clearly under the direct influence of the philosophical and particularly Stoic conception of the θεῖος σοφός. This observation is further documented in the general descriptions of Moses' divine or semi-divine status. The title ἄνθρωπος θεοῦ which Philo draws from Deut. 33:1 serves to indicate Moses' role as the mediator of τὸ ἀγαθόν to the people (Mut. 125-128). This rank is clearly a step above that of the one who is still making moral progress (ὁ προκόπτων) and is reserved for the perfect (ὁ τέλειος: Mut. 24-25), yet it falls short of true divine status:

> "Moses then describes the perfect man (ὁ τέλειος) as neither God nor man, but as I have said already, on the border-line between the uncreated and the perishing form of being. While on the other hand, the man who is on the path of progress (ὁ προκόπτων) is placed by him in the region between the living and the dead" (Som. II 234).

Philo clarifies his differential in rank still further:

> "The wise man (σοφός) is said to be a god to the foolish man, but in truth he is not God. ... for when he is compared to the Existent One, he will be found to be a man of God (ἄνθρωπος θεοῦ) ; but when compared with a fool, he will be a god in appearance and opinion" (Det. 162).

Moses' own stature as god is generally limited to this level of playing the role of God to the fool. Yet Philo is clearly intrigued by the Exodus passages where the title θεός is used of Moses. It is as the bearer of the divine mind

that Moses is regarded by Philo as god to Aaron and Aaron is
his prophet (Ex. 4:16; Det. 39-40, Mig. 81, 84, 169). This
mind "dwelt in his body like an image in a shrine" and the
observer had to ponder "whether it was human or divine or a
mixture of both" (ἀνθρώπειος ἢ θεῖος ἢ μικτὸς ἐξ ἀμφοῖν:
Mos. I 27). The noetic criterion is consistent. Moses'
divine status rests upon his rank as σοφός . He is god to
Pharaoh (Ex. 7:1) because the mind is god of the unreasoning
part (Leg. All. I 40, Sac. 9).

The title θεός is reserved for Moses, although others
such as the high priest can exceed human limitations (Som.
II 189). Moreover, Moses is called god because as a σοφός
he must perform the function of bringing the beneficence of
God to lesser men (cf. Det. 162, quoted above, Quod Omn.
Prob. 43-44, & Mut. 129: "this same man is a god, because
he is wise (σοφός) and thus the ruler of every fool"
particularly as intercessor for the trangressors, for
"beneficence is the peculiar province of a god").

Sac. 9-10 deserves special comment:

> ἀλλ' εἰς θεὸν αὐτὸν ἐχειροτόνει πᾶσαν τὴν περὶ τὸ σῶμα
> χώραν καὶ τὸν ἡγεμόνα αὐτῆς νοῦν ὑπήκοα καὶ δοῦλα ἀποφήνας
> "δίδωμι γάρ σε" φησί "θεὸν Φαραώ" (Ex. 7:1)· θεὸς δὲ
> ἔλλειψιν ἢ πρόσθεσιν οὐκ ἀνέχεται πλήρης καὶ ἰσαίτατος
> ὢν ἑαυτῷ. παρὸ καὶ τὴν ταφὴν λέγεται μηδὲ εἷς εἰδέναι
> τούτου (Deut. 34:6).

"But He appointed him as god, placing all the bodily
region and the mind which rules it in subjection and
slavery to him. "I give thee," He says, "as god to
Pharaoh" (Ex. 7:1); but God is not susceptible of
addition or diminution, being fully and unchangeably
himself. And therefore we are told that no man knows

his grave (<u>Deut</u>. 34:6).[42]

Philo appears to desert his usual caution of maintaining that Moses is merely god to the less perfect. <u>Sac</u>. 8 seems to imply a pre-existence for Moses: "He sent him as a loan to the earthly sphere;" and the argument in this passage suggests that Moses' nature is immutable because he is divine. The point that Philo is making in this context, however, is not exceptional: "Thus you may learn that God prizes the wise man (σοφός) as the world" (<u>Sac</u>. 8). Consequently even when Moses' status as god is elaborated, it is his possession and representation of virtue that documents his divine stature.

The assertion that the σοφός shares the attributes of God is completely possible within the Stoic conceptual framework. The traditional philosophical view of the sage as the friend of God and thus the possessor of all[43] is the basis of Philo's interpretation of <u>Exodus</u> 33:11,[44] and

---

[42]Trans. F.H. Colson and G.H. Whitaker, <u>Philo</u> II (Loeb edition: Cambridge and London, 1928), p. 101. Cf. their note on p. 488.

[43]Cf. <u>Diog</u>. <u>Laert</u>. 6.72: "All things belong to the gods. The gods are friends to the wise (σοφοί) , and friends share all property in common; therefore all things are the property of the wise." Cf. <u>Dio</u> <u>of</u> <u>Prusa</u> 69.4. Although the doctrine is attributed to Diogenes the Cynic by Diogenes Laertius, I see no reason to regard this idea a peculiarly Cynic.

[44]Cf. <u>Quis</u>, <u>Her</u>. 21, <u>Som</u>. I 232, <u>Mos</u>. II 163 where the <u>Exodus</u> text is followed closely and friendship is defined in terms of intimate communication with God. For Philo's discussion of the other biblical passages where Moses' unique communication with God is discussed, cf. on <u>Numbers</u> 12; 6-8:

126

provides Moses with particular qualities (cf. Quod Omn.

Prob 44: πάντως ὤφειλεν εὐδαιμονεῖν). The text of Mos. I

156-158 deserves special mention since here Moses is described

both as friend of God and prophet (φίλος δὲ ὁ προφήτης ἀνείρηται

θεοῦ: 156) as well as god (158). Most noteworthy is the

fact that as God's friend, he not only is heir to the whole

world (155) but further:

> "each of the elements obeyed him as a master, altering
> its natural property and was obedient to his command;
> even this is perhaps no wonder"[45]
>
> τοιγαροῦν ὑπήκουεν ὡς δεσπότῃ τῶν στοιχείων ἕκαστον
> ἀλλάττον ἣ εἶχε δύναμιν καὶ ταῖς προτάξεσιν ὑπεῖκον.
> καὶ θαυμαστὸν ἴσως οὐδέν:(156).

Subsequent discussion will show that Philo could treat the

miracles God performed in terms of the transmutation of

elements according to Stoic physics; but in this context, it

must be observed that it is Moses ὁ φίλος θεοῦ, ὁ σπουδαῖος,

ὁ κοσμοπολίτης (156-157) who is given such a special charism.

Philo's reference to Moses as "prophet" arises from his

interpretation of the direct communication with God which the

---

Leg. All. III 103, Quis Her. 262; on Deut. 34: 10-12: Quis
Her. 262. There is no mention of Moses' performance of
miracles in these interpretations.

[45]The last phrase could perhaps be translated, "and
nothing is equally marvelous." But the context argues in
favor of translating the adverb as "probably" or "perhaps"
since Philo goes on to point out that this authority is the
rightful possession of God's friends. For Philo's use of ἴσως
as a mild disclaimer, cf. Harry Austryn Wolfson, Philo:
foundations of Religious Philosophy in Judaism, Christianity,
and Islam (Cambridge, 1947), vol. I, pp. 125-126.

Exodus 33:11 text to which he is referring asserts. But the rationale for his possession of the power to alter the physical world rests on Moses' status as a wise man who shares in divine perogatives as God's friend.

Philo's de vita Mosis is a systematic attempt to portray Moses as at once the ideal king, law giver, high priest and prophet (I 334, II 2-7, 187, 292, cf. Praem. 53). Since the work is a comprehensive encomium, it is perhaps a bit futile to attempt to decide whether the office of prophet[46] or that of king[47] is of primary significance with the other functions being secondary. Philo himself insists that the four are like the virtues and he who has one possesses all (Mos. II 7; cf. Diog. Laert. 7.125). What is particularly valuable to observe, however, is that Philo verifies Moses' claim to these offices by appealing the same criterion that he used to authenticate the other patriarchal wise men as prophets, priests, and kings, i.e. the possession of virtue.

Philo's lengthy discussion of these offices would allow for a detailed analysis of each in turn, yet the

---

[46]Ibid., vol. II, p. 18.

[47]E. Goodenough, By Light, Light, op. cit., p. 188. Howard M. Teeple, The Mosaic Eschatological Prophet (JBL Monograph Series X; Philadelphia, 1957), pp. 36-37. It is probably correct that Philo stresses the office of ruler in this treatise, just as he can emphasize one virtue, piety, (cf. Praem. 53); but the mutuality of the offices and the virtues is his major theme.

qualification of the office holder is consistently the same. The best legislator is he who possesses "all the virtues fully and completely" (Mos. II 8) and only Moses met this standard (Mos. II 10). "The chief and most essential quality required by a priest is piety" (εὐσέβεια: Mos. II 66) which is in Philo's catalogue the chief of the virtues (cf. Praem. 53). This priestly service of God is the special privilege of the sage (Mos. II 67) whose moral purity must be unquestionable (Mos. II 68). Even in his description of priestly garments, Philo's Moses is the instructor in virtue (Mos. II 181-186). Moses the ₍ ᵥᵒhet is qualified like the other prophets in Philo by his being a wise man and possessor of virtue (cf. Quis Her. 259-260, discussed above). In this role he is ἀληθόμαντις (Mos. II 269) and the possessor of ἡ προγνωστικὴ δύναμις (Mos. II 190, cf. 269). Although Philo's understanding of prophecy can not be explained on the basis of Stoic parallels alone, Moses' skill in divination and his predictive powers must not be represented as magical-miraculous performances.[48]

---

[48]Cf. note 22. In Mos. II 191-288, Philo itemizes the great prophetic moments of Moses. He strongly emphasizes the elements of prediction, but this God inspired prediction always awaits God's confirmation.

In Mos. I 56-57, there is a perplexing discussion of Moses as the champion of justice in behalf of the daughters of the priest of Midian, leading up to a prophetic seizure. The difficulty lies in an obscure threat when Moses refers to himself as allied with a mighty hand against wrongdoers (καὶ γάρ εἰμι σύμμαχος ταῖς ἀδικουμέναις μετὰ μεγάλης χειρός). This could be construed as an argument that Moses the prophet is "equipped with a magically powerful hand." [Cf. the use of the hand in miracles and magic in O. Weinreich, Antike.

As with the Stoics, such divination is merely further
documentation of the sage's piety and of his clear understanding of the divinely ordained harmony of the universe.
The inspired prophet is in tune with the divine will, but
his prophecies do not miraculously produce the event. He
merely anticipates God's action which may confirm the
prediction in a miraculous way (cf. Mos. II 253, 262, 263,
269, 284). Even when God acts with a most miraculous
display of divine intervention, Philo interprets the event as
God's verification of the prophet's possession of the queen
of the virtues, piety (ἀπέφηνε τὴν εὐσέβειαν τοῦ προφήτου:
Mos. II. 284). Thus Moses' role as prophet is not an
exception, but like the other offices, rests upon his
possession of virtue as the necessary qualification:

> πᾶσαι μὲν οὖν αἱ ἀρεταὶ παρθένοι, καλλιστεύει δὲ ὡς ἐν
> χορῷ παραλαβοῦσα τὴν ἡγεμονίαν ἡ εὐσέβεια, ἣν ἐκληρώσατο
> διαφερόντως ὁ θεολόγος Μωυσῆς, δι' ἣν μετὰ μυρίων ἄλλων,
> ἅπερ ἐν τοῖς γραφεῖσι περὶ τοῦ κατ' αὐτὸν βίου μεμήνυται,
> τεττάρων ἄθλων ἐξαιρέτων τυγχάνει, [τυχὼν] βασιλείας,
> νομοθεσίας, προφητείας, ἀρχιερωσύνης.

> "Now all the virtues are virgins, but the fairest among
> them all, the acknowledged queen of the dance, is piety,
> which Moses, the teacher of divine lore, in a special
> degree had for his own, and through it gained among a

Heilungswunder (Religionsgeschichtliche Versuche und
Vorarbeiten, Band VIII, Heft 1; Giessen, 1909), pp. 1-66].
The frequent Old Testament references to the "mighty hand of
God," however, particularly as the agent of the exodus,
suggests that Philo's Moses is merely claiming that he is an
ally of the God who avenges injustice. Apart from the biblical
image, such a statement would be fully appropriate for any
of the Cynic or Stoic philosophers who saw themselves as
agents of the god.

multitude of other gifts, which have been described in the treatises dealing with his life, four special rewards, the offices of king, legislator, prophet and high priest" (Praem. 53).[49]

As this passage shows, Moses' role as a king is also inextricably related to his other offices (cf. Mos. II 2ff, Praem. 56), and the qualification for this office in particular is frequently stated by Philo in terms of Moses' possession of virtue. Moses receives the kingship "on account of his virtue and noble behavior (ἀρετῆς ἕνεκα καὶ καλοκἀγαθίας) and his good will for all, which he continually practiced," and it was his just reward from God the lover of virtue and nobility (φιλάρετος καὶ φιλόκαλος: Mos. I 148). All of which leads up to an extended list of the things Moses truly treasured, a catalogue of his virtues which might well be called Philo's "aretalogy" of Moses:

ταῦτα δ' ἦσαν ἐγκράτειαι, καρτερίαι, σωφροσύναι, ἀγχίνοιαι, συνέσεις, ἐπιστῆμαι, πόνοι, κακοπάθειαι, ἡδονῶν ὑπεροψίαι, δικαιοσύναι, προτροπαὶ πρὸς τὰ βέλτιστα, ψόγοι καὶ κολάσεις ἁμαρτανόντων νόμιμοι, ἔπαινοι καὶ τιμαὶ κατορθούντων πάλιν σὺν νόμῳ.

"These were displays of self-restraint, continence, temperance, shrewdness, good sense, knowledge, endurance of toil and hardships, contempt of pleasures, justice, advocacy of excellence, censure and chastisement according to law for wrong-doers, praise and honor for the just as the law furthermore suggests." (Mos. I 154)

The contrast between Moses ὁ τέλειος σοφός and Aaron ὁ προκόπτων further illustrates the consistency of the criteria with which Philo treats Moses as a "divine man."

---

[49]Trans. by F.H. Colson, Philo VIII (Loeb edition: Cambridge and London, 1939), p. 343.

Aaron is the model of gradual moral improvement or progress
(cf. Leg. All. III 140, 144, Som. II 234, 237) whose virtue
comes by practice (ἀσκητής). His inability to follow the
true sage in complete ἀπάθεία leads him to the
cultivation of moderation (μετριοπαθεία: Leg. All. III
131-132).[50] Yet Philo prevents his paradigm of virtue from
becoming an unattainable ideal which is completely removed
from those like Aaron who are pursuing virtue.[51] When Philo
uses the term θεῖος ἀνήρ in an apparent reference to Moses,
he immediately appends a discussion of Moses' gentle
training of those who aspire to lead a blameless life
(Virt. 177-178). Again this "perfect man is neither God nor
man (τέλειος οὔτε θεὸς οὔτε ἄνθρωπος) but is on the border
between the uncreated and corruptible nature. While the man
of progress (ὁ προκόπτων) is in the area between the living
and the dead, the living being those who abide with reason,
and the dead those who rejoice in foolishness" (Som. II 234).
Thus the ascending scale is established which measures prox-

---

[50]For the Stoic doctrine of the sage as apathetic, cf.
Diog. Laert 7.117 and S.V.F. #443-445.

[51]Moses is an approachable paradigm and one who can be
copied by those who yearn for virtue: In himself and his
life, "he has set before us, like some well-wrought picture,
a piece of work beautiful and godlike, a model (παράδειγμα)
for those who are willing to copy it" Mos. I 158, cf. Mos.
II 10, 17. Thus following Moses in obedience is the definition of virtuous conduct for the Israelites (Mos. I 329).
Moses is the archetype and model (ἀρχέτυπον παράδειγμα)
for all future rulers (Virt. 70). Cf. previous section for
discussion of the issue of the sage as an unattainable ideal
in Stoicism.

imity to God ranging from the fool to the man of progress,
to the divine man whose display of divine presence is
inferior in degree only to that of the divine word and of
God himself (cf. Som. II 237), and this graduated series is
scored according to the measure of the progression of virtue
(cf. Quis Her. 19).

Once moral virtue is established as the criterion which
Philo uses to document levels of divine presence in men,
his attempts to recast biblical accounts of miraculous
events become more understandable. The instances where he
allegorizes or rationalizes such stories ought not be too
quickly disregarded as attempts to assimilate the Scripture
to "Greek sensibilities."[52] "The burning bush is a symbol
of those who were wronged and the flaming fire of those who
committed the wrong" (Mos. I 67). The bitter spring may
have been sweetened by a tree with a previously unknown
natural quality" (ἐκ φύσεως δύναμις: Mos. I 185). The
rock that yielded water may have held a hidden source of
spring (Mos. I 211). The rod cast down is the serpent
pleasure but picked up is schooling in virtue (Leg. All.
II 90-93). When Aaron's rod swallows the rods of the
Egyptians, "all the arguments of the sophists are devoured"
(Mig. 85).

Yet as Wolfson has shown,[53] Philo is not trying to

---

[52]Moses Hadas, Hellenistic Culture (New York, 1959), p. 90.

[53]Wolfson, Philo, op. cit., vol. I, pp. 122-126, 347-356.

"explain away" these stories. Even when using the Stoic
theory of the transmutation of the elements as the physical
explanation of such phenomena,[54] he still regards the
biblical accounts as reliable. As brute facts, the miracles
may document the majesty of God; but their reliable value
for the life of virtue and for understanding the lives of
the paradigms of virtue can be discovered by assessing such
events in philosophical categories.

Philo's starting point is that everything is possible
for God, including those things that are impossible and
insuperable for men (ὅσα ἐν ἀμηχάνῳ καὶ ἀπόρῳ κεῖται παρ'
ἀνθρώποις: Abr. 175, cf. Abr. 112). The most amazing
display of God's miraculous power is the orderly creation
next to which "miracles and apparently incredible events are
child's play for him" (τὰ παράδοξα δὴ ταῦτα καὶ παράλογα
θεοῦ παίγνιά ἐστιν: Mos. I 212, cf. II 267, Op. 46). God
is master of the whole world and of its parts and the
elements are obedient to the point of assuming qualities
and functions not usually theirs (the air produces manna,
Mos. I 201-202; the miracles of Egypt are caused by an
"upheaval of the elements:" (νεωτερισμὸς τῶν στοιχείων:
Mos. I 216; the flame from heaven may have been caused by

---

[54]R. Grant, op. cit., p. 185, "We may conclude that
Wisdom's theory of miracle is based primarily on the work of
Cleanthes, perhaps through Posidonius. Given the basic
assumption that the stories of the exodus are history
rather than legend, the explanation ... is not 'unscientific.'"
Grant argues this is also Philo's theory of miracle.

"air resolved into fire by natural conversion of the elements":
μεταβολῇ τῶν στοιχείων: Mos. II 154).

It has already been observed that this mastery of the
elements also extends to God's friend Moses: "each element
obeyed him as its master, changed its natural properties and
submitted to his command" (Mos. I 156). Furthermore Philo
follows the Exodus 7 account in arguing that the miracles
(τέρατα) in Pharaoh's court were intended to persuade those
who had disbelieved Moses' words (Mos. I 90). Although these
factors show that Philo is seeking ways to document the
reliability of the biblical account, they do not demonstrate
that the miracles provide a primary basis for Philo to authenticate Moses as a "divine man."

Philo's discussion of the role of Aaron as miracle
worker provides good evidence that the miracles prove little
about the true "divine man." It has already been seen that
Aaron is in a distinctly secondary position compared with
the perfect sage Moses. In de vita Mosis, while Moses had been
in exile in training for kingship, Aaron was being prepared
by the providence of God for obedience (πειθαρχία: Mos. I
85). Nevertheless, Philo does not reserve the power to work
miracles to Moses, but he follows the Exodus account in
detailing Aaron's activity, even expanding upon Aaron's role
as a miracle worker.

First of all, Aaron casts down his staff in Pharaoh's
court turning it into a serpent. It must be observed that
Philo refers to Aaron's act as the first example of Moses'

display of the wonders he had been taught to perform (<u>Mos</u>. I
90). Thus it could be argued that Philo regards Aaron merely
as Moses' agent, as the Exodus text suggests. Yet no
mention is made of Aaron's action being commanded by Moses
which was the scenario as programmed in <u>Exodus</u> 7:9.
Furthermore, when Aaron's rod/serpent devours those of the
Egyptian wizards and magicians, the event is described as
brought about by a "diviner power (δύναμις θειοτέρα) to which
every feat is easy" (<u>Mos</u>. I 94). But this is not Moses the
Hellenistic θεῖος ἀνήρ who documents his divine status
with the performance of miracles. First of all, Philo has
followed the <u>Exodus</u> account by attributing the miracle to
Aaron.[55] Secondly, Philo neglects the biblical note that
Aaron was acting on Moses' command. Thus the same Hellenistic
author who is so explicit in demonstrating the superiority
of Moses as a perfect sage in contrast to Aaron who is only
making progress in virtue does not point up the primacy of
Moses in this miraculous performance even to the degree that
the <u>Exodus</u> text maintains his role as the one who commands
the act. Finally, the "diviner power" is really the possession
of neither Aaron nor Moses. In this instance, it is working
through the agency of Aaron's rod; but it is God who is
"showing his will by the proofs of signs and wonders"
(<u>Mos</u>. I 95).

---

[55]Contrast this with Josephus who completely neglects
Aaron's role (cf. <u>Antiq</u>. 2:279-284).

Again Philo ascribes the first three plagues directly
to Aaron. To be sure, Aaron's plagues deal with the lower,
denser elements (στοιχεῖα) of earth and water while those
of Moses belong to the elements most productive of life,
air and fire (Mos. I 97, 113) so that Moses' superiority is
protected. Yet Philo treats the first three miracles as
"committed to the brother of Moses" (ἐφεῖς τῷ Μωυσέως
ἀδελφῷ: Mos. I 97) and regards these plagues as due to
Aaron's agency: "Such were the punishments which were done
through the agency of the brother of Moses" (τοιαῦται
μὲν αἱ διὰ τοῦ Μωυσέως ἀδελφοῦ τιμωρίαι: Mos. I 113).
While the biblical account repeats in each instance that
Aaron receives the command to perform the miracle from Moses
(Exodus 7:19, 8:5, 8:16), Philo merely reports that Aaron
did the first by "divine command" (προστάξει θείᾳ: Mos. I
99), the second "when commanded" (κελευσθείς: Mos. I 103),
and the third when "God appointed the same agent of
punishment" (ἐπισχὼν ὁ θεὸς τὸν αὐτὸν κολαστὴν: Mos. I 107).
Moses does not figure in these miracles as directly as he
did in Exodus.

Philo is not merely prevented from developing the image
of Moses as the miracle worker by his close reading of the
biblical text which attributes some of the miracles to Aaron.
Philo actually neglects four explicit statements in the
text that Aaron was acting on Moses' command with the result
that Aaron's role in the performance of miraculous acts is
enhanced and Philo can describe an equal number of plagues as

belonging peculiarly to each brother in turn, only reserving
the more ethereal raw materials for Moses. Thus Moses'
superiority to Aaron as the τέλειος σοφός or "divine man"
versus Aaron ὁ προκόπτων does not rest on his superior
ability to perform miracles.

Philo does find the miracles persuasive and can regard
them as verifying the reliability of God as a speaker (Mos.
I 82: burning bush), proof that God is present (Mos. II
154: first from heaven), and verification of the axiom
that "God's way is not man's way" (Mos. II 173). In one
instance, a miracle helps to verify Moses' essential virtue,
piety (Mos. II 284); but even in that case, it is God's act,
not Moses', and it serves at the same time to vindicate
God's own word. Thus such phenomena verify God's power,
but are only secondary documentation of Moses' peculiar
status.

Since Philo schematizes the biblical account in order
to assign an equal number of plagues to Aaron and to Moses,
a mere recitation of such phenomena, an aretalogy of miracles,
would not show Moses' superiority in divine status to Aaron.
The moral and intellectual criterion is decisive. Because
he is a τέλειος σοφός , one who possesses all the virtues,
Moses outstrips Aaron who is still on the path of moral
progress; and only Moses stands as prophet, priest,
legislator, and king in closer proximity with God, ὁ
μόνος σοφός.

B.   Some Pre-Philonic Depictions of Moses

The large quantity of Philonic literature that has been
preserved permits a measure of confidence in the conclusion
of the previous section that the characterizations of the
heroes of the Greek philosophical traditions as "divine men"
can be regarded as the primary framework for Philo's
glorification of Moses as "the divine wise man." But it is
difficult to attempt to decide whether Philo's thoroughness
and consistency in this regard were exceptional since the
sources for pre-Philonic Hellenistic Jewish presentations of
Moses are very fragmentary. Yet even our meager lectionary
of pre-Philonic Hellenistic Jewish texts allows the observation
that Philo was not the first to make such a correlation.

Eupolemus, whose citation by Alexander Polyhistor[56] is
preserved in Eusebius' Praeparatio Evangelica 9, and who may
have been an ambassador for Judas Maccabeus,[57] identifies

---

[56]Since Alexander Polyhistor is the primary source for
the literature of Eupolemus, pseudo-Eupolemus, Ezekiel the
Tragedian, and Artapanus, his life provides the terminus
ante quem for the authors considered in this chapter, except
for Aristobulus (cf. notes 61 and 62 below). Alexander's
release by Sulla c. 80 B.C. provides the most clearly fixed
date, although a good case has been made for identifying the
period c. 65 B.C. as the height of Alexander's literary
productivity, cf. Felix Jacoby, Die Fragmente der Griechischen
Historiker, III a (Leiden, 1964), pp. 248-251.

[57]The precise dating and identification of Eupolemus are
uncertain and of passing interest for this study. The
identification of this author with the Eupolemus mentioned in
I Macc. 8:17, II Macc. 4:11 and Josephus Antiq. 12:415 has
been defended by J. Freudenthal, Hellenistische Studien, Heft
1 and 2: Alexander Polyhistor (Breslau, 1875), pp. 123-130.
This identification is also defensible in terms of the
chronography suggested by Clement of Alexandria [Strom. I

Moses as "the first sage" (πρῶτος σοφός : F.Gr.Hist. III
723, Eusebius P.E. 9.25.4, Clem. Al. Strom. 1.153.4). The
fact that Eupolemus connects his identification of Moses
as the "first wise man" with a claim that he was "the first
to teach the Jews letters" (γράμματα) [58] so that the
Phœnicians and Greeks are dependent on Moses, and with the
immediate mention of Moses' role as the Jews' first lawgiver
(νόμους τε πρῶτον Μωσῆν τοῖς 'Ιουδαίοις) [59] suggests
that Eupolemus view of Moses might not have been problematic
for Philo. The difficulty of describing Eupolemus'
perspective in any definitive way, however, is compounded
by the almost unanimous agreement of modern scholars with
Freudenthal's suggestion that the fragment in which Abraham
is described as the inventor of astrology should be attributed

---

141.4: cf. Felix Jacoby, Die Fragmente der Griechischen
Historiker (F. Gr. Hist.) III, #723, F. 4, p. 677 (Leiden:
E.J. Brill, 1958). The identification was opposed by Willrich,
Juden und Griechen (Göttingen, 1895), pp. 157-161. But M.
Hengel, Judentum und Hellenismus (Wissenschaftliche Unter-
suchungen zum Neuen Testament, 10; Tübingen, 1969), pp. 169-
175 restates the identification, bolstered by the important
study of the Maccabean period done by V. Tcherikover,
Hellenistic Civilization, op. cit.

[58]For the possible religious significance of the giving
of letters, particularly as developed by other Hellenistic
Jewish authors, cf. Georgi, op. cit., pp. 167-171.

[59]Clement of Alexandria Strom. I 153.4 omits the Greeks,
and he omits the reference to Moses as the "first lawgiver."
Furthermore, it is difficult to decide whether the text
should be read, "Moses was the Jews' first lawgiver," or
"Moses wrote the laws for the Jews first", implying the other
cultures also depended on his legislation but were second in
line to the Jews. Certainly the Eusebius text suggests this
note of cultural dependence, but the focus of the verse appears
to be an emphasis on the primacy of Moses.

to pseudo-Eupolemus.[60] With this limited lectionary, the
Moses whom Eupolemus elsewhere describes as "prophesying"
(προφητεῦσαι : Eusebius P.E. 9.30.1) can only be viewed as
Moses the wise man. Thus it must be allowed that the terms
σοφός and προφητεῦσαι may have had other connotations in
Eupolemus' complete work, but the general correlation between
Moses' roles as wise man, lawgiver, and prophet corresponds
neatly with Philo's treatment of Moses.

A similar and even stronger case can be made for
Aristobulus. Once the earlier scholarly arguments for the
priority of Philo to Aristobulus were laid to rest by Walter,[61]
the continuity between Aristobulus and Philo could be seen
in their mutual dependence on Stoic allegorical methods of

---

[60]A notable exception to this scholarly consensus is
A. Schlatter, Geschichte Israel[3] (Stuttgart, 1925). The
argument for the pseudo-Eupolumus authorship of the Abraham
fragment has also been attacked recently in a paper by
William Poehlmann and E. Jeff Miller, "Pseudo Eupolemus," New
Testament Seminar 201, Harvard Divinity School, April 27, 1970.
But the significance of (pseudo-)Eupolemus' depiction of
Abraham as the inventor of astrology (P.E. IX 17.8) is not
self-evident. Not only does this author suggest that the
real inventor of this art may have been Enoch (ad loc.), but
the legend of Abraham's knowledge of astrology is open to
diverse interpretations (cf. Artapanus in P.E. 7.18.7, an
anonymous fragment in P.E. 9.18.2, Josephus Antiq. I 155-156,
167). Philo associates the legend with Abram's study of
nature (Gig. 62-63, 70-71, 76, Abr. 82-84) prior to the
patriarch's departure from Chaldea and attaining the new name
Abraham and the status of a wise man (cf. Leg. All. III 83-
84, 244; Cher. 4; Mut. 66-76).

[61]Nikolaus Walter, Der Thoraausleger Aristobulus (Texte
und Untersuchungen, Band 86; Berlin, 1964), pp. 58-86. Cf.
also Albert-Marie Denis, Introduction aux pseudépigraphes
grecs d'ancien testament (Studia in Veteris Testamenti
pseudepigrapha, 1; Leiden, 1970), pp. 277-283.

interpretation.[62] Walter characterizes Aristobulus as more
"primitive" in his use of these methods than Philo, but the
tendency of explaining mythical and anthropomorphic statements
about God by pointing to what is "really" (φυσικῶς: P.E.
8.10.2, cf. Clem. Strom. 6.138.1: τῷ ὄντι)   meant corresponds
well with what has been seen in Philo.

The image of Moses that Aristobulus draws also fits
this specific interpretative framework. From the fragments
of Aristobulus that are extant (cf. note 62), this writer
appears to be more interested in presenting the laws, practices, and scriptures of the Jews in a good light to a philosophically enlightened audience than in composing an
encomium on Moses. Since Aristobulus sees these elements
originating in the words of Moses, he must also praise the
lawgiver of the Jews. The figure that is drawn is that of
Moses the sage[63] who instructs the Greek poets and

---

[62]Cf. Hengel, op. cit., p. 298 and literature cited in
note #371 ad loc. I am indebted at several points to the
work of Adela Yarbro and Daniel Fraikin, "The Fragments of
Aristobulus," New Testament Seminar 201, Harvard Divinity
School, May 28, 1970. Unless it can be shown that the
fragments are an unrepresentative selection, which was made,
for example, to support the fiction (?) that Aristobulus was
an instructor of Ptolemy (cf. Eusebius P.E. 9.6.6; 8.9.38),
the consistency of these extant fragments with the author's
intention must be assumed.

[63]Cf. ps. Aristeas 139: "the lawgiver, a sage equipped
by God for knowledge of all things" (σοφὸς ὢν ὁ νομοθέτης,
ὑπὸ θεοῦ κατασκευασμένος εἰς ἐπίγνωσιν τῶν ἁπάντων) . The
question of the possible lines of dependence between Aristobulus
and the epistle of pseudo-Aristeas need not be discussed in
this context. Cf. Walter, op. cit., pp. 88-103. The high
incidence of striking parallels both in subject matter and
methodology, however, invite comparisons. Little is said
about Moses himself in ps. Aristeas, but it is Moses the sage
and instructor in virtue whom Aristeas presents (cf. 131, 144,
148, 151, 153, 160, 162), not Moses the miracle worker.

philosophers, including Plato and Pythagoras (P.E. 8.10.4;
13.12.1-2). As with Philo and Eupolemus, Moses' role as a
prophet is viewed in immediate connection with his impressive
wisdom: "those who understand well are amazed at his wisdom
and divine inspiration on account of which he has been
proclaimed a prophet" (οἷς μὲν οὖν πάρεστι τὸ καλῶς νοεῖν,
θαυμάζουσι τὴν περὶ αὐτὸν σοφίαν καὶ τὸ θεῖον πνεῦμα, καθ' ὃ καὶ προφήτης
ἀνακεκήρυκται : P.E. 8.10.4). The precise connotation that
the title "prophet" has in this context is admittedly
elusive, but it appears that the θεῖον πνεῦμα upon which
this status of "prophet" depends is to be viewed as
sufficiently in concert with rational and ethical criteria
so that philosophers admire it and that any apparent irration-
ality (ἀλογία : P.E. 8.10.6) lies with the interpreter
rather than with Moses.

The particular bent of Aristobulus can perhaps be best
assessed by the way in which he uses the term "power" or
"divine power", especially in references to the "hand" of
God. Weinreich has described the peculiar function that was
frequently associated with the hand as the agent in the
performance of miraculous or magical feats.[64] But Aristobulus
appears to be consciously "demythologizing"[65] such

---

[64]Cf. note 48 above.

[65]In the light of the variety of understandings of
"demythologizing" held in modern scholarship, Aristobulus
should be allowed to speak for himself: "I wish to encourage
you to take the interpretations in their real sense (φυσικῶς)

associations with respect to their value for understanding the "real" sense of Moses' words.

The term δύναμις is used with enough frequency to suggest a self-conscious application by Aristobulus (cf. P.E. 8.10.1; 10.5; 10.7; 10.8; 10.15; 13.12.4; 12.7). The hypothesis that Aristobulus is attempting to focus attention on the concept of "power" can be documented by his use of the word even when his source uses another expression. When the Exodus text he cites in P.E. 8.10.8 refers to the "mighty hand" (ἐν χειρὶ κραταιᾷ) and his pseudo-Orphic poet speaks of God's "mighty hand" (κρατερός) and his "might" (κρατερόν: P.E. 13.12.5), Aristobulus discusses these in terms of δύναμις, insisting that this δύναμις must be fittingly interpreted so as to avoid all mythical anthropomorphisms which are inappropriate to a proper conception of God (P.E. 8.10.2-3).

The first method of arriving at such an interpretation is to demonstrate that Moses (i.e. the book of Exodus) has merely chosen an appropriate metaphor. The military forces of a king (δυνάμεις: P.E. 8.10.7) are said to be his "hands", and thus a reference to God's "mighty hand" is merely a metaphor for his δύναμις. Aristobulus would certainly quail at any suggestion that God's hand was actually the agent by which a magical or miraculous act was performed.

---

and to grasp the fitting conception of God and not to fall away into the mythical and anthropomorphic conception" (εἰς μυθῶδες καὶ ἀνθρώπινον κατάστημα: P.E. 8.10.2).

This is further verified by his characterization of those
who miss the real point of the text by clinging to its
literal sense as those "devoid of power and understanding"
(δύναμις καὶ σύνεσις: P.E.   8.10.5).

Aristobulus offers another avenue for arriving at a
fitting conception of "divine power" in his description of
the manifest descent of God upon the mountain in fire.
While the δύναμις of fire is normally displayed in a
localized blaze that consumes everything, Aristobulus
insists that this fire could be seen everywhere in a huge
area and that it did not consume anything which proves that
the descent of God is not localized (τοπική) because God is
everywhere (P.E. 8.10.13-17). This description of the
"divine power" as unlocalized which is based on a view of
the all pervasive character of God bears striking
resemblance to the Stoic conception of the divine fire that
penetrates all of nature (cf. D.L. 7.147, 156-157). Even
if Aristobulus is not consciously opposing a magical-
miraculous interpretation of "divine power", his description
of θεῖα δύναμις as that which governs all things (P.E.
13.12.4) and that which pervades all things (P.E. 13.12.7)
could come directly out of a Stoic handbook describing the
ὀρθὸς λόγος: cf. D.L. 7.88, "The right reason which pervades
all things (διὰ πάντων ἐρχόμενος), and is identical with
this Zeus, lord and ruler of all that is." The peculiar
connotation of the term "divine power" is thus clearly

Stoic, although the precise reason for the concentration on the word δύναμις remains conjectural.[66]

Aristobulus' interpretation of the "voice of God not as words spoken but as arrangement of things" (P.E. 13.12.4) also merits brief scrutiny. Not only is the aversion to unfitting statements about God's "words" obvious, but the emphasis on "voice" as a "arrangement of things" (ἔργων κατασκευή) is explicable in terms of Stoic teaching: "Voice (φωνή) is a body (σῶμα) according to the Stoics, as Archedemus says in his treatise On Voice, Diogenes, Antipater and Chrysippus in the second book of his Physics" (D.L. 7.55). The contrast with primitive descriptions of God as "speaking" is even more explicit in Philo who insists that God has no need of a mouth, tongue and windpipe to produce a voice that is audible to the mind (Decal. 32-35) and that God's voice is an articulate and silent form (Mos. I 66) which is "seen" by the powers of sight residing in the soul (Mig. 49, cf. also Som. I 236, Spec. Leg. IV 132). But Aristobulus is following the same line of interpretation when he calls on Pythagoras, Socrates and Plato "who said that they heard the voice of god (φωνῆ θεοῦ) when they were contemplating the arrangement of the universe" (P.E. 13.12.4) and when he approvingly cites his pseudo-Orphic poet who instructs to

---

[66]Cf. pseudo Aristeas 236 and 252 for similar usages of "divine power." Compare with ps. Aristeas 248, 255, 266, 268. Cf. note 63 above.

"look to the divine word" (εἰς δὲ λόγον θεῖον βλέψας:
P.E. 13.12.5). Thus the peculiar reticence to accept the
Exodus account of God as "speaking" is shared by Aristobulus
and Philo.

In spite of our fragmentary sources for Aristobulus,
therefore, it is possible to proceed with some confidence
in describing the continuity in interpretative framework between
Aristobulus and Philo. The Moses whom Aristobulus presents
may be a "divine man" in so far as he possesses the "divine
spirit" (θεῖον πνεῦμα: P.E. 8.10.4), but there is no basis
for suggesting that this writer would have been any more
anxious than Philo to highlight Moses' role as a miracle
worker in an attempt to verify his divine stature.

The picture that Artapanus paints of Moses is
dramatically different. The fascinating suggestion that
this work which is preserved in fragmentary form in Eusebius'
Praeparatio Evangelica 9 and in Clement of Alexandria
Stromateis I 154.2 comes from the same hand as pseudo-
Aristeas[67] is untenable. As Dalbert has observed, next to
works like pseudo-Aristeas, Aristobulus, or Philo, Artapanus
appears naive and uncritical, "a primitive mixture (Gemisch)
of history, legend, traditions of faith, and fantasy."[68]
Certainly his depiction of Moses is enough of a complex

---

[67]Cf. Freudenthal, op. cit., pp. 143-174. For Eusebius'
text of Artapanus on Moses, cf. Appendix II, p. 321. Cf. also
F. Gr. Hist. for a critical Greek text.

[68]Dalbert, op. cit., p. 44.

concotion to prevent its hasty classification as a "romance"[69] or "aretalogy"[70] or βίος of a θεῖος ἀνήρ .[71]

The argument for a line of continuity between Artapanus and Philo on the basis of a shared conception of Moses as a θεῖος ἀνήρ has been stated most precisely by Georgi.[72] The propagandistic intention of Artapanus' depiction of Moses is no less obvious than that of Eupolemus or Philo. Furthermore the work may display Artapanus' acquaintance with a larger context of propaganda and polemic. For example, Artapanus is aware of the traditions also found in Diodorus of Sicily (depending on Hecataeus?, cf. Diod. I 46.8)[73] that the great heroes of Greek antiquity such as Orpheus, Musaeus, Homer, Plato, and Hermes were dependent on Egyptian

---

[69]Cf. I. Heinemann, "Moses", PW XVI (1935), col. 367. Braun, op. cit., pp. 26-27. A sober and cautious classification of this work as a "romance" is offered in a recent study which has been of considerable help to this analysis: John Collins and William Poehlmann, "Artapanus", New Testament Seminar 201, Harvard Divinity School, April 6, 1970, p. 50.

[70]M. Hadas, Hellenistic Culture, op. cit., pp. 90-91, 172.

[71]Otto Weinreich, Gebet und Wunder (Stuttgart, 1929), p. 141. Reprinted from the Festschrift Genethliakon Wilhelm Schmid (Tübinger Beiträge zur Altertumswissenschaft 5; Stuttgart, 1929), p. [307].

[72]Op. cit., pp. 148-162.

[73]The numerous parallels between Artapanus and Diodorus with respect to Egyptian religious culture argue in favor of a common source of traditions. Hecataeus could have been this source, but the difficulty of identifying precise points of dependence of Diodorus upon Hecataeus, coupled with the lack of verbal parallels between Artapanus and Diodorus, cautions against final judgements. After all, Diodorus reports

customs and learning (Diod. I 96, cf. also I 16, I 23.8-24.4;
P.E. 9.27.3-6), and he includes Moses' invention of philosophy
in the list of his other practical discoveries such as
ships, devices for laying stones, weapons, and devices for
drawing water and waging war (P.E. 9.27.4).[74] The
description of Moses in his old age as "tall, ruddy, with
long grey hair and dignified bearing" (ἀξιωματικός: P.E.
9.27.39), which probably represents an expansion of Deut.
34:7, could also be viewed as a fitting characterization of
the Moses portrayed by Eupolemus, Aristobulus, or Philo.
Doubtless Artapanus is aware of certain literary conventions,
but these elements are too general to suggest an
interpretative continuum between Artapanus and those authors
who have depicted Moses as a divine wise man.

Consideration must be given to the evidence that
Artapanus is responding to anti-Jewish polemics. Halévy[75]

---

that he himself visited Egypt (I 44.1; I 83.8) and thus may
have had access to other Egyptian sources.

[74]The theme of the "discoverers" (εὑρεται) of diverse
benefits for humanity is too wide-spread as to permit precise
identification. As Hengel points out (op. cit., p. 552),
however, Artapanus' use of the motif does demonstrate that
this propagandistic work is intended to place Moses in a
favorable light next to other great legendary figures. Cf.
Weinreich, op. cit., p. 134 [300]. But the fact that philosophy
is merely listed as another discovery alongside of devices
for drawing water suggests a context of discourse in which
philosophical criteria are not primary.

[75]M.A. Halévy, Moïse dans l'histoire et dans la légende
(Judaisme VI; Paris, 1927), pp. 54-55, 61.

and Vermes[76] argue that the exceptional elements in the
depiction of Moses can be adequately perceived as the attempts
of a loyal Jew to defend his tradition before a pagan
audience as a system of religious philosophy by assuming the
terms of the debate from his opponents, while a writer like
Josephus refuses to accept any common ground with the anti-
Semites he is refuting.

Braun also sees the work as a response to anti-
Semitism, but he regards it as a popular expression which is
directed to an audience composed of oppressed Jews who need
encouragement.[77] Braun's work must be regarded as something
of a breakthrough in that it illustrates the difference in
propagandistic context between those who debate on a literary
and educated level, such as Manetho and Josephus, and those
who celebrate the mighty deeds of the heroes of their
tradition in a less sophisticated attempt to preserve a
sense of national integrity and pride in the face of the
loss of national independence:

> "This popular narrative literature is the spiritual
> bread without which no proud people can stand the
> pressure of alien domination, and it is individual
> heroic figures in whom the feeling and longing of the
> masses come to a concentrated expression."[78]

---

[76]Geza Vermes, "La figure de Moise au tourant des deux
testaments," Moise, l'homme de l'alliance (ed. H. Calles et
al, special issue of Cahiers Sioniens; Paris, 1955), pp. 68-
73. Cf. Heinemann, op. cit., col. 369.

[77]Braun, op. cit., pp. 26-27. Cf. V. Tcherikover,
"Jewish Apologetic Literature Reconsidered," op. cit.,
pp. 132-133, 192-193.

[78]Braun, op. cit., p. 3.

Such "romanticizing"[79] of national heroes was apparently

a widespread phenomenon in the Hellenistic world, cf.

Plutarch Isis and Osiris 24 (360 B):

> "Mighty deeds of Semiramis are celebrated among the
> Assyrians, and mighty deeds of Sesostris in Egypt, and
> the Phrygians, even to this day, call brilliant and
> marvelous exploits 'manic' because Manes, one of their
> early kings, proved himself a good man and exercised a
> vast influence among them."[80]

Some literary authors were highly critical of such

popular legends.[81]

What is particularly striking in Braun's analysis,

moreover, is his demonstration of the way in which feats

ascribed to one hero in romantic legend can be attributed to

a series of national figures as their exploits are recited.

The founder of Meroe, for example, can be claimed to be

Semiramis (Diod. II 14.4, ps. Callisthenes III 18), Cambyses

(Diod. I 33), and Moses (Artapanus, P.E. 9.27.16) in turn.[82]

---

[79]In light of scholarly disagreement concerning the
origins of the romance as a genre of literature, it seems
prudent to avoid Braun's terminology of "Nectanebus Romance,"
"Alexander Romance," and "Moses Romance;" but Braun argues
very cogently for the formal similarity of such collections
of legends and makes a good case for the continuity between
these narratives and later romance literature.

[80]Trans. by F.C. Babbitt, Plutarch's Moralia V (Loeb
edition: Cambridge, 1936), p. 57.

[81]Cf. Josephus, c. Ap. I 142. Braun, op. cit., p. 15,
suggests that Manetho did not include the Sesostris legend
out of his low opinion for such material but that "in
Apion, at a later stage, Graeco-Egyptian scholarship has
fallen almost to the level of the legend and pseudo-
historical folk story." Cf. c. Ap. II 132).

[82]Ibid., p. 17.

Furthermore, as the previous chapter of this study has argued,[83] the emphasis that pseudo-Callisthenes places on Alexander the Great's powers to work miracles is best explained by the dependence of such accounts on the specifically Egyptian romantic legends about Nectanebus.

The Egyptian provenance of Artapanus' treatment of Moses and its ties with popular romantic legends can be highlighted in a brief review of the text.[84] After situating Moses in Egyptian history (27.1-3), Artapanus reports that the king's daughter Merris[85] adopted (ὑποβαλέσθαι) the Jewish child Moses, whom the Greeks called Musaeus (27.3). Perhaps Artapanus is responding to the charge that Moses was not a Hebrew but an Egyptian,[86]

---

[83]Cf. previous chapter, circa notes 152-153.

[84]Whether Artapanus was himself an Egyptian Jew may have to remain an open question, but the numerous contacts with Egyptian cultural practices at least demonstrates his acquaintance with sources knowledgeable about Egypt. Whether he was merely dependent upon a handbook such as that of Hecataeus can only be decided by an orientalist who is much better versed in this culture than I. The question merits further study.

[85]Josephus gives her name as Thermuthis (Antiq. II 224, 232, 236, 243; cf. Jubilees 47:5 where she is called Tharmuth) which represents a logical tie with Egyptian culture since Thermuthis is known in some texts as the goddess of wet nursing [cf. Hans Bonnet, Reallexikon der Ägyptischen Religionsgeschichte (Berlin, 1952), pp. 803-804]. Note, however, that both Jubilees and Josephus follow the story of Exodus 2:8-9 by having Moses nursed by his own mother. This detail is omitted in Artapanus.

[86]For the extensive lectionary of texts which record this opinion, cf. Gager, op. cit., pp. 7, 47 ff, 220 ff.

but he makes no attempt to provide an aetiology for such a
non-Jewish opinion as Philo does when he credits the king's
daughter with an elaborate ruse to pass off Moses as her own
son (γνήσιος) and not adopted (ὑποβολιμαῖος: Mos. I 19).
Artapanus appears to be merely giving a rather free version
of the biblical account of Moses adoption by the king's
daughter.

The identification of Moses as Musaeus "by the Greeks"
may be logically connected with the next line where Moses is
called "the teacher of Orpheus" (27.4). Weinreich points to
an orphic tradition where Mousaios was identified as the
teacher of Orpheus,[87] and Diodorus I 23 records the complex
tradition of Orpheus' role in transferring the birthplace of
Osiris to Thebes. Thus Orpheus was not only a founder of
Greek culture who learned from the Egyptians (Diod. I 96),
but he was also credited with influencing the foundation of
an Egyptian cult. His teacher, Moses, is once again shown
by Artapanus to be the ultimate "master of Egyptian
civilization."[88]

The bland inclusion of philosophy as one of the
practical discoveries of Moses does not establish that
Artapanus aims to depict the Jewish benefactor of Egypt as
a "divine wise man" as did Eupolemus, Aristobulus, and

---

[87]Weinreich, op. cit., p. 134 [300]. Cf. O. Kern Orphic
Frag. p. 14 t. 44. Cf. also Denis, op. cit., pp. 255-257 and
note 43.

[88]Halévy, op. cit., p. 55.

Philo.[89] Nor is Artapanus appealing to a general image of
the θεῖος ἀνήρ. The Moses he presents is in direct
competition with traditional Egyptian benefactors who gained
immortality and divine status because of their practical
sagacity (σύνεσις) and benefits to men (εὐεργεσία:
Diod. I 13.1). Particular attention should be paid to the
romantic legends about Sesostris and the legendary accounts
of benefits which Isis bestowed upon Egypt.

The practical benefits credited to Moses show striking
parallels to those of Sesostris. Sesostris is remembered
as the military genius (cf. Diod. I 54-56; 94.4; Herodotus II
102-106) and is specifically credited with being the first
Egyptian to build warships (Diod. I 55.2; cf. Herod. II
102; cf. Artapanus 27.4). His role in providing for the
building of stone temples and irrigation canals (Herod. II
108; Diod. I 57) appears to be outdone by Artapanus' Moses
who invented devices for laying stones and drawing water
(27.4). Both Moses (Artapanus 27.4) and Sesostris (Diod. I
54.3) are in turn credited with dividing Egypt into 36 nomes.
Sesostris' care for observing local religious customs by
building "in each city in Egypt a temple to the god who was
specially revered by its inhabitants" (Diod. I 56.2)

---

[89]Cf. note 74 above and note that Artapanus never calls
Moses either "sage" or "legislator", the two favorite
designations used by those who were appealing to the philosophical criteria of the true "divine man". In Artapanus,
Moses is only a legislator in so far as he orders Egyptian
civilization.

corresponds to Moses' apportionment of a god to be worshipped
in each nome (27.4). Artapanus' claim that Moses designated
a certain precinct of land for the priests (27.4) may also
correspond to the legend that Sesostris gave allotments of
land to his commanders (Diod. I 54.6) as well as to every
Egyptian (Herod. II 107).[90] The report of the love of the
multitudes for Moses (27.6) is probably too general a motif
to provide compelling evidence for the connection between
Artapanus and romantic Egyptian legends, yet the image of
the great ruler who is a beloved benefactor of the masses
and inaugurates a period of secure peace and prosperity for
all his people is a strong theme in the legends which
conquered peoples cultivated about their national heroes
(on Sesostris, cf. Diod. I 54.2; 55.12; 56.1-2; 57.2;
Herod. II 109).

Even Artapanus' report that the Egyptian priests regarded
Moses as worthy of being honored like a god (ἰσοθέου τιμῆς
καταξιωθέντα: 27.6) places Moses in direct competition

---

[90]Both Diodorus and Herodotus are particularly interested
in the military aspect of the portrait of Sesostris, but they
also regard the priests as the primary defenders of the
memory of this benefactor (cf. Diod. I 58.3,4; Herod. II
102, 107, 110). Thus the fact that neither Diodorus nor
Herodotus mentions special districts for the priests is
probably not significant. The reference by Artapanus to the
appointment of sacred letters (ἱερὰ γράμματα) to the
priests does not appear to have parallels in the Sesostris
legend, although Diodorus (I 55.7) mentions that Sesostris
inscribed his victory stelae with "Egyptian letters which
are called sacred" (Αἰγυπτίοις γράμμασι τοῖς ἱεροῖς
λεγομένοις).   Cf. the discussion of Isis as a transmitter
of Demotic letters below.

with a romantic hero like Sesostris, whose revered position
in the cult was eagerly defended by the priests (<u>Herod</u>. II
110; <u>Diod</u>. I 58.4). This correspondence with the Sesostris
legend is particularly striking since there it is reported
that the priests refused to let Darius place his statue
before that of Sesostris in the temple since he had
"achieved nothing equal to the deeds of Sesostris the
Egyptian" (<u>Herod</u>. II 104, cf. <u>Diod</u>. I 58.4) while Artapanus
claims that it was the priests who regarded Moses as worthy
of divine honor.

The identification of the "divine Moses" with Hermes on
the basis of his interpretation of Hieroglyphics finds
resonance in the traditions about Isis. Yet Moses is a
step above the goddess. While Isis was taught by Hermes
(<u>Diod</u>. I 17.3; I 27.4; Isis inscription from Ios, line 5:
Deissmann)[91] and was co-inventor (εὗρον) with Hermes of
Demotic letters for special (sacred?) applications,[92] Moses
is <u>identified</u> with Hermes (<u>Artapanus</u> 27.6) and is alone
credited with giving the sacred letters to the priests
(27.4).[93] Even in those texts where Hermes-Thoth was

[91]A. Deissmann, <u>Light from the Ancient East</u> (New York,
1927), p. 139. Cf. chapter I of this study, note 3.

[92]<u>Ibid</u>., lines 6-8: "I devised with Hermes demotic
letters in order that all things might not be written with the
same (letters)" For Hermes-Thot as the inventor of writing,
cf. <u>Diod</u>. I 16.1; Philo of Byblos, Eusebius <u>P.E</u>. I 9.31d;
Cicero <u>de</u> <u>nat</u>. <u>deorum</u> III 22. Cf. Hengel, <u>op</u>. <u>cit</u>., pp. 171
390.

[93]For the general importance of the "sacred script" in
Hellenistic religious propaganda, cf. Georgi, <u>op</u>. <u>cit</u>., p. 202.

recognized as the father of Isis (Plutarch <u>Isis</u> <u>and</u> <u>Osiris</u>
355 F - 356 A: 12), her subordination was clear. Hermes,
whose name Diodorus (I 16.1) also derives from ἑρμηνεία,
attained his divine status due to his practical sagacity
and beneficence to men (<u>Diod</u>. I 13.1-2; 15.9; 43.6) including
the discovery of the arts of learning (<u>Diod</u>. I 43.6; Cicero
<u>de</u> <u>nat</u>. <u>deorum</u> 3.22)[94] and the giving of law to the
Egyptians (<u>Diod</u>. I 94.1; Cicero <u>loc</u>. <u>cit</u>). Thus although
Artapanus does not feature Moses as the one who gives the
law to the Jews, he portrays him as the one who taught the
Egyptians their letters and instituted law and order in
Egypt. As such, he is worthy of the divine rank of Hermes,
a status superior to that of Isis.

The reference to the ἀρετή of Moses (27.7) which
Chenephres envied is problematic. Nothing is said in
Artapanus of Moses having superior moral virtue and the
catalog of his magical-miraculous acts which appears later
in the work does not appear to be intended as documentation
of this ἀρετή. Georgi suggests that it is no accident that
Artapanus mentions Moses' ἀρετή in the line following his

---

[94]Diodorus, <u>loc</u>. <u>cit</u>., indicates that it was the priests
who relate that Hermes was the "discoverer of the branches
of learning and of the arts (εὑρετὴς τῶν μὲν παιδειῶν καὶ
τῶν τεχνῶν). Although "philosophy" is not explicitly
mentioned, it seems reasonable to regard Artapanus' reference
to Moses' discovery of philosophy (27.4) in this light.
Philosophy is merely one of the practical benefits that
Hermes-Thot-Moses bestows.

reference to the divine status of Moses.[95] Doubtless
Artapanus intends this verse be connected with the
preceding section in so far as it provides further
documentation of Moses' exalted status; but since this verse
introduces the episodes where Chenephres opposes Moses, the
connotation of the term ἀρετή may be more precisely
grasped by looking at the subsequent verses where Moses is
shown to be militarily superior to the king (27.7-8).

Once again an incident from the romantic legends of
Sesostris furnishes an interpretative context. In I 58.1-2,
Diodorus describes the subjection of kings and potentates
(βασιλεῖς καὶ οἱ ἄλλοι ἡγεμόνες) to the point that they
took the places of horses in pulling Sesostris' chariot to
a city or temple. This bit of theatrics was the most
fitting display of Sesostris' majesty (μεγαλοπρεπέστατον),
and exhibited to all men that these rulers who were famous
for their ἀρετή   were unable to compete with Sesostris
for the prize of superiority (εἰς ἅμιλλαν ἀρετῆς).   The
concept of ἀρετή appears similarly specific for Artapanus.
Even when the priests have declared him to be a divine
Hermes on the basis of his benefits to Egypt, his
superiority or ἀρετή which the king envies is documented
not by a list of moral qualities or miracles but by an
incredible display of military prowess, accomplished with

---

[95]Op. cit., p. 150.

the unlikely aid of an army of farmers.[96]

A war with the Ethiopians is featured in several of the romantic legends about national heroes.[97] The Babylonian heroine Semiramis subdued Ethiopia (Diod. II 14.4), and Cambyses is charged with an imprudent and unsuccessful campaign against the Ethiopians (Herod. III 17-26). Diodorus (I 55) points out that Sesostris began his wars of military conquest ($\dot{\epsilon}\pi\grave{\iota}$ $\pi\rho\acute{\omega}\tau\upsilon\upsilon\varsigma$) with the defeat of the Ethopians, which apparently relegated his earlier defeat of the Arabs (Diod. I 53.5 & 10) to a training mission. At any rate, Sesostris gained a reputation as the first man to conquer the Ethiopians (Strabo 16.4.4) and as "the only Egyptian king who also ruled Ethiopia" (Herod. II 110). Operating under the handicap of a non-professional army, Moses' victory against the Ethiopians is just that much more glorious than that of the other national heroes.

Josephus' version of this non-biblical legend of Moses the military conquerer of Ethiopia (Antiq. 2.238-253) also indicates that this was the first campaign of the young

---

[96]The reason for the king's envy is clearer in Josephus Antiq. 2:255 since Moses has already displayed his military prowess. This appears to be a more direct version of the legend. But Moses victory is glorified in Artapanus by the fact that the king, out of envy, is plotting Moses' death by sending him into battle with an untrained army. Cf. below and note 98 for Josephus' view of the victory as a display of $\dot{\alpha}\rho\epsilon\tau\acute{\eta}$.

[97]I am indebted to the paper of Collins and Poehlmann, op. cit., p. 26, for several of these references.

Moses and increases the magnitude of the victory by having
Moses called in when the Ethiopians are on the verge of
conquering all of Egypt. Furthermore, Josephus introduces
the story with the comment:

> "When he had come of age, he made his superiority
> manifest (φανερά) to the Egyptians and showed that he
> was born for their humiliation (ταπείνωσις) and for the
> advancement of the Hebrews." (Antiq. 2.238)[98]

Thus in the legends of Sesostris and Moses, the campaign of
the hero leading an army (δύναμις: Diod. I 55.1; Artapanus
27.7) in victory against the Ethiopians provides primary
evidence of his military superiority (ἀρετή).

Weinreich stresses the frequency of aetiological
arguments in Artapanus' account of Moses.[99] Certainly the
reference to the founding of Hermopolis as "Hermes city"
and the abbreviated reference to the establishment of the
cult of the ibis (27.9)[100] are attempts to document Moses'
stature as the master of Egyptian civilization. The
aetiology of the Ethiopian practice of circumcision (27.10)
could also represent a response to the un-Jewish view that

---

[98]This section of Josephus reproduces the legend in
more detail than does Artapanus, including the marriage of
Moses to the daughter of the Ethiopians (252-253) and the
details of the importance of the ibis for the victory (245-
246). No doubt the problem of sources is insoluble with
respect to much of this legendary material (cf. Heinemann,
op. cit., col. 367), but the view of the military strength
of the hero as the documentation of his ἀρετή must have
been a common feature in such sources.

[99]Op. cit., pp. 135-136 [301-302].

[100]Cf. Josephus Antiq. 2.245-246 and note 98 above.

the Jews learned circumcision from the Egyptians and
Ethiopians (cf. especially Diod. I 28.3). But the precise
reason for mentioning circumcision at this point may have
been that a discussion of the origin of the rite was
embedded in the romantic legends of Sesostris. One of the
arguments for the extent of the conquests of Sesostris which
is recorded both in Herodotus (II 103-104) and in Diodorus
(I 55) is the widespread practice of circumcision which is
claimed to be of Egyptian or Ethiopian origin. Whether or
not Artapanus' version of the romantic legend of Moses
arises from an explicit awareness of the Sesostris legend,
the continuing practice of circumcision in Ethiopia could
have been used in the same way by Artapanus as evidence of
the veracity of his account of Moses' conquest.

Artapanus' attitude toward the animal cults of Egypt is
not easily assessed. Clearly these cults were an important
aspect of Egyptian culture;[101] and Moses, the master of that
culture, must be credited with the benefits associated with
those cults. Thus, unlike a writer such as Aristeas (cf.
134-139),[102] Artapanus does not attack the cults. In fact,
he apparently credits Moses with the distribution of a god to

---

[101]Cf. Diod. I 86-90 where explanations as to the origin
of such practices range from myths that the gods once
assumed animal disguises, to their symbolic value as military
standards, to the utility of animals, and to their value for
organizing primitive Egyptian society.

[102]Cf. Dalbert, op. cit., p. 44.

each nome, including cats, dogs, and ibises (27.4).[103] This
is part of Moses' practical efforts in the ordering of
Egyptian culture which might be seen as consistent with the
sociological explanation of the origin of such cults that
Diodorus gives (I 90). Moses is also credited with
consecrating the ibis (τὴν ἶβιν καθιερῶσαι: 27.9) because
of the usefulness of the bird to man (cf. Diod. I 87).

Although his Moses is thus responsible for the assets
of the cults, Artapanus is not unequivocally approving of
them. The first sign of this comes in his aetiology of the
Apis cult (27.12). First of all, Moses is given credit for
identifying oxen as beneficial to mankind because of their
use in plowing. Apparently this prompts Chenephres to found
the Apis cult with a temple in Memphis (cf. Diod. I 85.3;
88.4; Plutarch Isis and Osiris 359 B: 20). Thus Moses is
ultimately but indirectly credited with the founding of this
cult. But then the king orders that the animals which Moses
had consecrated be buried there in order that Moses'
inventions (ἐπινοήματα) might be covered up. By this
device, Artapanus gives Moses all the credit for the useful
discoveries but reduces the competition between the cults
to the level of personal jealousy. His own view of the

---

[103]The text is murky at this point: καὶ ἑκάστῳ τῶν νομῶν
ἀποτάξαι τὸν θεὸν σεφθήσεσθαι τὰ ἱερὰ γράμματα τοῖς ἱερεῦσιν,
εἶναι δὲ καὶ αἰλούρους καὶ κύνας καὶ ἴβεις   (27.4).
Freudenthal, op. cit., p. 147, is probably correct that τὸν θεόν
is to be read distributively with ἑκάστῳ.   The same verb
probably also governs the list of animals, each is god of a
separate nome.

inadequacy of the animal deities is also seen in his conception of Moses' God as "the Lord of the world" (ὁ τῆς οἰκουμένης δεσπότης: 27.22) which can be contrasted to the treatment of the animal gods as being distributed by Moses, one to each nome, (27.4). Thus when the showdown comes, it is no surprise that the Egyptians who brought along their animal gods (27.35) are destroyed by fire and flood (27.37).

The death of Merris (27.15) occasions another plot on Moses' life, climaxed by his murder of Chanethotes in self-defense (27.18) and flight into Arabia (27.17 & 19). Whether this account represents a further correspondence with the legends of Sesostris who also went from Ethiopia into Arabia (Strabo 16.4.4; cf. Diod. I 53.5)[104] remains hypothetical. But the correlation between the burial of Merris and the founding of Meroe (27.16) puts Moses into direct competition with other national heroes whose legends credit them with the foundation of this city.[105]

The reported honor or worship of Merris "not less than that for Isis" (27.16) is perplexing. Weinreich's explanation that this is an aetiology for ruler worship in an attempt to make such a cult palatable to Jews seems

_____

[104]The order is reversed in Diodorus who sends Sesostris on a training mission into Arabia before his conquest of Ethiopia. Yet Diodorus (I 55) counts the Ethiopian campaign as the first of Sesostris' conquests in his policy of world imperialism.

[105]Braun, op. cit., p. 17.

promising, but lacks support in the text.[106] Isis was generally regarded as buried in Memphis,[107] but she was also apparently the chief goddess of Meroe (cf. Strabo XVII 2.3; Diod. III 9).[108] Artapanus' acquaintance with Isis worship at Meroe invites the further question of whether he was aware of a competing local cult which claimed that its patron was buried at Meroe.[109] At least, Artapanus is attempting to fortify his claim that Moses founded the city with an aetiology based on the similarity of the names "Merris" and "Meroe". Even this detail that Moses founded Meroe and named it after his foster mother whom he buried there has intriguing parallels with the legends of Cambyses. Diodorus reports that Meroe "was founded by Cambyses and named by him after his mother Meroe" (I 33.1), and Strabo indicates that "the name was given by him to both the island and the city, it is said, because his sister Meroe - some say his wife - died there. The name, at any rate, he

---

[106]Op. cit., p. 136 [302].

[107]Cf. Diod. I 21, where a tradition is also cited that Isis may have been buried on an island in the Nile near Philae.

[108]Cf. Bonnet, op. cit., "Meroe," pp. 456-457.

[109]Strabo 17.2.3 mentions that the inhabitants of Meroe worship "Hercules, Pan, and Isis in addition to some other barbaric god." It is doubtful that this vague reference to a god can be directly applied to the goddess Merris, but it allows for the possibility that the identity of every member of the local pantheon was not unequivocally clear. Any debate about the identity of a god whose grave was known would have invited interpretations by tendentious historians like Artapanus. Nevertheless, the point remains conjectural.

bestowed upon the place in honor of the woman" (17.1.5). It appears likely that Artapanus has adapted a version of this legend and applied it to Moses.

In 27.21 Moses' God appears for the first time and the orientation of Artapanus' account of Moses seems to have changed. Perhaps the shift in perspective should be recognized in 27.20 where Chenephres is reported to have died from elephantiasis because of his persecution of the Jews. Verses 20-38 are clearly concerned with the conflict between the Egyptians and Jews and their respective champions. To this point, Moses has been identified as the benefactor of the Egyptians in competition with Chenephres, and the only indication of the oppression of the Jews is the mention that Palmanothes, the father-in-law of Chenephres, treated the Jews badly (27.2).

In addition to the appearance of Moses' God and the new focus on the oppression of the Jews, this section is characterized by a series of miraculous events and magical performances without parallel in verses 1-19. The death of Chenephres is doubtless intended to be interpreted as miraculous evidence of divine retribution, although neither God nor Moses is credited with the miracle. But when Moses prays to God on behalf of the tribes, a detail not found in the Exodus account, a fire blazes from the earth which not only consumes nothing, as Exodus 3:2 also reports, but goes on burning although there is no fuel or wood in the place (27.21). Thus Artapanus' account of the fire has heightened

the miraculous element in the biblical story of the burning
bush. Furthermore, Artapanus shares none of the reticence
that Aristobulus and Philo have shown in referring to the
"divine voice" (θεῖα φωνή:27.21 & 30).[110] The "divine
voice" merely commands, and Artapanus includes none of the
Stoic overlay that such a message is only heard when it is
seen (cf. P.E. 13.12.4; Philo Mig. 49).

Nor is Artapanus particularly cautious about maintaining
that Moses is subservient to God in all that he does. After
a very brief mention of his initial fright before the
miraculous fire (27.21), Moses "took courage and determined
to lead a hostile force against the Egyptians" (21.21). To
be sure, he is acting on command of the "divine voice" now
further identified with "the Lord of the world" (27.22),
but Moses runs his own show until the "divine voice" commands
him to divide the Red Sea (27.36).

His first performances are most noteworthy because they
are completely without biblical parallel. When imprisoned
by the king, he escapes when the doors open of their own
accord (αὐτομάτως: 27.23).[111] This is not intended to be

---

[110]Cf. previous discussion of "divine voice" in Aristobulus
and Philo. Here my analysis differs markedly from Dalbert,
op. cit., p. 45, who cites Philo for parallels to Artapanus.

[111]This section of Artapanus is also paralleled in Clement
of Alexandria, Strom. I 154.2, but his version has eliminated
many of the magical-miraculous elements, including the
substitution of κατὰ βούλησιν τοῦ θεοῦ for αὐτομάτως.
For the argument that Clement's version is secondary, cf.
Weinreich, op. cit., p. 137 [202].

interpreted as an accident, but as a miraculous event.[112]
Some of the guards die while the others sleep and their
weapons are broken. From the prison, Moses proceeds directly
through opened palace doors and past more sleeping guards
into the king's chamber (27.24). The miraculous character
of the events merely underlines Moses' complete mastery
of the situation.

These performances provide the primary basis for
Weinreich's classification of Artapanus' account of Moses as
a βίος of a θεῖος ἀνήρ, [113] but the correlations
between Artapanus' depiction of Moses and nationalistic
legends about a variety of popular heroes are also multiplied
by these expansions of the biblical account. In particular,
the parochial legends of Egyptian national heroes ought to
be examined before citing Artapanus as evidence of the
emergence of a general Hellenistic conception of the divine
man.

Once again, the Sesostris legends as cited in Herodotus

---

[112]Ibid., p. 58 [224].

[113]Op. cit., p. 138 [304]. The motif of a miraculous
escape from prison does invite comparison with a wide range
of escape stories of antiquity. The parallels with Acts 12:
6-11, including the passing of two sets of guards and the
opening of the barred door "by its own accord" (αὐτομάτη:
Acts 12:10), are striking, cf. also Acts 16:25-30.
Philostratus' Life of Apollonius also has a story of a
miraculous escape from a fetter which proved he was divine
since he didn't even offer a prayer (7.38), and this work
includes an account of Apollonius' miraculous disappearance
from the emperor's court in a "divine and not easily explained
manner" (δαιμόνιόν τε καὶ οὐ ῥᾴδιον εἰπεῖν τρόπον: 8.5).

and Diodorus include a story with comparable features.
Herodotus (II 107) tells a rationalized version of Sesostris'
escape from a fire which the king's brother set around his
house. Herodotus reports that Sesostris is saved by building
a human bridge over the fire with the bodies of two of his
sons. But Diodorus (I 57.7-8) records that Sesostris was
"miraculously saved (σωθεὶς παραδόξως) by "raising both
hands and praying for the safety of his wife and children"
as he dashed through the flames.

The Moses legend does not parallel this escape story
closely enough to suggest any direct associations, but the
marvelous escape of the romantic hero is fully consistent
with the expectation of such popular legends that the hero
would be confirmed by miraculous and magical displays. The
importance of such performances in popular Egyptian legends
for authenticating the divine king[114] has already been
discussed in the first chapter with reference to the
treatment of Alexander the Great by pseudo-Callisthenes and
the Nectanebus cycle of legends. It is worth noting in

---

[114]Diodorus ends his account with these words: "When he
had been miraculously saved, he honored the other gods (οἱ
ἄλλοι θεοί) with offerings, as stated above, and Hephaestus
most of all since it was by his intervention that he had
been saved" (I 57.8). The reference to "the other gods" may
be merely an anticipation of the mention of Hephaestus. But
if Hephaestus is counted as a member of this group of "other
gods" who deserves special mention, the text may refer to
Sesostris' own divine status. Thus he honored his fellow gods
and Hephaestus in particular for their aid. The status of
Sesostris in the temple cult, which the priests were eager to
defend (Herod. II 110; Diod. I 58.4) would be consistent
with such an intimation of Sesostris' divinity in this text.

passing, however, that Sesostris' own son is featured in a
miraculous healing legend. Herodotus (II 111) and Diodorus
(I 59) report that this king was blinded for impiously
hurling a spear into the flooding Nile and was only cured
when he was eventually able to follow the oracle's instruction
of washing his eyes in the urine of a woman who had never
had intercourse with any man but her husband. Apparently
Egyptian religion did not share the aversion to miraculous
or magical legends which has been described as characteristic
of Greek philosophical idealizations of the divine wise
man,[115] and thus such tales were regarded as appropriate in
popular characterizations of the parochial heroes who were
thought to have had divine status.

The magical power that Moses possesses because of his
knowledge of the name of God gives him a mastery over the
king and priests of Egypt which admits no challenge. When
Moses whispers the name in his ear, the king falls down mute
and Moses must "revive" him (ἀναβιῶσαι: 27.25).[116] The
priest who ridicules the divine name that Moses wrote on a
tablet dies in a convulsion (27.26). This connection
between Moses' knowledge of the ineffable name and his

---

[115]Cf. Bonnet, op. cit., "Magie," pp. 435-439, and
"Zauber," pp. 875-880.

[116]Perhaps Moses "brought the king to life again" from
death. The fate of the priest who dies for mocking the
divine name (27.26) might support this stronger reading of
ἀναβιῶσαι. But if Artapanus wishes to suggest that Moses
performed a re-vivification of a dead man, his description
of the king as "mute" (ἄφωνος) seems too mild.

possession in Egypt of the power to work miracles may also

be found in Josephus:

> "Moses, unable to doubt the promises of the Deity, after
> having seen and heard such confirmation of them, prayed
> and entreated that he might be given this power (δύναμις)
> in Egypt; he also asked that he not be denied the
> knowledge of his name (ὀνόματος αὐτῷ γνῶσις τοῦ ἰδίου).
> . . . Then God revealed his name to him, which had not
> previously reached men, concerning which it is not
> fitting for me to speak. And Moses found these miracles
> (σημεῖα) available to him not only then, but at all
> times when there was need" (Antiq. II 275-276).[117]

The repeated allusions to Moses in the magical papyri

document the importance of this knowledge for his authent-

ication as a great miracle worker.[118]

In the syncretistic sphere of magic, particularly as

represented by the magical papyri, it is almost impossible

---

[117]Since Exodus 3-4 reports that Moses received the divine
name and the power to work miracles in this encounter at the
burning bush, it is difficult to decide whether Josephus is
merely following the biblical account or suggesting an
integral connection between the knowledge of the name and the
power to work miracles. Josephus merely states that Moses
"also asked that he not be denied the knowledge of his name
... so that, when sacrificing, he might invoke him by name"
(Antiq. 2:275). Thus the magical power of the name is clear
in Artapanus and the magical papyri (cf. note 118), but
Josephus' attitude toward the name appears more complex, cf.
notes 218 and 227 below.

[118]Cf. PGM II 126-128: "I am him who met you and you
gave to me as a gift the knowledge (γνῶσις) of your
greatest name." PGM III 158-159: "I am him whom you
encountered and to whom you granted knowledge (γνῶσις) of
your greatest name and of its sacred pronunciation" (ἐκφώνησις).
PGM XII 92-94: "I am him whom you encountered at the foot of
the sacred mountain and you granted knowledge (γνῶσις) of
your greatest name which I will keep and transmit to no one
except to fellow initiates in your sacred mysteries." PGM V
108-118: "I am Moses your prophet to whom you committed
your mysteries which are celebrated by Istrael" (sic).
Gager, op. cit., pp. 280-281, argues convincingly that the
speaker who claims status before God on the basis of his
knowledge must be Moses.

and somewhat pointless to attempt to decide what is Jewish
and what is pagan in origin,[119] but Gager is probably correct
in asserting that "the greatest contribution of Judaism to
the syncretistic world of magic was the divine name which
appears so frequently in the papyri, Iao, Sabaoth, Adonai."[120]
Gager also showed that this Moses of the magical papyri is
far removed from the Moses known to more cultured or literary
pagans. The Moses whose reputation as a miracle worker or
magician rested on his knowledge of the divine name was so
glorious that his own name "guaranteed the efficacy of magical
charms and provided protection against the hostile forces of
the cosmos."[121]

There is no evidence that Artapanus regarded Moses'
name as having magical power, but even his inclusion of these
episodes of the power of the divine name which Moses knows
indicate that Artapanus is interested in a cycle of legends
about Moses and his miraculous power which Aristobulus,
Eupolemus, and Philo would have regarded as alien to their
portraits of Moses the wise man, law giver, and prophet.

Artapanus' fascination with the rod of Moses is

---

[119]Cf. the schema proposed by Goodenough, Jewish
Symbols, op. cit., vol. II (1953), p. 206, for grouping the
charms of the papyri from those composed predominately by
pagans to those composed predominately by Jews. The
classification only helps to document the complexity of the
syncretism that is involved.

[120]Gager, op. cit., p. 277.

[121]Ibid., p. 312.

additional evidence of his interest in Moses as a miracle
worker. In verses 27-36, Artapanus mentions the rod nine
times, always in reference to a miraculous occurence. While
Philo carefully follows the Exodus text in observing that it
was Aaron who cast his rod down before the king turning it
into a serpent (Mos. I 90) and Aaron who smote the river with
his rod turning it to blood (Mos. I 99), brought forth the
frogs with his rod (Mos. I 103) and brought forth the
insects with his staff (Mos. I 107), Artapanus credits
Moses and his rod with all of these.

Other writers such as Ezekiel the tragic poet[122] and

---

[122]Ezekiel suggests that Moses worked all of the
plagues with the rod (P.E. 9.29.442a). Grant, op. cit.,
p. 183 observes that Ezekiel admits the incredibility of the
miracles of the exodus but "illustrates how far literary men
could go in stressing miracles." A good example of this
stress on the miraculous is found where Ezekiel has the
Egyptian messenger report: "and then their leader Moses took
God's rod (ῥάβδον θεοῦ) by which he previously worked
evil signs and wonders (σημεῖα καὶ τέρατα) in Egypt and
struck the waves." The Egyptian also reports sighting a
mighty fire ahead of the Egyptians. Here Ezekiel diverges
from his usual scrupulous attendance to the biblical text (cf.
Hadas, Hellenistic Civilization, op. cit., p. 100), and the
parallels with Artapanus' account of the crossing of the Red
Sea (also attributed to Egyptian, Heliopolitan, witnesses)
suggest that Ezekiel was using a source for this legend like
Artapanus. Ezekiel does elevate Moses to a lofty status in
other contexts, even having him assume the sceptre, crown and
throne of God on Mount Sinai (P.E. 9.29, 440a). But Ezekiel's
tragedy must be studied thoroughly against the background of
its close attention to the biblical text and its relationships
with contemporary tragic verse before Ezekiel's particular
perspective on Moses can be assessed. Cf. John Strugnell,
"Notes on the Text and Metre of Ezekiel the Tragedian's
'Exagoge'," HTR 60 (1967), pp. 449-457. Jerry Robertson,
"Ezekiel the Tragedian," Harvard Divinity School: New
Testament Seminar 201, May 8, 1970. Until this more extensive
study of Ezekiel has progressed further, it seems prudent
merely to note such features as Ezekiel's references to the

pseudo-Philo, the author of the Biblical Antiquities,[123] were also intrigued by the importance of Moses' rod in the performance of miracles. Artapanus, however, deals with the rod in two ways which merit special scrutiny.

First he sets up the competition between Moses and the Egyptian magicians in terms of a test of Egyptian religion. The Egyptians accomplish the production of a serpent and the alteration of the Nile as they did in Exodus 7:11 and 22,[124] and Artapanus reports that they did these wonders by "certain magical means and incantations" (διά τινων μαγγάνων καὶ ἐπαοιδῶν: 27.30). This is neither a clear denigration of the arts of the Egyptians nor necessarily an attempt to defend Moses against the literary polemicists such as Apollonius Molon and Lysimachus who call him a charlatan and imposter (γόης καὶ ἀπατεῶν: Josephus Ap. II 145). Josephus himself points out that the issue in the accusation of the

rod of Moses and to refrain from reading all of Ezekiel in this light, heeding Robertson's warning (Ibid., p. 57): "any attempt to assess the work ought not to base its judgment on one isolated facet of the whole. My objections at this point lie primarily with those who have 'seized' different features of Ezekiel's work in order to support their own projects and theses. But these in turn have a tendency to reflect back upon the work from which they were taken, and to distort it."

[123]In the Biblical Antiquities 19:11, pseudo-Philo sees the rod as being preserved by God as a witness of God's covenant with Israel, just as the rainbow was a reminder of the covenant with Noah. Ps. Philo also stresses Moses' role as a miracle worker in 9:7 and 12:2.

[124]Note that the Exodus text allows the Egyptian opponents to accomplish one more trick, the bringing forth of frogs (Ex. 8:7), but Artapanus omits this.

polemicists was whether Moses taught vice or virtue (Ap. II
145), and he makes no reference or defense of Moses as a
miracle worker in that context. Furthermore, the Exodus
text itself describes the Egyptians as sorcerers who work by
(magical) charms: "But the magicians of Egypt did the same
by their secret arts" (RSV) (καὶ ἐποίησαν καὶ οἱ
ἐπαοιδοὶ τῶν Αἰγυπτίων ταῖς φαρμακίαις αὐτῶν ὡσαύτως/

וַיַּעֲשׂוּ גַם־הֵם חַרְטֻמֵּי מִצְרַיִם בְּלַהֲטֵיהֶם כֵּן

Exodus 7:11, 22; 8:7). Artapanus appears to be merely
following the biblical tradition that the Egyptians worked
by magic without any explicit denial that the rod was a
magical instrument.

Moses' superiority in power, however, is used to
humiliate Egyptian religion. Artapanus suggests that the
king brought in magicians who were priests,[125] and the king
threatens to kill them and destroy their temples if they are
unable to match Moses' power (27.30). These non-biblical
details pit Moses and his rod against Egyptian religion;
and whether or not Artapanus regarded the rod as a "magical"[126]

---

[125]Numenius of Apamea (II A.D.) reported that Moses'
opponents named Jannes and Jambres were Egyptian sacred
scribes (ἱερογραμματεῖς)   "men judged inferior to none in
magic" (μαγεῦσαι)   and that they stood up successfully to
the worst that Mousaios "the leader of the Jews and a man
most powerful (δυνατώτατος) in prayer" could offer (cited in
Eusebius P.E. 9.8.1-2). Numenius is also credited with the
remark that Plato is merely Moses speaking Attic (Μωσῆς
ἀττικίζων: P.E. 9.6.5).

[126]The term "magic" has a pejorative connotation in
much of the secondary literature, but I see no evidence that
Artapanus is attacking the Egyptians' methods because they
are "magical" except that this is another aspect of their

instrument, the report that Moses brings hail and earthquakes
upon Egypt so that "all the houses and most of the temples
were destroyed" (27.33) resolves the contest. The religion
of Egypt has been humiliated before the power of Moses.

Secondly, the rod is expressive of the mastery of Moses
over Isis. The equation of Isis with the earth (27.32),
which was apparently well known in Egyptian religion,[127]
gives Artapanus an occasion to show Moses' forcing Isis to
yield up frogs, locusts and lice by striking her (i.e. the
earth) with his rod. Whether rods were actually dedicated
in Egyptian temples or to Isis as Artapanus claims is not
known, but Moses is presented as in command of the goddess
and this reference to cultic practices could be Artapanus'
attempt to verify the historicity of his story by an appeal
to contemporary practices.

The argument that Artapanus is responding to anti-
Jewish polemicists of the educated or literary class has not
been well-supported by this analysis. To this point, Braun's
contention seems corroborated that Artapanus' treatment of
Moses arises from a popular nationalism where the hero is

----

religious culture which Moses surpasses with his power. For
a good discussion of the misuses of the term "magic" in
modern literature, cf. Goodenough, Jewish Symbols, op. cit.,
vol. II, pp. 155-161.

[127]Cf. Bonnet, op. cit., p. 328. Note that Bonnet sees
this role for Isis as particularly prominent in the later
period of Egyptian religion (720-525 B.C.) when her image
was becoming merged with that of the goddess of the harvest
Thermuthis. This would bear closer scrutiny since Thermuthis
is the name that Josephus gives for the king's daughter who
adopted Moses. Cf. note 85 above.

hailed as the complete master of a repressive culture and
superior in every way to the nationalistic heroes and gods
of that culture. The account of the appropriation of Egyptian
goods and the Memphite rationalized version of the crossing
of the Red Sea may suggest further that if Artapanus was
aware of the charges of the literary polemicists, he was not
concerned to respond apologetically to them.

Josephus, who is aware of the charges of Manetho (Ap.
I 248-250) and Lysimachus (Ap. I 309-311; cf. Tacitus Hist.
5.5) that Moses plundered Egypt and burned its temples,
maintains that the Egyptians honored the departing Hebrews
with gifts (δῶρα: Antiq. II 314). This represents a clear
softening of the Exodus 12:35-36 account where the
extortion involved is transparent: "the Egyptians let them
have what they asked (ἔχρησαν: וישאלו') and they despoiled
(ἐσκύλευσαν: וינצלו') the Egyptians."

Artapanus mentions this episode which Josephus and the
literary polemicists debated, but he does not appear to be
sensitive to any charges of impropriety. He does not
develop the suggestion of the biblical tradition that the
Egyptians "gave" the Jews the goods, which Josephus uses to
exonerate them. He merely reports that they "appropriated"
(χρησάμενος: 27.34,35) the items. He maintains, moreover,
that the Egyptians pursued the Jews to the Red Sea "because
the Jews were carrying off the property which they had
appropriated from the Egyptians", while Exodus 14:5 suggests
that the king came after the Jews in order to retrieve them

as slaves. If Artapanus was responding to an anti-Jewish
polemic, he adopted the unusual tact of pushing the
confiscation of Egyptian treasure into the center of the
discussion. Thus it appears more plausible that he was
writing for an audience which would have cheered the
plundering of Egypt, and a Jewish population which was in
danger of losing its national identity under Egyptian
domination would fit this description admirably.

Artapanus was not totally unaware of literary conventions.
Weinreich has analyzed the two versions of the crossing of
the Red Sea where in the first account the Memphites (μέν)
report that Moses knew the country and waited for the water
to ebb, and in the second the people of Heliopolis (δέ)
tell the more dramatic version (27.35). Doubtless Weinreich
is correct that this represents a nod to the conventions of
Hellenistic historiography by offering an alternative
rationalistic explanation and separating the two accounts
with a μέν/δέ construction.[128] But it is only a gloss
for Artapanus. The climax of his whole account depends on
the Heliopolitan version[129] with all of its marvelous elements.
The king and his army, accompanied by the consecrated

---

[128]Weinreich, op. cit., p. 140 [306].

[129]Since Artapanus does not indicate the extent of the
Heliopolitan story, it must be assumed that he intended the
reader to think it was an alternate account to the Memphite
version of the crossing of the Red Sea. Thus verses 35b-37
are referred to here as the "Heliopolitan version".

animals,[130] are rushing at Moses and the Jews (27.35), when
Moses, instructed by the "divine voice" (cf. 27.21) strikes
the water with his rod and the Jews cross on dry land
(27.36) while the Egyptians who pursue them are miraculously
destroyed by a fire and flood (27.37). The non-biblical
elements of Moses striking the sea and the fire of
destruction dramatically enhance the climax of this
romantic legend of the humiliation of the Egyptians at the
hands of Moses.

Artapanus probably would have been happy to hear Moses
called a "divine man", particularly if he heard it from an
Egyptian (so also Josephus, Ap. I 279). It is the Egyptian
priests, after all, who have honored him as a god and have
called him Hermes (27.6). But Moses is the nationalistic
hero of the Jews precisely because he shows himself as the
legendary master of Egypt and its gods. Moses is not the
divine wise man who instructs Israel in the life of virtue
by giving the law. He is the leader of an oppressed people
who controls the animal cults, strikes terror in the heart
of the king, commands the great goddess Isis, and surpasses
the accomplishments of the heroes of romantic Egyptian
legends at every turn.

---

[130]Cf. the discussion of Artapanus' view of the animal
cults above, c. notes 101-103.

C. The Figure of Moses in Palestine from 157 B.C. to 70 A.D.

The importance of the figure of Moses as a focus of the
nationalistic and religious hopes of oppressed Jews is by no
means original with or limited to Artapanus. In order to
deal with a variety of phenomena which appeared in Palestine
in the historical period between the rise of the Maccabees
and the fall of the second temple, two distinct factors must
be highlighted in older biblical traditions.

The first is the general importance of the exodus motif
for the religion of Israel and its national identity. As
von Rad observes, "the praises with which later Israel
celebrated the deliverance from Egypt and the rescue at the
Red Sea are a vast chorale surpassing all the praise she gave
for all other divine actions."[131] Furthermore, although
the portrait of Moses was drafted in very diverse ways in the
separate traditions, the sources of the Hexateuch which have
been identified have a common feature: "the figure of
Moses everywhere stands at the center of the historical
events from the Exodus down to the end of the wandering in
the wilderness."[132] Thus it was perfectly natural that a

---

[131]Gerhard von Rad, Old Testament Theology, trans. by
D.M.G. Stalker, vol. I (New York, 1962), p. 12.

[132]Ibid., p. 289. Von Rad's characterization of the
particular portrait that each of the sources draws of Moses
(cf. pp. 289-296) bears some fascinating resemblances to the
diversity that this study aims to identify in the Hellenistic
period. It is particularly striking to read that in E as
contrasted with J and D, "Moses is now the miracle worker,
in fact to the point of being a magician" (pp. 292-293).

people whose very identity had been forged in the recitation
of the exodus deliverance should treasure the memory of Moses
and look for rescue in their own periods of crisis in terms
of a repetition of the exodus events, and the continual
recurrence of the exodus motif in the writings of the prophets
documents this understanding of the significance of the
exodus events. A good example is found in the way in which
Micah tempers his gloomy predictions with a promise of
eventual restitution: "As in the days when you came out of
the land of Egypt, I will show them marvelous things"(7:15)[133]
[cf. also Hosea 2:15, 12:9; Isaiah 11:11, 63:11-12;
Jeremiah 32:20 (LXX 39:20); and Ezekiel 20 and passim].
Perhaps no prophet used the theme of the exodus with more
force than II Isaiah, who gives encouragement on the basis
of the accounts that water flowed from the rock in the
desert (48:21) and the arm of the Lord dried up the depths
of the sea (51:10). All of which is seen as pointing to a
return to Zion which will be more glorious and effortless
than the first exodus (cf. 51:11; 52:3-5, 12; 55:12-13).
There is even a remote possibility that II Isaiah may be
drafting his portrait of the "Servant" after a particular
image of Moses.[134]

---

[133]The possibility that this section may have been a
secondary addition from the time of the exile would only
make the use of the exodus motif more compelling. Cf. Otto
Eissfeldt, The Old Testament, trans. by Peter R. Ackroyd
(New York, 1965), p. 412.

[134]This argument, which may be defensible on the basis
of post 70 A.D. rabbinical traditions of Moses as suffering
(cf. Jeremias, "Μωυσῆς," op. cit., pp. 863-864), seems
difficult to support in the period of the exile. The case

The second element in biblical traditions which must be carefully noted is the prediction in <u>Deut</u>. 18:15, 18 of the prophet like Moses. In view of the almost complete lack of direct references to this motif in pre-Christian literature, scholars have long argued as to whether the concept of a "prophet like Moses" was a viable focus of Jewish expectations of the Messiah.[135] The problem is complicated both by the frequent introduction of concepts of "the Messiah" which belong to the Christian era[136] and by confusions as to with which "Moses" the "prophet" in question is to be compared. Furthermore, <u>Deut</u>. 13:1-5 and 18:9-14 portray a counter-type to the prophet like Moses who also works "signs and wonders" but leads the people astray. Thus any figure who was presented or proclaimed himself as the "prophet like Moses" on the basis of the performance of miracles would have been immediately open to the criticism of his opponents that he was "leading the people astray."

Nevertheless, it appears that it would have been almost impossible for a Jew of the Hellenistic period to conceive an image of Moses which did not include the aspect of miracle working. Perhaps the general prevalence of this feature in diverse portraits of Moses can be best high-lighted by a brief examination of two sources which lie just

---

for this suggestion is made by A. Bentzen, <u>Messias-Moses redivivus-Menschensohn</u> (Zürich, 1948), pp. 64-65.

[135]Cf. Jeremias, "Μωυσῆς," <u>op</u>. <u>cit</u>., p. 858, note 125 for a review of this debate.

[136]Cf. M. de Jonge, "The Use of the Word 'Anointed' in the Time of Jesus," <u>Novum Testamentum</u> 8 (1966), pp. 132-148.

outside the period that is of central concern here, Ben
Sira, which can be dated with confidence in the second
century B.C. before the rise of the Maccabees, and the
Biblical Antiquities of pseudo-Philo, which may have been
composed in the period from 70-100 A.D.[137]

In his chapters on the praise of Israel's heroes (44-
50), Ben Sira includes a relatively brief section on Moses,
44:23 - 45:5. The text is difficult in the verses (45:2-3)
which are of special interest here; but on the basis of the
fragmentary Hebrew, it probably should read:

> v. 2 "And He (God) made him (Moses) as glorious as God
> (ὡμοίωσεν αὐτὸν δόξῃ ἁγίων/   ‎ד'‎ ‎ה‎ ‎אכ‎‎בי‎‎ו‎כ‎נ‎ ‎'‎ ‎‎ל‎‎)) 138
> And mighty in awe-inspiring deeds (reading ‎ד'‎‎ארו‎‎פנ‎‎ד‎
> with the Hebrew margin and the Syriac against ‎ד‎‎נו‎ור‎‎בנ‎
> in the text/ ἐν φόβοις ἐχθρῶν).
> v. 3ab "By his words He (or he) brought signs (σημεῖα)

---

[137]The dating of this document appeared to be firmly
established on the basis of the destruction of "the place
where they shall serve me" on "the 17th day of the 4th month"
(ps. Philo 19:7) which Leopold Cohn, "An Apocryphal Work
ascribed to Philo of Alexandria," JQR 10, old series (1898),
pp. 277-332, linked with rabbinical dating of the fall of
Jerusalem, and on the basis of the work being "a product of
the circle from which both Baruch and IV Esdras emanated" as
argued by M.R. James, The Biblical Antiquities of Philo
(London, 1917), p. 58. Daniel Joseph Harrington, Text and
Biblical Text in Pseudo-Philo's Liber Antiquitatem Biblicarum
(Unpublished doctoral dissertation: Harvard University,
October, 1969), pp. 167-182, supports 100 A.D. as the
terminus ad quem for the work, on the basis of the biblical
text type, but argues that the work may have been written
prior to 70 A.D., in which case the reference to the 17th day
may be an allusion to the plundering of the temple by Antiochus
Epiphanes in the second century B.C. (cf. p. 172). Harrington
also demonstrates the priority of pseudo-Philo to II Baruch
and IV Esdras. Cf. also Pierre Bogaert. Apocalypse de Baruch
(Sources Chretiennes, #144, 145; Paris, 1969). Thus Harrington
must at least be credited with having countered the arguments
upon which previous certainty about the post-70 A.D. dating
had rested.

[138]For the frequent insertion of δόξα in the Greek text
(9:11; 49:8; 50:7) and the argument for the secondary
character of the Greek version, cf. Rudolf Smend, Die Weisheit
des Jesus Sirach (Berlin, 1906), p. 426.

swiftly to pass and He emboldened him in the presence
of the king."

The uncertainty as to who brought the signs to pass is
not crucial. Since God is the subject of all the other
action in vv. 2-5, it seems more likely that God is the
subject of verse 3a who acts through the agency of Moses'
words.[139] In any case, the passage is noteworthy in that it
links Moses' glory in his role as god with his function as
the agent of wonders. It has already been observed that
this connection was suggested in Exodus 4:16 and 7:1, but
the Ben Sira passage documents an awareness of this linkage
in the period prior to the rise of the Maccabees.

The importance that pseudo-Philo attached to the rod of
Moses in the performance of miracles has been previously
discussed (cf. 10:5-6; 19:11).[140] But the image of Moses as
a worker of miracles is most clear in the predictions of his
birth and in the situation when the people believe that
Moses has departed permanently. Before Moses' birth, God
pronounces a special blessing on Moses' father, Amram:

> "that which is begotten of him shall serve me for ever
> and by him will I do wonders (mirabilia) in the house of
> Jacob and will do by him signs and wonders (signa et
> prodigia) for my people which I have done for no other,

---

[139]Here this analysis differs slightly from that of
R.H. Charles, The Apocrypha and Pseudepigrapha of the Old
Testament, vol. I Apocrypha (Oxford, 1913), p. 485, and Smend,
op. cit., ad loc. To be sure, the Greek text is corrupt and
the intention of the passage is to set forth Moses' power.
But when emended, the Greek text still presents Moses in this
light while it lacks a reflexive pronoun which would clearly
establish that Moses accomplished these signs by his words.

[140]Cf. note 123.

and will perform in them my glory and declare unto them my ways." (9:7)[141]

And in a dream God speaks to Moses' sister Maria (sic = Miriam),

> "Go tell thy parents: behold, that which shall be born of you shall be cast into the water, for by him water shall be dried up, and by him will I do signs (signa), and I will save my people, and he shall have the captaincy thereof alway." (9:10)[142]

In Exodus 32:1 when Moses has not returned from the mountain, the people say to Aaron,

> "Up, make us gods who shall go before us; as for this Moses, the man who brought us up out of the land of Egypt, we do not know what has become of him."

But pseudo-Philo reports their words differently:

> "Make us gods that we may serve them as other nations also have. For this Moses by whom the wonders were done before us, is taken from us." (12:2)[143]

In spite of the predictions of the wonders that God will do by him and the fact that the departed Moses is remembered, at least by the dissidents, as the wonder worker, the most important role that Moses plays for pseudo-Philo is his function as God's spokesman and intercessor for the people. Pseudo-Philo also can be described as attempting to attribute the miracles to God, de-emphasizing Moses' role, as can be seen in particular in his description of the 10 plagues (10:1), the drying of the Red Sea (10:5, "and when Moses did all this, God rebuked the sea", cf. also 10:6), and the

---

[141]Tran. by M.R. James, op. cit., p. 101.

[142]Ibid., p. 102.

[143]Ibid., pp. 116-117.

miracles in the wilderness (10:7). And when at the end of his life Moses is elevated to receive the revelation of God's timetable for Israel (19:7, 14-15, cf. II Baruch 59 and IV Ezra 14:3ff), he also predicts the yearning for a second Moses in terms of his role as intercessor:

> "But then both ye and your sons and all your generation after you will arise and seek (complain of) the day of my death and will say in their heart: Who will give us a (another?) shepherd like Moses, or such another judge to the children of Israel, to pray for our sins at all times, and to be heard for our iniquities?" (19:3)[144]

In the years between the literary activity of Ben Sira and that of pseudo-Philo, the sectarian community which has been identified as Essene[145] lived in the Judean desert in the vicinity of Wadi Qumran. Throughout its checkered history of varying degrees of disaffection with the Maccabees, the Hasmoneans and their Roman allies, and the Roman procurators, the community interpreted its retreat into the desert in terms of a new exodus. The flight to the desert is a separation "from the midst of the habitation of perverse men" for the purpose of "the study of the law which

---

[144]Ibid., p. 127. The conjecture of reading "another shepherd" was suggested in a private conversation with Professor John Strugnell.

[145]This identification and approximate dating of the origins of the group to 100-150 B.C. appear firmly established by current scholarship. Cf. F.M. Cross Jr., The Ancient Library of Qumran (New York, 1961), pp. 51-52, 72 note 33, 121-122. J.T. Milik, Ten Years of Discovery in the Wilderness of Judaea, trans. by J. Strugnell (Studies in Biblical Theology #26: Naperville, 1959), pp. 44-98. A later dating which must be rejected on the basis of the paleography of the scrolls is defended by C. Roth, The Historical Background of the Dead Sea Scrolls (Oxford, 1958), who also argues for a Zealot identification of the sect.

He (God) has promulgated by the hand of Moses" (<u>IQS</u> 8:12-16,
cf. <u>4QpPs</u> 37 2:1).[146] This secession from the nation was
not a mystical return to the glories of the days of the
desert sojourn, but the "time when the way is being prepared
in the wilderness" (<u>IQS</u> 9:19-20), a time of training and
purification and testing in which the community is "imitating
the ancient desert sojourn of Mosaic times in anticipation
of the dawning Kingdom of God."[147] Furthermore in entering
upon this "probationary period,"[148] the community organized
itself in groups numbered by thousands, hundreds, fifties
and tens (<u>IQSa</u> 1:14-15, <u>IQM</u> 4:1-4, <u>CD</u> 13:1-2)[149] in direct

---

Cf. also G.R. Driver, <u>The Hebrew Scrolls</u> (Oxford, 1951).

[146]Trans. by A. Dupont-Sommer, <u>The Essene Writings from
Qumran</u> (Cleveland and New York, 1962), p. 92.

[147]Cross, <u>op</u>. <u>cit</u>., p. 78. This point is also made very
clearly by Shemaryahu Talmon, "The 'Desert Motif' in the
Bible and in Qumran Literature," <u>Biblical Motifs Studies and
Texts</u>, vol. III, ed. Alexander Altmann (Cambridge, 1966),
pp. 31-63, who emphasizes that the sectarians took a "gloomy
view of the desert trek" (p. 37) and maintains that the view
that the community had of the wilderness period was heavily
dependent on that of <u>Ezekiel</u> and <u>II Isaiah</u>. Cf. also Paul A.
Riemann, <u>Desert and Return to Desert in the Pre-exilic
Prophets</u> (Unpublished doctoral dissertation; Harvard University,
1964).

[148]Cf. F.F. Bruce, <u>Biblical Exegesis in the Qumran
Texts</u> (Grand Rapids, 1957), p. 27.

[149]Jeremias, "Μωυσῆς," <u>op</u>. <u>cit</u>., p. 861, had observed
this correspondence on the basis of the Damascus Document
before the discovery of the Qumran library. To be sure, the
methodological problem of describing a group's theology on
the basis of the discovery of its library is a constant
caution against focusing the whole analysis on a given text.
In the case of <u>CD</u>, however, both its consistency with other
material from the library and the fact that it was found in
seven copies in the central library and in private collections
documents its importance for the group. Cf. M. Baillet,

correspondence to the ordering of the wilderness generation
of the first exodus by Moses (Ex. 18:21-25; Deut. 1:15). The
constitution of these ranks of members into "camps"
also arises from the military ordering of the tribes by Moses
in Numbers 2.[150] As Fensham puts it, "the sect regarded
themselves as the ancient Israel wandering in the desert
until they are able to take the Holy Land by force."[151]

It must be emphasized, however, that no matter how
loudly the sectarians rattled their sabres in their literature
as they dreamed of the great battle, they were quietists
with respect to the forces that ruled Palestine and
occasionally oppressed them. As they waited for the day when
God would intervene and lead them in battle, they invested
their energies in purifying themselves, in the study of the
law and in fortifying their alliances with the angelic powers
together with whom they were preparing to war against the
forces of darkness led by Belial. In the meantime, memories

"Fragments du documents de Damas,grotte 6," Revue Biblique 63
(1956), pp. 513-523. For the importance of the forty year
periodization, cf. Milik., op. cit., pp. 115-116.

[150]This term is used most frequently in CD and IQM.
Cf. the complete list of passages in Y. Yadin, The Scroll of
the War of the Sons of Light against the Sons of Darkness
(Oxford, 1962), p. 47, notes 2 and 3. Cf. also Karl Georg
Kuhn, Konkordanz zu den Qumrantexten (Göttingen, 1960).
Karl Georg Kuhn, "Nachträge zur Konkordanz zu den
Qumrantexten," Revue de Qumran 4 (1963-1964), pp. 163-234.

[151]F.C. Fensham, "'Camp' in the New Testament and
Milhamah," Revue de Qumran 4 (1963-1964), p. 560. Cf. also
F.F. Bruce, Second Thoughts on the Dead Sea Scrolls (Grand
Rapids, 1961²), p. 113.

of past struggles with those evil powers provided a paradigm for the community's current skirmishes with Belial as well as verification of the cosmic dimensions of the struggle.

One of the forms that such relatively minor encounters with the forces of darkness took was that of healings or exorcisms. The Essenes have long been known from Josephus for having cultivated ancient traditions on the treatment of diseases and for "making investigations into apotropaic roots and the properties of stones" (ῥίζαι τε ἀλεξητήριοι καὶ λίθων ἰδιότητες: B.J. 2:136).[152] The discovery of the Qumran scrolls has further verified the testimony of Josephus. From the description of Abraham's healing of Pharaoh in the Genesis Apocryphon 20 and of the healing of Nabonidus in the Prayer of Nabonidus, it seems clear that such stories were cultivated as examples of the supremacy of the sons of light over the demonic powers. The clues to this reading of these texts lie in the correlation of the healing of Pharaoh with the "driving out" (גער) of an "evil spirit" by the laying on of hands (IQGen. Apoc. 20:28-29) and the healing of Nabonidus by an exorcist (גזר) who is a Jew and "one of the exiles" (4QNab 1:4).[153]

---

[152]The word ἀλεξητήριος could merely refer to "medicinal roots," but the connection of the healings and exorcisms in the texts discussed below supports the stronger reading. Furthermore the magical root from Solomon's ring which Eleazar is reported to have used to exorcise a demon (Josephus Antiq. 8:46) documents the power that such charms were known to possess in Palestine in this period. Cf. also the apotropaic root in B.J. 7:178-185.

[153]The translation of both of these passages has been

Another account of the conquest of demonic powers by an ally of God, which was apparently well-known at Qumran[154] and is of direct interest to this study, is the story of the exodus in _Jubilees_. The whole of chapter 48 is an extended account of the battles that "the angel of the

---

disputed. For a discussion of the problems and a defense of this interpretation cf. H. Kee and Dupont-Sommer as cited above in note 30 where the text of these verses from the _Genesis Apocryphon_ is also given. Cf. also A. Dupont-Sommer, _The Essene Writings_, _op. cit._, p. 322, note 3, and D. Flusser, "Healing through the Laying on of Hands in a Dead Sea Scroll," _Israel Exploration Journal_ 7 (1957), pp. 107-108.

[154]Although fragments of up to ten manuscripts of _Jubilees_ have been found in caves I, II and IV at Qumran (cf. Milik, _op. cit._, p. 32), the view that this work originated from the community must rest on other grounds. One of the more impressive pieces of evidence is the correspondences between the calendar at Qumran and that of the book of _Jubilees_ including "the insistence on a special form of solar calendar and on fixed dates for the main festivals" (Milik., _Ibid._). Furthermore the identification of the arch-rival of the sect as Belial appears focal at Qumran: "Belial occurs thirty-three times in the Dead Sea Scrolls; twelve of those are in the DSW (=IQM), five in DSD (=IQS), ten in DST (=IQH) and six in CDC (=CD). This proves that the members of the sect were greatly interested in Belial, who in their view led all their enemies" (Yadin, _op. cit._, p. 232). Belial is also explicitly labelled the "angel of hatred" (=mastemah IQM 13:11, cf. also IQM 13:4; 14:9; IQS 3:23). Against this background, the references in _Jubilees_ to Beliar (_sic_) are to be noted, particularly in Moses' prayer for the people when he says, "Let thy mercy, O Lord, be lifted up upon thy people, and create in them an upright spirit, and let not the spirit of Beliar rule over them to accuse them before Thee, and to insnare them from all the paths of righteousness so that they may perish from before Thy face" (1:20, trans. by R.H. Charles, _The Apocrypha and Pseudepigrapha of the Old Testament_, vol. II, _Pseudepigrapha_ (Oxford, 1913), p. 12, cf. also 15:23). This is precisely the role played by the figure Mastema (=angel of enmity?) in _Jubilees_. He and his forces lead astray the sons of men (10:8), bring calamities (11:5, 11), oppose Abraham in the story of the sacrifice of Isaac (17:16; 18:9, 12) and provide continuous opposition to Moses (cf. chapter 48 discussed below). The Qumran references

presence" (cf. 2:1) and Moses wage against "prince Mastema,"
who has been identified by the author of Jubilees as the
leader of the demonic forces (10:8) and is probably "the
angel of hatred" (mastemah) who opposes the Qumran community.[155]
Moses is saved by his angelic ally from a murder plot of
Mastema (48:3) so that he may serve as the Lord's agent of
vengeance against the Egyptians by the performance of signs
and wonders (48:4-9). When Mastema helps the Egyptian
sorcerers who are his allies (48:10), Moses and the angel of
the presence proves to be more than an adequate match for
their power until the struggle is won:

> 48:10 "the evils indeed we permitted them to work, but
> the remedies we did not allow to be wrought by their
> hands."

> 48:13 "And I (the angel) stood between the Egyptians
> and Israel, and we delivered Israel out of his (Mastema's)
> hand, and out of the hand of his people, and the Lord
> brought them through the midst of the sea as if it were
> dry land."

> 48:18-19 "And on the fourteenth we bound him (Mastema)
> that he might not accuse the children of Israel on the
> day when they asked the Egyptians for vessels and
> garments, vessels of silver and vessels of gold, and
> vessels of bronze, in order to despoil the Egyptians in
> return for the bondage in which they had forced them to
> serve. And we did not lead forth the children of Israel
> from Egypt empty handed."[156]

Although elsewhere in Jubilees Moses was presented
primarily as the one who transmitted the laws to Israel, this
dramatic account of the struggles of the exodus illustrated

---

to this "angel of enmity" (mastemah) would suggest that the
term "mastemah" in Jubilees is also a descriptive title rather
than a proper name.

[155]Cf. previous note.

[156]Trans. by Charles, Pseudepigrapha, op. cit., p. 79.
Cf. Halévy, op. cit., p. 98.

the kind of opposition that the true believers faced. The
only sure protection was the scrupulous observence of the
law: "ye were eating the passover in Egypt, when all the
powers of Mastema had been let loose to slay all the first-
born in the land of Egypt" (49:2).[157] Only such purity
would end the dominion of the evil forces:

> 50:5 "And the jubilees shall pass by, until Israel is
> cleansed from all guilt of fornication, and uncleanness,
> and pollution, and sin, and error, and dwells with
> confidence in all the land, and there shall be no more
> a Satan or any evil one, and the land shall be clean
> from that time for evermore."[158]

Whether or not _Jubilees_ was written by a member of the
Qumran community, it fits their understanding of their life
in the desert. The Essenes at Qumran regarded the period in
the desert as the time of the dominion of Belial, and they
looked for the protection from the forces of evil that was
afforded those who observe the laws:

> "This is what they shall do, year by year, during all
> the time of the dominion of Belial" (_IQS_ 2:19)[159]

> "And we, the re[mnant of Thy people,] [shall praise] Thy
> Name, O God of favours, who hast kept the Covenant with
> our fathers, and during all our generations lettest Thy
> favours fall upon the remn[ant of Thy people]. [For]
> during the dominion of Belial and amid the Mysteries of
> his hostility they have not driven [us] from Thy
> Covenant; and Thou hast caused his spirits of [des]
> truction to depart from [us]". (_IQM_ 14:8-10)[160]

> "And in all those years Belial shall be unleashed

---

[157]Ibid., p. 80.

[158]Ibid., p. 81.

[159]Dupont-Sommer, _The Essene Writings_, op. cit., p. 76.

[160]Ibid., p. 190.

against Israel" (CD 4:12-13)[161]

The persistence of the correlations between the period of trial in the desert of the Israelites of the first exodus generation and the situation of the community of Qumran as they interpreted it makes it probable that the sectarians also regarded their leader as a new Moses.[162] One of the texts that is most suggestive of this view is CD 5: 17-20:

> "For formerly Moses and Aaron arose by the hand of the Prince of Lights but Belial raised up Jannes and his brother, in his cunning when Israel was saved for the first time. And in the time of the desolation of the land, the removers of the bounds rose up and led Israel astray."[163]

From the similarity of description of the opponents "in the time of the desolation of the land" to the depiction of the opponents of the sect in CD 1:13-16, it seems safe to conclude that the writer is comparing the time of Moses to the situation of the community. If this reading is correct, the verses which follow this mention of Moses are probably a description of the appearance of the lawgiver at Qumran with a direct comparison between the situations of this leader and of Moses. Thus by a word play on the term מחוקק, which can mean either "rod" or "lawgiver", the

---

[161]Ibid., p. 128.

[162]This suggestion was defended by Jeremias, op. cit., p. 861 before the discovery of the scrolls on the basis of the Damascus Document alone. With the broader lectionary at his disposal, the idea was pursued vigorously by N. Wieder, "The 'Law-Interpreter' of the Sect of the Dead Sea Scrolls: the Second Moses," Journal of Jewish Studies 4 (1953), pp. 158-175.

[163]Dupont-Sommer, The Essene Writings, op. cit., p. 130.

the author identifies the new lawgiver in a pesher on

Numbers 21:18:

> "'The well which the princes dug which the nobles of
> the people delved with a rod' (Numbers 21:18)
> The well is the Law and those who dug it are the
> converts of Israel who went out from the land of Judah
> and were exiled in the land of Damascus; all of whom
> God called princes, for they sought Him and their
> (glory) is denied by the mouth of no man. And the rod
> (the lawgiver) is the Seeker (=interpreter) of the
> Law" (CD 6:3-7).[164]

On the basis of this text plus the identification of

"the interpreter of the Law" with the star prophesied in

Numbers 24:17 (CD 7:18) and the citation in the Testimonia

5-8 of the Deuteronomy 18:18-19 prediction of a prophet like

Moses, Wieder believes he has demonstrated the identity of

the law interpreter as the "prophet like Moses." The

argument is risky, however, since the Testimonia appear to be

collected proof texts, but the Deuteronomy prediction is not

explicitly linked to a Qumran figure. Even more questionable

is Wieder's interpretation of the equation 7וזכ התורה = כוכב

as a cipher for an identification of Moses and the new Moses

with the Greek god Hermes, whose name also means "interpreter"

and who is frequently identified with a heavenly body.[165]

Of course if he were correct, this could be read as evidence

that Moses and the second Moses of Qumran were regarded by

the sect as "divine men" who rivaled Hermes.

Such a possibility ought not be discounted out of hand

164Ibid., p. 131.

165Wieder, op. cit., p. 166.

on the basis of a view of Palestinian Judaism as untainted
by Hellenistic influences,[166] but the evidence for such an
apotheosis is simply lacking.[167] Furthermore, Wieder's
methodology of appealing to Greek equivalents in order to
explain a cipher used at Qumran is quite unjustified. Thus
there is still a significant lack of evidence of a direct
connection between the depiction of Greek Hellenistic
charismatic heroes and the portrayal of Moses or the Law
Interpreter at Qumran.

For the purposes of this study, however, a few summary
observations will suffice. First of all, it seems clear
that the community interpreted their desert sojourn in terms
of their understanding of the period of the desert wanderings
of the exodus generation as a time of testing and struggle
against demonic forces in preparation for inheriting the
land. Secondly, they interpreted the role of their leader
in terms of their view of Moses as the lawgiver who struggles
against the evil powers and leads an exodus into the
wilderness, whether or not they referred to their lawgiver

---

[166]This is what I take to be the thrust of Jeremias'
constant discrimination between Palestinian and Hellenistic
Judaism, "Μωυσῆς," op. cit. For a good summary of
scholarship of the penetration of Palestinian Judaism by
Hellenism, cf. Morton Smith, "Palestinian Judaism in the
First Century," Israel: Its Role in Civilization (ed.
Moshe Davis; New York, 1956), pp. 67-81.

[167]Cf. Hengel, Judentum, op. cit., p. 71, note 4 and
the sober rebuttal to those scholars who regard the
Righteous Teacher as having divine status by Jean Carmignac,
Christ and the Teacher of Righteousness, trans. by Katharine
Greenleaf Pedley (Baltimore, 1962), pp. 32-47.

as the "prophet like Moses." Yet in spite of the fact that
Jubilees and the Damascus Document illustrated the kind of
struggle that was involved by pointing to the alliance
between Belial or Mastema and the magicians of Egypt, the
primary correspondence that was drawn between Moses and the
leader of the community was based on their functions as law
givers. This is documented by the observation that Jubilees
emphasizes that the lasting protection of the Israelites
rests with their observance of the law and the Damascus
Document interprets the victory of the leader of the
community over the forces of Belial by pointing to his office
of lawgiver. Furthermore, although Wieder's argument that
Moses and the lawgiver of Qumran were being presented as
rivals of Hermes is doubtless wrong, there is evidence that
special reverence was paid by the community to the lawgiver.
As Josephus reports, "After God they hold most in awe
(σέβας μέγα) the name of their lawgiver, any blasphemer of
whom is punished by death" (B.J. 2:145). Whether the
reference is to the leader of the community or Moses,[168]
this high regard is focused on the one who gives the law.
Both of these figures were regarded by the community as
allies of the angels of God who assured protection to God's
people from the power of the forces of Belial in the present
and in the imminent cosmic battle for which they were

---

[168]Cf. discussion by Carmignac, op. cit., pp. 45-47, who
believes this is a clear reference to Moses, at least in
Josephus' view of the Essenes.

preparing. Since the only fail-safe protection came from the observance of the law, the elevated status of Moses and the leader of the community rested on their reliability as lawgivers.

The work which is generally called The Assumption of Moses[169] should also be mentioned in this context. This book, which probably was assembled in its present form sometime in the first century A.D. after the death of Herod the Great and before the fall of Jerusalem, presents Moses as the mediator of God's law (1:14; 3:11-12) who reveals the apocalyptic timetable of Israel's history, with particular attention to the period of the Maccabees and beyond. The work is singular in the respect that no mention is made of Moses' role as a miracle worker.

Chapters 9 and 10 of this book are of particular interest. They refer to "Taxo" and his seven sons who retreat "into a cave which is in the field" (agro), choosing to die "rather than transgress the commands of the Lord of Lords, the God of our fathers" (9:6). The passage is intriguing first of all because the events described, which have long been recognized as corresponding to the situation of the Hasidim in the Maccabean period,[170] may be a veiled reference

---

[169]The text which is extant should more properly be called the Testament of Moses, cf. Charles, Pseudepigrapha, op. cit., pp. 407-408.

[170]Ibid., p. 420, where Taxo is taken as an allusion to Eleazar (II Macc. 6:18) and the seven brothers who were martyred (II Macc. 7).

to the retreat to the desert caves led by the lawgiver of
Qumran. The clue to this allusion may lie in the name
Taxo.[171] Since the Latin version of this text which is
extant is generally accepted as being a translation from
the Greek which depended on a Hebrew or Aramaic text,[172]
the name Taxo probably reflects a Greek ταξω or
ταξων could be a translation of the Qumran title for the
leader of the community מחוקק (cf. CD 6:3-7 cited above).
Secondly, even if no direct tie with the Qumran sect can be
established, the retreat of Taxo and his sons is clearly
regarded as an act of purification which is a prelude to
the cosmic battle against the forces of evil and lawlessness
which God and his angel will wage successfully (10:1-10):

> "For if we do this and die our blood shall be avenged
> before the Lord (9:7). And then His kingdom shall appear
> throughout all His creation, and then Satan shall be
> no more" (10:1).[173]

Thus whether this work came from the hand of a "quietistic
Pharisee"[174] or an Essene, it reflects the perspective which
has been identified in the Qumran literature where the
sojourn in the desert is a retreat from a lawless and evil
society in passive anticipation of the ultimate victory over

---

[171]This suggestion was made by Professor John Strugnell
in a lecture at Harvard Divinity School in December of 1967.
Cf. also Eissfeldt, op. cit., p. 624.

[172]Cf. Charles, Pseudepigrapha, op. cit., p. 410.

[173]Ibid., p. 421.

[174]Ibid., pp. 407, 411-412.

the powers of evil which God and his angelic and human allies
would wage and win.

Not all of the Jews of Palestine who found in the
figure of Moses a focus for their nationalistic or religious
hopes interpreted the exodus motif in a light which resulted
in a retreat from political activity or a quietism in the
face of oppression. Unfortunately, only the anti-Zealot,
Josephus, provides any extensive documentation for the variety
of revolutionary "prophets" who enjoyed varying degrees of
popular support in the first century of the Christian era.[175]
But given that limitation, it appears probable that several
of these figures appealed to nationalistic sentiments of
liberation associated with Moses and the exodus and attempted
to organize revolutionary movements by leading a new exodus
while documenting their claims to charismatic leadership
by promising to repeat the miracles associated with the
first wilderness generation.

Some of the more intriguing accounts that Josephus gives
of these figures merit scrutiny. The first who is worthy

---

[175]Care must be exercised to avoid the methodological
error of assuming that all such figures were Zealots. The
problem is not resolved by referring to them as para-Zealots
as does S.G.F. Brandon, Jesus and the Zealots (Cambridge,
1967). Doubtless these "prophets" were carried along with
the same rising tide of popular revolutionary activity that
furnished the Zealots with surging success in the latter
half of the century, but it is not possible at present to
describe an organizational connection between the Zealots and
several of these figures.

of noting in this context is the Samaritan who led an armed
band out of a Samaritan village towards Mount Gerizim during
the procuratorship of Pilate (c. 26-36 A.D.):

> "Neither was the Samaritan nation exempt from dis-
> turbance. For a man, who had little concern about lying
> and manipulated everything according to the whim of the
> crowds, rallied them with the command to accompany him
> to Mount Gerizim, which is regarded by them to be the
> most sacred of mountains. He vigorously insisted that
> when they arrived he would show them the sacred vessels
> which were buried there where Moses had deposited
> them. Since they regarded the story as credible, they
> armed themselves (ἐν ὅπλοις) and established them-
> selves in a certain village called Tirathana, taking in
> others who could be collected since they planned to
> make the ascent to the mountain as a great multitute.
> Pilate appeared and blocked their ascent with a detach-
> ment of cavalry and armed infantry, who killed those
> whom they engaged in a battle as they were gathered in
> the village and took prisoner many of those who fled,
> of whom Pilate killed the leaders and those who were
> most influential." (Josephus Antiq. 18:85-87)[176]

The procuratorship of Cuspius Fadus (c. 44-48 A.D.) was
marked by the rise of a "prophet" named Theudas:

> "While Fadus was procurator, a certain fraud (γόης
> τις ἀνήρ) named Theudas persuaded the majority of the
> masses (τὸν πλεῖστον ὄχλον) to gather their
> possessions and follow him to the Jordan river. He
> claimed to be a prophet (προφήτης) and that at his
> command the river would divide and provide easy passage
> for them. He misled (ἀπατᾶν) many by saying these
> things. But Fadus did not allow them to thrive on such
> folly. He sent a squadron of cavalry against them
> which fell on them unexpectedly and killed many and took
> many prisoners. Having captured Theudas himself, they
> beheaded him and took the head to Jerusalem" (Josephus
> Antiq. 20:97-98)

In spite of chronological inconsistencies, it seems likely

---

[176]M. Gaster, The Samaritans (London, 1925), pp. 90-91,
regards this passage as an allusion to the Samaritan Taheb,
a prophet like Moses who will perform wonders with Moses'
rod and will discover the hidden vessels of the temple.

this is the same Theudas mentioned in Acts 5:36:

> "For before these days, Theudas arose, giving himself
> out to be somebody (λέγων εἶναί τινα ἑαυτόν), and
> a number of men, about four hundred joined him; but he
> was slain and all who followed him were dispersed and
> came to nothing."[177]

Felix, who was the Roman procurator from 52 to sometime

between 55 and 60 A.D.,[178] also had his problems with

revolutionary activities in the desert. After mentioning the

rise of the Sicarii, Josephus reports:

> "In addition to these, another band of villains arose
> whose hands were purer but whose intentions more
> impious and who destroyed the calm of the city no less
> than the assassins. Deceivers and imposters, promoting
> revolutions and changes under the guise of divine
> inspiration (πλάνοι γὰρ ἄνθρωποι καὶ ἀπατεῶγες,
> ὑπὸ προσχήματι θειασμοῦ νεωτερισμοὺς καὶ μεταβολὰς
> πραγματευόμενοι), they persuaded the masses to act
> possessed (δαιμονᾶν) and led them into the desert
> ᾽(ἐρημία), since there God was to show them signs of
> deliverance (σημεῖα ἐλευθερίας). Since he believed
> this to be the foundation for a revolution, Felix sent
> his cavalry and armed infantry against them and
> slaughtered a large number.
> The Egyptian false prophet (ψευδοπροφήτης) dealt
> the Jews a blow that was even worse. Having appeared
> in the countryside and passed himself off as a prophet
> (προφήτης) this fraud (ἄνθρωπος γόης) gathered
> about 30,000 of those who were misled (ἀπατᾶν) and

---

[177]Cf. A.C. Headlam, "Theudas," Hastings Dictionary of
the Bible IV (1903), p. 750 who uses the discrepancies
between Acts and Josephus, most notably the divergence as to
whether Judas the Galilaean was before or after Theudas, to
argue against the dependence of Acts on Josephus. In private
conversation, Professor John Strugnell offered the intriguing
conjecture that the indefinite relative pronoun may not be
original in Acts 5:36. If the text reported that Theudas was
trying to promote himself as Joshua ('Ἰησοῦν) the
Christian scribe might have construed this name as "Jesus"
and thus substituted the indefinite τινα to protect the
name of Jesus.

[178]Cf. Dieter Georgi, "Zur Frage der Chronologie," Die
Geschichte der Kollekte des Paulus für Jerusalem (Theologische
Forschung, 38: Hamburg, 1965), pp. 91-96.

led them around on a route from the desert (ἐρημία)
to the mountain called the Mount of Olives. From there
he planned to enter Jerusalem by force and seize the
Roman garrison in order to rule the city as a tyrant,
using those who fell in with him as bodyguards. But
Felix anticipated his attack and encountered him with
the Roman infantry and the whole city aided in the
defense. The result of the engagement was that the
Egyptian and a few of his followers escaped, but most
of those with him were killed or taken prisoner, while
the rest were dispersed and stole back to their own
homes." (Josephus B.J. 2.258-263)

"While the deeds of the brigands filled the city with
such unholiness, the frauds and deceivers (οἱ δὲ γόητες
καὶ ἀπατεῶνες ἄνθρωποι)   persuaded the crowd to follow
them into the desert (ἐρημία).   For they promised to
show them clear signs and wonders accomplished in accord
with God's providence (δείξειν γὰρ ἔφασαν ἐναργῆ
τέρατα καὶ σημεῖα κατὰ τὴν τοῦ θεοῦ πρόνοιαν γινόμενα).
And many, having been persuaded, paid the penalty for
their foolishness. For when they were brought to
Felix he punished them. And a certain Egyptian came to
Jerusalem at this time claiming to be a prophet
(προφήτης).   He advised the masses to accompany him
᾿to a mountain called the Mount of Olives, which lies
opposite the city at a distance of five furlongs. For
he claimed that he wanted to show them from there that
the walls of Jerusalem would fall at his command,
promising to provide entrance to the city through them.
When Felix was advised of this, he commanded his
soldiers to take up their arms; and accompanied by a
large cavalry and infantry, he rushed from Jerusalem
and fell on those with the Egyptian, slaying four
hundred and taking two hundred prisoners. The Egyptian
himself was not to be found since he had run from the
battle."   (Josephus Antiq. 20:167-172)[179]

---

[179]If this Egyptian is the same man whom the Romans
believed Paul to be in Acts 21:38, it may be that this
"prophet" was known as one of the Sicarii. Since Acts speaks
of him stirring up a revolt and leading 4000 Sicarii out into
the wilderness, these may have been the hard core revolutionaries
of the 30,000 Josephus believes to have been involved (B.J.
2:261). The possible identification of this Egyptian with the
Egyptian Ben Stada mentioned in the Talmud (Shabbat 104b)
and the subsequent confusion of Ben Stada with Jesus are of
passing interest to this study. Cf. J. Gutmann, "Ben
Setada," Encyclopaedia Judaica IV (1929), pp. 72-73.

Festus, the successor of Felix, receives only a brief
treatment by Josephus, but he apparently had to deal with the
same kind of wilderness rebels:

> "Festus also sent a force of cavalry and infantry
> against those who had been misled (ἀπατᾶν)   by a certain
> fraud (ἄνθρωπος γόης)   who promised salvation (σωτηρία)
> and rest from troubles, if they would follow him into
> the desert (ἐρημία).   Those who were sent killed both
> the deceiver (ἀπατᾶν) himself and the followers.'
> (Josephus Antiq. 20:188)

As Josephus tells it, the unholy alliance between the
revolutionaries and such prophets of salvation was also
maintained in the beseiged Jerusalem and was ultimately
responsible for its destruction:

> "The cause of their destruction was the appearance of a
> certain false prophet (ψευδοπροφήτης τις) who arose on
> that day proclaiming to those in the city that God
> commanded them to ascend to the temple to receive the
> signs of salvation (τὰ σημεῖα τῆς σωτηρίας). And many
> ˋprophets were subverted by the tyrants at that time to
> encourage the people to await help from God."
> (Josephus B.J. 6:285)

Once Jerusalem had fallen, such activity did not
immediately cease. From what Josephus relates about Jonathan
of Cyrene, c. 73 A.D., the motif of the wilderness miracle
worker was a part of Jewish revolutionary activity as far
away as North Africa:

> "The madness of the Sicarii even touched the cities
> around Cyrene like a disease. Jonathan, a most evil man
> and a weaver by trade who had taken refuge there,
> convinced many of those without resources to listen to
> him and he led them into the desert (ἔρημος) promising
> to show them signs and apparitions (σημεῖα καὶ φάσματα).
> His knavish activity was not noticed by others, but
> the Jews who were in high positions in Cyrene reported
> his exodus (ἔξοδον) and preparations to Catullus, the
> governor of the Libyan Pentapolis. He sent his cavalry
> and infantry which quickly overcame the unarmed, most
> of whom were killed in the encounter, and some of whom
> were taken prisoner and brought to Catullus. At that
> time, Jonathan the leader of the plot escaped, but was

caught after a long and very meticulous search of the country." (Josephus B.J. 7:437-441)

It is, of course, very difficult to attempt any generalizations on the basis of such episodes which occurred in divergent locations over a period of forty to fifty years and which are reported by an extremely polemical author. Perhaps the prophets in besieged Jerusalem should not even be included in this collection since they were obviously not in a position to be desert prophets, but they do illustrate the connection that Josephus wants to emphasize between revolutionary activity and prophets who affected the populace. Furthermore, even after the temple had fallen, the survivors proposed to Titus that they be allowed to "withdraw to the desert" (B.J. 6:351). In spite of such limitations, however, certain aspects of these portrayals merit scrutiny.

The motif of an exodus into the wilderness is clearly an important feature of several of these revolutionary actions. Only in the case of Jonathan, does Josephus explicitly call the retreat to the desert an "exodus" (B.J. 7:439), and it is possible that the word could merely be translated "departure." But it seems more likely that the desert sojourn of the first exodus generation had a more symbolic value for such figures since the desert was the place where the nation was marshaled for the conquest of the land. At least Josephus interprets the actions of "the frauds" who led the crowd into the desert during the procuratorship of Felix as having chosen that location

because <u>there</u> (ὡς ἐκεῖ: <u>B.J</u>. 2:259) God would give "signs
of deliverance" (cf. also <u>Antiq</u>. 20:168). His view that the
Egyptian prophet led the people on a "circuitous route"
(περιάγειν: <u>B.J</u>. 2:261) from the desert to the Mount of
Olives may also be evidence of the particular significance of
the desert. The fraud whom Festus killed also made his
assurances of salvation contingent upon his being followed
into the desert (<u>Antiq</u>. 20:188). And Jeremias is convinced
that Theudas in promising to divide the Jordan was also
planning a new exodus into the desert.[180] But none of these
figures appear to have shared the Qumran view of the exodus
as a retreat. At least as Josephus presents them, they are
only congregating in the desert in anticipation of an
immanent forceful conquest.

The importance of miracles as a means of authenticating
these figures is obvious but raises the problem of the
reliability of the source. Josephus appears to be fully
conscious of the predictions in <u>Deut</u>. 13:1-5 and 18:9-14 of
a false Mosaic prophet who will work "signs and wonders" but
for the purpose of leading the people astray. Thus he
continually tries to characterize these figures as "misleading the people" (cf. <u>Antiq</u>. 20:98; <u>B.J</u>. 2:259, 261-262;
<u>Antiq</u>. 20:167, 188) and always treats them as victimizing the
masses. His frequent use of the terms γόης (<u>Antiq</u>. 20:97;
<u>B.J</u>. 2:261; <u>Antiq</u>. 20:167) and ψευδοπροφήτης (<u>B.J</u>. 2:261;

---

[180] "Μωυσῆς," <u>op</u>. <u>cit</u>., p. 862.

6:285) must also be regarded as evidence that Josephus is
describing these figures in the terms of the very antithesis
of true prophecy.[181] Thus it may be that Josephus is laying
stress on their attempts to perform signs and wonders in order
to discredit them along the lines of the Deuteronomic
prediction of the false prophet.

Nevertheless, the specific miracles that are promised
appear to be significantly tied to the performances of the
wilderness generation. It is notable that the two figures of
this group who are reported to have referred to themselves
as "prophets", Theudas (Antiq. 20:97) and the Egyptian (B.J.
2:261, Antiq. 20:169) promise very specific displays of power
associated with the first period of conquest.

The issue of whether such attempts to re-enact the
experiences of the wilderness generation document an appeal
to the prophecy of a prophet like Moses is not easily resolved. On the one hand, both the dividing of the Jordan and

---

[181]Josephus does admit that Theudas and the Egyptian
regarded themselves as prophets but immediately calls them
"frauds" (γόης). The direct opposition of these terms is
also seen in Philo Spec. Leg. I 315 in a passage which
appears to be a direct reference to Deut. 13. It ought to be
noted, however, that Josephus uses the term γόης to describe
a variety of his opponents with whom no miraculous performances
have been associated (cf. John of Gischala, B.J. 4:85;
Castor, B.J. 5:317-330, and his reference to Justus the son
of Pistus as having "a fraud's tricks of oratory" (γοητεία
καὶ ἀπάτη ἡ διὰ λόγων: Life 4). Thus the mere use of the
word γόης does not establish that these figures claimed to
be miracle workers, and there seems to be no justification
for arguing that when Josephus uses the term γόης he has a
"nomadic sect of healers in mind" as is maintained by R.
Eisler, ΙΗΣΟΥΣ ΒΑΣΙΛΕΥΣ ΟΥ ΒΑΣΙΛΕΥΣΑΣ, vol. II (Heidelberg,
1930), p. 190. Cf. Brandon, op. cit., p. 100, note 2, p. 109.

the destruction of city walls are actually part of Joshua's repertoire[182] (Joshua 3:7-13; 6:1-21). Thus the actions of Theudas and the Egyptian would appear to have been attempts to authenticate them as figures like Joshua. On the other hand, even the Samaritan and Jonathan, who may fit the Moses typology more closely, appear from Josephus to have been retreating only to prepare to attack. Therefore, the distinction between a Joshua and a Moses typology may only be misleading, particularly since the book of Joshua identifies Joshua as the true successor of Moses by introducing his parting of the Jordan as God's verification that he is Moses' successor.

> "This day I will begin to exalt you in the sight of all
> ˎIsrael, that they may know that as I was with Moses, so
> I will be with you." (Joshua 3:7)

At most, these figures wanted to be regarded as the true successors of Moses. Furthermore they were all apparently more interested in the conquest phase of the exodus than in the retreat from Egypt. The Samaritans even armed themselves before ascending Mount Gerizim to verify the claim of their leader (Antiq. 18:86). Thus although the miracles appear from Josephus to have been the primary mode of authenticating these figures, it is perhaps irrelevant to attempt to describe what their view of Moses himself might

---

[182]E. Fascher, ΠΡΟΦΗΤΗΣ (Giessen, 1927), pp. 162-163, correlated the parting of the river to the Elijah/Elisha cycle of I Kings 2. But neither of those prophets led a host of people through the water.

have been. Even if Theudas and the Egyptian were presenting
themselves as "the prophet like Moses," it seems clear that
Joshua the successor of Moses who led the conquest by
miraculously parting the Jordan and destroying the walls of
Jericho was their primary model.[183]

Given the sources currently available, it is also
impossible to maintain that such figures regarded Moses or
themselves as divine. Certainly they all claimed a special
alliance with God,[184] and apparently understood the miracles
as documentation of such a connection. On that count alone,
these "prophets" of the revolution were operating on a
thought frequency quite different from that used by Philo,
Aristobulus and Eupolemus in communication with the Greek
philosophical tradition. But it also appears doubtful that
they shared the view of Artapanus and the magical papyri of
Moses as the miracle worker and magician of divine power.

---

[183]This conclusion stands in rather marked contrast with
that of Jeremias, "Μωυσῆς," op. cit., and Vermes, op. cit.,
who find strong evidence for the expectation of a "second
Moses" in Josephus' accounts of these figures. The text
that Vermes, p. 85, cites from the Slavonic version of
Josephus' Wars, saying of Jesus, "This is our first legislator
who has risen from the dead and who has shown many cures and
proofs of his knowledge," is intriguing, but appears to have
no real claim to having come from Josephus. Cf. also Ferdinand
Hahn, Christologische Hoheitstitel (Forschungen zur Religion
und Literatur des Alten und Neuen Testaments, Heft 83;
Göttingen, 1963), pp. 218-220.

[184]The same can be said of the founder of the Zealot
movement, Judas of Gamala, who assured the people that in
spite of the apparent impossibility of revolt, they could be
confident that heaven (τὸ θεῖον) would be of aid (Antiq. 18:5).

D. Josephus

Writing in the last decades of the first century A.D.
after the fall of Jerusalem, Josephus draws a rather
grandiose portrait of Moses. If his varied descriptions of
this figure are viewed together, Moses appears at a glance
to be the sage, law giver, miracle worker, prophet, and
military genius, and he is even explicitly called a θεῖος
ἀνήρ (Antiq. 3:180). But rather than regard Josephus as
collecting all these features from the biblical and
legendary accounts of Moses in order to make his Moses
correspond to a general hellenistic image of the θεῖος ἀνήρ,
the methodology of this study suggests that it may be more
fruitful to analyze Josephus' portraiture of Moses with an
eye to the particular facets of the picture that this
historian highlights in order to make Moses as appealing as
possible to his audience.

A point of departure for finding a path through the
maze of Josephus' statements about Moses has been provided
by the research which Professor George MacRae has done on
Josephus' understanding of miracles. After a detailed
analysis of Josephus' accounts of miracles in the Antiquities,
MacRae concludes:

> "As a Jew, Josephus does not balk at accepting the
> miraculous whenever he encounters it because what he
> sees in it are God's πρόνοια and δύναμις. But as a
> Hellenist, he does not hesitate to offer a pseudo-
> scientific or pseudo-philosophical explanation as well
> whenever one comes to mind."[185]

---

[185]George MacRae, "Miracles in The Antiquities of

Seen in the larger context of MacRae's analysis, it is clear
that Josephus is a Jew in so far as he is a loyal believer
in the reliability of the biblical record and shares the
belief in God as the master of human history, and he is a
Hellenist in that he feels obliged to adjust his account to
make it palatable to the Hellenists of literary and philosophical tastes.

Perhaps the best method of demonstrating how this
discrimination applies to Josephus' treatment of Moses is
to begin with the contra Apionem, where Josephus' apologetic
interest is most clear and his confessional concerns are less
focal. Although the work is a response to a variety of
polemical charges by the literary anti-Semites, the interpretation of the figure of Moses is clearly one of the primary
issues in Josephus' mind.

In his refutation of slanders against Moses, Josephus
seeks to present him as the virtuous lawgiver of the Jews
who rivals and excels the heroes of virtue of the Greek
tradition. Unlike Artapanus and the author of Jubilees who
apparently took some delight in the idea that the Jews
despoiled Egypt,[186] Josephus is writing for a cultured non-
Jewish audience and must defend Moses against charges that

Josephus," Miracles: Cambridge Studies in their Philosophy
and History (ed. Charles F.D. Moule; London, 1965), p. 142.

[186]Cf. Artapanus in Eusebius P.E. 9.27.34-35 and
Jubilees 48:18-19 discussed above.

he was an evil leper (Ap. 1:237-250, 304-308) who organized
the outcast Jews with the advice to attack the Egyptian
population, "to show goodwill to no man,[187] to offer not the
most noble but the worse counsel, and to overthrow any
temples and altars of the gods they encountered" with the
result that these scurrilous lepers "maltreated the people
and plundered and burned temples until they reached Judaea"
(Ap. 1:309-310). Since the context of Apion's anti-Semitism
is identified with a reference to the exclusion of Egyptians
and Jews from the cultured circles of Alexandrian citizenship
(Ap. 2:28-32),[188] Josephus responds by depicting the Jews as
model citizens and subjects who are scrupulous in observing
the Mosaic law, insisting that Moses is the noblest
instructor in virtue who trained the Jews in gentleness and
humanity (φιλανθρωπία) and specifically "prohibited even the
plundering of fallen combatants" and the burning of the
enemy's country (Ap. 2:211-213).[189]

---

[187]This particular charge that the Jews were enemies of
mankind is also mentioned in Ap. 2:121-122 and in Tacitus
Hist. 5:5: "adversus omnes alios hostile odium."

[188]For a credible analysis of the class struggle involved
in this controversy, cf. V. Tcherikover and A. Fuks, Corpus
Papyrorum Judaicarum, vol. I (Cambridge, 1957), pp. 1-111.

[189]There appear to be no such injunctions in the Mosaic
law, although the other items that Josephus mentions in this
context do derive from the law. Thus Josephus is probably
stretching the law to include responses to the specific
charges. His choice of terms is particularly revealing since
the LXX reports that the Israelites "despoiled" (σκυλεύειν)
the Egyptians" (Ex. 12:36), while Josephus argues that the
law prohibits the "despoiling (σκυλεύειν) of fallen
combattants" (Ap. 2:212). The hypocrisy is all the more
striking in the light of Josephus' reports in the Antiquities
of Moses ordering the stripping of the corpses of the enemy

Apion has also charged that the Jewish nation has not produced any "illustrious men" (θαυμαστὸς ἀνήρ) such as "inventors of certain arts or men distinguished in wisdom" (τεχνῶν τινων εὑρεταὶ ἢ σοφίᾳ διαφέροντες), men who can compare with Socrates, Zeno, Cleanthes or Apion himself (Ap. 2:134, cf. also 2:148). Josephus counters with the assertion that has been frequently sounded by others who were promoting Judaism to cultured audiences to the effect that Pythagoras, Anaxagoras, Plato and the Stoics learned from Moses (Ap. 2:168, 257, 281, cf. also 1:162-165). And in attempting to show how the Greek sages depended on the illustrious lawgiver of the Jews, Josephus puts Moses' conception of God in a distinctively Greek philosophical dress and emphasizes the universality of Mosaic legal principles:

> "He (Moses) displayed Him (God) as One, unbegotten and eternally immutable, surpassing mortal forms (ἰδέα) in beauty, and known to us in power, although unknowable in essence" (κατ' οὐσίαν: Ap. 2:167)

> "Just as God permeates the whole cosmos, so the law has moved among all men" (καὶ ὥσπερ ὁ θεὸς διὰ τοῦ κόσμου πεφοίτηκεν, οὕτως ὁ νόμος διὰ πάντων ἀνθρώπων βεβάδικεν: Ap. 2:284).[190]

But Josephus' most striking presentation of Moses as an "illustrious" figure is found in his description of the ambivalence of the Egyptians toward Moses:

---

after a battle (Antiq. 3:59, cf. also 4:93, and 4:162).

[190]Cf. Cleanthes' "Hymn to Zeus", Stobaeus Eclogae I.112 and Acts 17:28.

> "The Egyptians regard this man as illustrious (θαυμαστός) and divine (θεῖος), but they choose to claim him for themselves with the incredible blasphemy that he was one of the Heliopolitan priests who was expelled from there for leprosy" (Ap. 1:279).

Here Josephus does not indicate his own view as to whether or not Moses was divine, but he is merely documenting Moses' role as a benefactor of human civilization by appealing to the Egyptian practice of deifying those who have made a lasting cultural contribution.[191]

The primary focus of Josephus' treatment of Moses in this treatise, however, is his defense of the most ancient lawgiver as a paradigm of virtue. A major section of his work (Ap. 2:145-296) can be regarded as a response to the charges that Moses was a "fraud and imposter" (γόης καὶ ἀπατεῶν) and that his law taught vice (κακία) instead of virtue (ἀρετή: Ap. 2:145, cf. also 161). The specificity of the issues involved in the debate is best highlighted by the precise definition of the virtue of lawgivers as being "insight to know what is best and the ability to persuade those who are to practice the laws he establishes" (Ap. 2:153) and by the observation that nowhere in this discourse

---

[191]This criterion for deification has been discussed in the material on Artapanus, but it may be helpful to point once again to the crucial text from Diodorus I.13.1: "And besides these there are other gods, they say, who were terrestrial, having once been mortals, but who, by reason of their sagacity and the good services which they rendered to all men, attained immortality, some of them having even been kings in Egypt." Trans. by C.H. Oldfather, Diodorus of Sicily I (Loeb edition: New York, 1933), p. 45.

does Josephus refer to Moses' ability to perform miracles.[192]

Moses is the most ancient of all lawgivers, next to whom
Lycurgus, Solon, and Zaleucus were only born yesterday (Ap.
2:154).[193] His first great achievement was his leadership
in the exodus. No mention is made of any of the plagues or
even of the crossing of the Red Sea, but his ability to
lead the people safely through inhospitable regions in spite
of opposition prompts Josephus to recite Moses' virtues:
"Through all this, he was the most excellent general, the
wisest adviser and the most conscientious of all guardians"
(Ap. 2:158). He never took advantage of his position of
authority to play the despot, but regarded it as necessary
for himself as leader to live piously (εὐσεβεῖν), since "he
believed this was the best way to exhibit virtue (ἀρετή)
and to provide for the lasting welfare (σωτηρία) of those who
had made him the leader" (Ap. 2:159). This life of virtue
was also the sine qua non of his privileged status with
God: "With this noble purpose and successful achievement of
great things, he properly (εἰκότως) believed he had God as
his guide and counselor" (Ap. 2:160).

The picture rivals Philo's portrait of Moses the divine

---

[192]It is once again worth noting that this distinction
corresponds to what Gager, op. cit., has observed in pagan
treatment of Moses. Those of cultured or literary circles
were interested in evaluating him as a lawgiver, even if
they were acquainted with his reputation as a miracle worker.

[193]For a discussion of the propagandistic value of the
claim to highest antiquity, cf. Georgi, Die Gegner, op. cit.,
pp. 169-172, 257.

wise man for consistency. Moses, the possessor of virtue,
is the one who attained the best conception of God (Ap.
2:163), and his prophecies are thoroughly trustworthy (Ap.
2:286).

> "He excelled greatly because his legislation was always
> naturally suitable for all men. For he did not make
> piety (εὐσέβεια) a part of virtue (ἀρετή) but made the
> virtues, such as justice, temperance, endurance, and the
> concord of all members of the community toward each
> other in all things, parts of piety" (Ap. 2:170).[194]

The ultimate proof of the virtue of Moses which Josephus
adduces is that his laws have stood the test of time:

> "Since time is the most truthful judge of worth, I would
> summon it as a witness of the virtue (ἀρετή) of our
> lawgiver and of the account of God that was transmitted
> by him" (Ap. 2:279).

Thus in his summation of the debate, Josephus states his
refutation of the cultured despisers of the Jews in terms of
the Stoic contrast between the sage or the possessor of
virtue and the worthless man:

> "They reviled our legislator as a most worthless man
> (φαυλότατος), but in the past God, and after Him, time,
> have been found as witnesses of his virtue (ἀρετή:
> Ap. 2:290).[195]

The image of Moses that Josephus drafts in the
Antiquities is more variegated and difficult to control. If
more precise methods could be found for identifying the kinds

---

[194]This emphasis on piety as the dominant virtue is also
clear in Philo and is counted as Moses' particular possession.
Cf. Praem. 53, Mos. II 66.

[195]For a discussion of Philo's use of Stoic categories
to describe the divine sage as completely removed from the
fool, cf. note 23 above and text ad loc.

of sources that Josephus had at his disposal and the way he
used such sources,[196] it would probably be possible to make
more accurate discriminations as to which features of his
portrait of Moses were essential in Josephus' own view and
which have been agglomerated from previous descriptions. It
is at least possible to observe, however, that certain aspects
of his picture of Moses stand out against the backdrop of
the biblical account.

The apologetic thrust of the Antiquities is stated
explicitly in the early paragraphs of the work:

> "Other legislators, in fact, following fables, have in
> their writings imputed to the gods the disgraceful
> errors of men and thus furnished the wicked with a
> powerful excuse; our legislator, on the contrary, having
> shown that God possesses the very perfection of virtue
> (ἀρετή), thought that men should strive to participate
> in it, and inexorably punished those who did not hold
> with or believe in these doctrines. I therefore entreat
> my readers to examine my work from this point of view.
> For, studying it in this spirit, nothing will appear to
> them unreasonable (ἄλογος), nothing incongruous with
> the majesty of God and His love for man; everything,
> indeed, is here set forth in keeping with the nature of
> the universe (πάντα γὰρ τῇ τῶν ὅλων φύσει σύμφωνον ἔχει
> τὴν διάθεσιν); some things the lawgiver shrewdly veils
> in enigmas, others he sets forth in solemn allegory;
> but whenever straightforward speech was expedient, there

---

[196] A good example of the problem involved is the scholarly
dispute as to whether Josephus had a written source of
haggadic traditions as is maintained by Salomo Rappaport,
Agada und Exegese bei Josephus (Wien, 1930), pp. xx-xxiii, or
was merely using oral tradition. Cf. G. Vermes, op. cit.,
pp. 87-88, who suspends judgement. Cf. also H. St.John
Thackeray, Josephus the Man and the Historian (The Hilda Stich
Stroock Lectures at the Jewish Institute of Religion: New
York, 1929), pp. 78, 81-82, 88 note 39. Louis H. Feldman,
"Hellenizations in Josephus' Portrayal of Man's Decline,"
Religions in Antiquity (Essays in Memory of Erwin Ramsdell
Goodenough, ed. Jacob Neusner: Leiden, 1968), pp. 336-353,
especially pp. 336-339 and notes ad loc.

he makes his meaning absolutely plain." (Antiq. 1:
22-24)[197]

Josephus also claims that he will not supplement or omit
anything that is written in the scriptures (Antiq. 1:17),
but this statement must be taken with a grain of salt since
he does not include some of the stories which show Moses in
a less favorable light, such as Moses' killing of the
Egyptian (Exodus 2:12), his grumbling and doubting before
the second miraculous quail feast (Numbers 11:11-23, cf.
Antiq. 3:295-299), his disobedience in striking the rock to
bring forth water (Numbers 20:10-12), and the story of the
golden calf which includes Moses' breaking the tablets of
the law (Exodus 32).[198] Josephus' frequent use of a rationalistic disclaimer in his conclusion of miracle stories (cf.
Antiq. 1:108; 3:81; 4:158; 10:281; 17:354) must also be
regarded as an apologetic nod to the cultured tastes of his
audience.[199]

---

[197]Trans. by H. St.J. Thackeray, Josephus vol. IV,
Jewish Antiquities I-IV (Loeb edition: Cambridge, 1930), p. 13.

[198]Cf. Feldman, op. cit., pp. 337-339, who indicates
that such omissions are by no means limited to the figure of
Moses (cf. also Rappaport, op. cit., p. xxviii), but Feldman
observes that Josephus' list of omissions does not correspond
precisely with the passages the rabbis (Megillah 25 a-b) left
untranslated. Cf. also his supplements from other sources
(also "writings"?) discussed below, c. note 204.

[199]Thackeray, Josephus the Man and the Historian, op. cit.,
p. 57, and Jewish Antiquities, op. cit., p. 52 note b, points
to the frequent use of this disclaimer by Dionysius of
Halicarnassus, "the unnamed model for our author's Jewish
Antiquities" (cf. Dionysius, Roman Antiquities 1.48.1, 4;
2.40.3; 2.74.5; 3.36.5) and a similar disclaimer by Lucian,
How to Write History 60. Delling, op. cit., p. 305, also
cites Pliny, Hist. nat. 9.18. Thus Josephus was clearly
using an established literary convention.

Delling[200] and MacRae,[201] however, have demonstrated that
Josephus does not include himself among those who doubt the
reliability of these accounts. Although he is frequently
willing to offer rationalizing explanations of how a miracle
was performed, Josephus' apologetic interests do not alter
his confidence in the authenticating value of miracles.[202]
A clear example of this confidence is his expansion of
Hezekiah's request for a sign to verify Isaiah's prophecy,
"For, he said, things that are beyond belief (παράλογα)
and surpass our hopes are made credible by things of a like
nature" (Antiq. 10:28).[203]

Furthermore, Josephus did not limit his trust in the
reliability of Jewish traditions to those stories found in
the biblical writings. He appears to have accepted the
veracity of a diverse group of additional stories from non-
biblical legends[204] as well as accounts of miraculous

---

[200]Op. cit., pp. 305-309.

[201]Op. cit., pp. 136-142.

[202]Josephus referred to himself as the servant of God
(διάκονος: B.J. 3:354; 4:626) and authenticated this
status with interpretation of dreams and predictions, cf.
B.J. 3:350-354, 399-408; 4:622-629; Life   208-209.

[203]Cf. MacRae, op. cit., p. 135.

[204]Cf. Feldman, op. cit., p. 339. Note, for example,
that the manna congeals around Moses' hands in Antiq. 3:26,
which Thackeray, loc cit., identifies as a midrashic addition.

phenomena in his own era.[205]

His account of Moses' early years in Egypt displays extensive dependence on such non-biblical legends. Although these stories are like those collected by Artapanus[206] and thus probably displayed little of the reticence of miracles that characterized the philosophical presentations of Moses as a divine sage, Josephus is clearly more cautious than is Artapanus in describing Moses as the possessor of magical and miraculous powers. On the other hand, the Jewish historian is willing to amplify the biblical account with such legends[207] in order to show that God had destined Moses to become the great military conqueror of Egypt, even stressing that the preservation of the infant Moses was due to God's miraculous intervention.

According to Josephus, the reason that the Egyptian king ordered the slaughter of male infants was that he was

---

[205]Cf. Delling, op. cit., pp. 294-296. S.V. McCasland, "Portents in Josephus and in the Gospels," JBL 51 (1932), pp. 323-335. Otto Michel, "Studien zu Josephus: Apokalyptische Heilsansagen im Bericht des Josephus (B.J. 6, 290f, 293-295); ihre Umdeutung bei Josephus," Neotestamentica et Semitica: Studies in Honour of Matthew Black (eds. E.E. Ellis and M. Wilcox; Edinburgh, 1969), pp. 240-244.

[206]The question of whether Josephus actually knew Artapanus' work or had access to common legends must be constantly kept in view, although a definitive answer is elusive. Cf. Freudenthal, op. cit., pp. 169-174.

[207]Julien Weill, Oeuvres complètes de Flavius Josèphe, tr. en francais sous la direction de Theodore Reinach (Paris, 1900 ff), collects a variety of rabbinic parallels to Josephus' account of Moses. Such parallels do not, however, resolve the question of whether Josephus had a written source for such legends or merely was acquainted with a range of haggadic tales.

forewarned of Moses' military prowess by a sacred scribe

(ἱερογραμματεύς):

> "He announced to the king that one was about to be born
> to the Israelites at that time who would humiliate
> Egyptian sovereignty and would exalt the Israelites when
> he had been reared and would surpass everyone in valour
> (ἀρετή) and would attain everlasting fame" (δόξα:
> Antiq. 2:205).

Perhaps Josephus is also appealing in this passage to the

image of Moses as the sage who possesses virtue (ἀρετή)

but the military threat posed by the birth of the child is

the focal concern.[208] This is also the case in the dream

vision that Moses' father, Amram, is reported to have when

he is assured by God that Moses will be miraculously

preserved to overcome the Egyptian slavemasters:

> "This child whose birth has caused the Egyptians to
> condemn the offspring of the Israelites to destruction
> will be yours, and he shall escape those who are watching
> to destroy him, and when he has been miraculously
> (παραδόξως) reared, he shall release the Hebrew race
> from their bondage by the Egyptians and his memory
> will endure not only among the Hebrews but also among
> other peoples as long as the universe endures" (Antiq.
> 2:215-216).[209]

Josephus also adds an excursus on the frailty of human reason

compared with the might and providence of God which documents

the real value that Josephus regarded the miracle to have:

---

[208]So also in Exodus 1:8-10 where the military strength
of the Israelites is feared, but the might of Moses is not
mentioned in that context.

[209]Contrast this emphasis with that of pseudo-Philo
(9:7, 10 cited above) where the predictions of Moses' birth
specifically mentioned the signs which God will perform
through him. In Josephus, Moses is miraculously reared, but
he himself is remembered for freeing the Hebrews from the
Egyptians.

"Then God also showed human intelligence (σύνεσις)
to be nothing and that everything He wills to do attains
its good end and that they fail who condemn others to
destruction for the sake of their own security even
while expending great effort to that end, while those
who take the risk, relying on the will of God, are
miraculously saved (ἐκ παραδόξου) and discover a safe
path out of the very midst of evils. In this very way,
what happened to the child displayed the might (ἰσχύς)
of God" (Antiq. 2:222-223).[210]

In spite of this little gibe at the intellectuals,

Josephus has not completely neglected his apologetic interest

in showing Moses as possessing the qualities of a great

sage. Thus he includes a small testimony to such attributes

in the account of Moses' childhood in Egypt:

"Admittedly he was the noblest (ἄριστος) of the
Hebrews with respect to magnitude of intellect (φρόνημα)
and contempt of toils (πόνος) in accord with God's
prediction" (Antiq. 2:229).

Furthermore, Josephus emphasizes that his understanding

(σύνεσις) developed at an unusually rapid rate, and he points

out the physical beauty of the child Moses (Antiq. 2:230-

231).[211]

But in this section, such apologetic interests are

overshadowed by the stress of the legends on the military

prowess of Moses and the threat that the Egyptians recognized

---

[210]This is one of the passages where Josephus' apologetic
veneer cracks and he engages in direct criticism of those
who are unwilling to accept the miraculous. Cf. also his
criticism of the Epicureans who reject the idea of divine
providence, and note that the criticism follows a miracle
story (Antiq. 10:277-280). Cf. also Antiq. 3:216 and MacRae,
op. cit., pp. 133, 139-140.

[211]Philo expatiates on the glories of the child Moses at
even greater length than does Josephus. Cf. Mos. I 18-24.

him to be. Thus when Moses is brought into the king's court
by his Egyptian foster-mother, Thermuthis,[212] and presented
as "a child of divine beauty (μορφῇ θεῖος) and noble
intellect" (φρονήματι γενναῖος) whom she "miraculously
(θαυμασίως) took from the river's bounty" (Antiq. 2:232),
Moses "childishly" (κατὰ νηπιότητα) tears off the crown the
king places on Moses' head, throws it to the ground and
tramples it (Antiq. 2:233). Although Josephus tries to
discount the action as "childish",[213] the significance of
the display is not lost on the Egyptians who recognize it as
an evil omen of what Moses will do to Egypt: "When he saw
it, the sacred scribe who had predicted that his birth would
lead to the humiliation of Egyptian dominion pushed forward
to kill him." Only the intervention of Termuthis and the
hesitance of the king which was prompted by God's providence
(πρόνοια) saves the child Moses (Antiq. 2:234-236).

Additional documentation of the importance of this
"childish" act is provided when Moses is selected by Egyptian

---

[212]Cf. Merris in Artapanus (27.3) and Tarmuth in
Jubilees 47:5 as discussed in note 85 above. The fact that
it is once again an Egyptian who refers to Moses as "divine"
is perhaps not accidental, cf. Ap. 1:279.

[213]It is difficult to believe that Josephus did not also
think this was an evil omen for Egypt. Thackeray, Jewish
Antiquities, op. cit., p. 267, points to two midrashic
parallels to the story which make the action even more wilful
by having Moses snatch the crown from the king's head. It
seems likely that Josephus refers to it as "childish" only to
avoid the unfavorable impression that Moses was an undis-
ciplined or malicious child. Philo's account of the respect
that Moses showed to his Egyptian foster parents exhibits, by
contrast, the way a more consistent picture of Moses as the
paradigm of moral virtue would be drawn (Mos. I 25-33,
especially 32-33).

oracles and divination, which were really directed by God
(Antiq. 2:241), to lead the Egyptian armies against the
Ethiopians. Josephus introduces the episode with these
words:

> "Moses then, having been born in the way previously
> described and having been reared and come to maturity,
> made his prowess manifest to the Egyptians (φανερὰν
> τοῖς Αἰγυπτίοις τὴν ἀρετὴν ἐποίησε)   and the fact that
> he was born for their humiliation and for the advance-
> ment of the Hebrews, by seizing this opportunity"
> (Antiq. 2:238).

After Moses' very successful military display of his ἀρετή,
the king joins the other conspirators in plotting on Moses'
life, "both out of envy for Moses' generalship (στρατηγία)
and from fear of humiliation" (ταπείνωσις: Antiq. 2:256).[214]
It is this assassination plot, not the killing of an
Egyptian,[215] which prompts Moses to flee Egypt for Madian
where he once more displays his prowess (ἀρετή: Antiq. 2:257)
by driving off the shepherds who were trying to jump claim on
Raguel's well (Antiq. 2:258-260).

Whatever sources Josephus was using for his version of
the episodes of Moses' youth in Egypt, the rest of his
treatment of Moses' life is a rehearsal of his ἀρετή
both in the sense of moral virtue as emphasized by authors
like Philo and in the sense of military prowess as in
Artapanus. But unlike Artapanus, Josephus abbreviates the

---

[214]For the close correlation with Artapanus in this
section, cf. notes 96 and 98 above and the text ad loc.
Note particularly Artapanus' report that the king plotted
against Moses' life because he envied the ἀρετή of Moses.

[215]Cf. above note 198 and text ad loc.

biblical catalog of Moses' miraculous performances and
emphasizes the subordination of Moses to God in such activity.

One of the more difficult and crucial texts is Josephus'
version of the story of the burning bush where God
establishes an alliance with Moses for the liberation of the
Hebrews. In conversation with the voice (φωνή) from the
bush, which Josephus identifies as God as does Exodus 3,[216]
Moses demurs from accepting the task since as "a common man
(ἰδιώτης) with no strength" (ἰσχύος) he would be unable to
persuade the people to follow him (Antiq. 2:271, cf. Exodus
3:11, 4:1, 10). Josephus follows the Exodus account very
closely in insisting that Moses is not operating under his
own power:

> "But God counseled him to take courage (θαρρεῖν),[217]
> by promising Himself to assist him and when there was
> need of words to provide persuasion and to furnish
> strength (ἰσχύς) when there was need of action"
> (ἔργον: Antiq. 2:272).

But Moses is only convinced when he sees the miracles of the
staff being changed into a snake, the leprous hand, and the
water transformed into blood (Antiq. 2:272-273, cf. Ex.
4:2-9):

> And while he marveled at these, God exhorted him to take
> courage (θαρρεῖν), to be assured of the continued
> presence of this mighty aid, and to make use of miracles

---

[216]Contrast this with the caution of writers like
Aristobulus and Philo in speaking about the "divine voice,"
and compare Artapanus, cf. note 110 above and text ad loc.

[217]Contrast this with Moses' surge of apparent self-
confidence in Artapanus 27.22: "Moses took courage (θαρρεῖν)
and determined to lead a hostile force against the Egyptians."

(σημεῖα) with all men to persuade them that 'having been sent by me you do all things in accord with my commands'" (Antiq. 2:274).

As in the book of Exodus, this is also the occasion when Moses receives the name of God, which Josephus reports to be ineffable:[218]

"Then God revealed his name to him, which had not previously reached men, concerning which it is not fitting for me to speak. And Moses found these miracles (σημεῖα) available to him not only then, but at all times when there was need. From all of which, trusting more the truth of the fire and believing God would be his gracious protector, he also hoped to save his people and to destroy the Egyptians with evils" (Antiq. 2:276).

The point that must be stressed is that the miracles convince Moses himself that God is going to intervene on Israel's behalf and He will back Moses as his agent. Moses' own role as a miracle worker is not at issue. It quickly becomes apparent that the noble Hebrews grasp the point very precisely. Like Moses, they only believe when they see the miracles, and then they immediately understand that God is going to champion their cause:

"The most noble Hebrews, having learned of his coming, encountered them (Moses and Aaron) as they came. Unable

---

[218]The fact that the mention of the receiving of the name is so directly tied to Moses' receiving the promise of the ability to work miracles is difficult to assess. Both are important factors in Exodus 3-4 for authenticating Moses' role, but Josephus clearly invests the name with a numinous quality by refusing to speak it. If this represents the knowledge of the magical power of the name as seen in Artapanus and the magical papyri, cf. note 118 above, it is crucial to observe that Josephus never depicts Moses as using the name in this way. On Josephus' attitude toward the divine name, cf. note #227 below.

> to be convincing to them by describing the miracles
> (σημεῖα), Moses performed them in their sight. And they
> took courage with amazement at the astonishing things
> they saw and were hopeful for the whole project because
> God was taking ·forethought (προνοουμένου)   for their
> safety" (Antiq. 2:279-280).

Of course this response also means that Moses has been
authenticated as God's agent, but both Moses and the noble
Hebrews "take courage" from these signs as verification of
God's providence for Israel.

Pharaoh, however, completely misses the point. Although
Moses tries to tell him that the miracles God had shown him
were intended to inspire confidence in God's commands and
that unbelief on the king's part would be an attempt to
impede God's purpose (Antiq. 2:283), the king writes off
Moses' performance of these signs as due to the deceit
(ἀπάτη)   of one who operates by wonderworking and magic
(τερατουργία καὶ μαγεία)   and explicitly rejects the idea
that Moses owed such talents to God (Antiq. 2:284-285). He
then has his priests transform their staves to serpents.
Once again, Josephus' Moses tries to make Pharaoh understand
that he is not merely dealing with another magician who
rivals the Egyptians, but with God:

> "To be sure, O king, he said, I myself do not disparage
> the cunning (σοφία) of the Egyptians, but I assert that
> the deeds done by me (ὑπ' ἐμοῦ) are as superior to
> their magic and skill (μαγία καὶ τέχνη) as divine acts
> (τὰ θεῖα) surpass human ones. And I will demonstrate
> that my acts are not displays done by wizardry (γοητεία)
> and deception (πλάνη) of true judgement but are due to
> God's providence (πρόνοια) and power" (δύναμις:
> Antiq. 2:286).

Yet even when Moses' staff consumes the staves of the

Egyptians "which looked like snakes" (Antiq. 2:287),[219]
Pharaoh disregards this display as due to Moses' cunning
(σοφία) and cleverness (δεινότητος) and increases the
oppression of the Hebrews (Antiq. 2:288).

The ensuing plagues document Moses' claim that Pharaoh's
opponent is actually God, not Moses. Neither Moses nor his
rod are even mentioned as agents of the plagues. These
miracles are accomplished at God's command (cf. Antiq. 2:294,
296, 300, 303, 304-306, 311). But Pharaoh refuses to accept
the point:

> "He only exasperated God more, thinking to impose on his
> providence, as though it were Moses and not He who was
> punishing Egypt on behalf of the Hebrews" (Antiq. 2:302).

> "Less from foolishness than from evil, he matched himself
> against God although he perceived the true cause of the
> miracles" (Antiq. 2:309).

Thus before the last plague, Moses reminds Pharaoh, "How long
will you disobey God's will? For God commands the Hebrews
be released" (Antiq. 2:309). But even after the Hebrews
have departed, Pharaoh changes his mind out of the fear that
"these things happened by the witchcraft (γοητεία) of Moses"

---

[219]Except for this mild insult, Josephus seems to believe
that the Egyptians really could perform magic since he
previously (#285) admits their staves became snakes and has
Moses grant them that they have real ability (cf.Delling,
op. cit., p. 297). But this is not a contest between Moses'
and the magicians. Note that they do not imitate the plagues.
Josephus is trying to show that God is responsible for the
miracles, although Pharaoh refuses to understand that. Thus
it is not merely a case of Josephus drawing a "broad contrast"
between Moses and the magicians, as is maintained by Wayne A.
Meeks, The Prophet-King: Moses Traditions and the Johannine
Christology (Leiden, 1967), p. 139.

(Antiq. 2:320).

The miracles are God's work, but they also confirm
Moses' role as God's spokesman. Josephus maintains that he
recounted all of the plagues[220] in order to show that "Moses
erred in none of his predictions (προεῖπεν) of them" and
that men should not provoke God (Antiq. 2:293). His extended
account of the miracle at the Red Sea also provides an
occasion for him to emphasize that the despondency of the
Hebrews before the miracle was due to the fact that:

> "they had forgotten the miracles that had been done by
> God for their liberation and thus met the prophet
> (προφήτης) who was encouraging them and promising
> salvation, with disbelief" (Antiq. 2:327).

Once again the miracle is God's act. Moses implores
the people to rely on God's providence (Antiq. 2:330):

> "For the Deity does not give His own aid to those he
> favours in minor affairs, but in those circumstances
> when He does not see that human hope can provide the
> improvement" (Antiq. 2:332).

Before the miracle, Moses offers an extended prayer to God
invoking His alliance and clearly indicating that only God
can save the Hebrews but that He could accomplish the rescue
by a variety of means, according to His pleasure (Antiq.
2:334-337). Even when Moses strikes the sea with his
staff[221] and it divides, Moses regards it as a "manifestation

---

[220]Actually he omits the plague on the cattle.

[221]This detail does not correspond directly to the
Exodus 14 account where Moses extends his hand and rod over
the sea (vv. 16, 21), but it does parallel the version of
the story found in Artapanus 27.36. Cf. also Exodus 17:5.

(ἐπιφάνεια) of God."[222] Moses' ability to work miracles is not at issue. Even his role in bringing the sea back upon the Egyptians (Exodus 14:26-27) is omitted. Both the people and Moses credit God with the miraculous rescue (Antiq. 2:345-346); and even in his rationalistic overture to the skeptics in his audience, Josephus does not mention Moses but puts the question of the miracle in terms of "whether it was by the will of God or by accident"(ταὐτόματον: Antiq. 2:347-348).[223]

The subordination of Moses to God in miracle working is also a consistent theme in the rest of Josephus' treatment of Moses. Moses' elevated status does not rest on his miracles. The only exception may be Josephus' version of Moses' holding his hands aloft to aid the troops in defeating the Amalekites (Antiq. 3:53, cf. Exodus 17:8-13), but even here Josephus dwells at some length on the military preparations (Antiq. 3:47-52), omits the mention of the rod (cf. Exodus 17:9), and prefaces the story with the remark that Moses "withdrew to the mountain, committing the battle to God and Joshua" (Antiq. 3:52), and the raised hands may

---

[222]On Josephus' vocabulary of miracle, cf. MacRae, op. cit., pp. 142-147.

[223]MacRae, op. cit., pp. 139-140, shows that Josephus is not indifferent about this question, but rejects the notion of the accidental or automatic. On this concept, cf. also Feldman, op. cit., pp. 341-344, who shows that Josephus regarded the automatic course of nature to have been disrupted by the fall of man. Note how Josephus also interprets the ambiguous oracle of the "automatic" opening of the temple gate during the seige of Jerusalem in B.J. 6:293-296.

merely illustrate Moses' role as intercessor. Elsewhere his
accounts of the sweetening of the bitter spring (Antiq.
3:5-9), the miraculous supply of quail and manna (Antiq.
3:13-32), and the water from the rock (Antiq. 3:33-38), are
marked both by frequent rationalizations[224] and by the
continual insistence that these are displays of God's
providence.[225] Perhaps this emphasis is best seen in Moses'
address to the people on the occasion of his descent from
Sinai. He pleads that they not scorn the words because they
are transmitted by a human tongue but that they notice that
the excellence (ἀρετή: Antiq. 3:85) of the words displays
God's majesty:

> "For it is not Moses, son of Amaram and Jochabad, but He
> who constrained the Nile to flow for your sake a blood-
> red stream and tamed with divers plagues the pride of
> the Egyptians, He who opened for you a path through the
> sea, He who caused meat to descend from heaven when ye
> were destitute, water to gush from the rock when ye
> lacked it, He thanks to whom Adam partook of the produce
> of the land and sea ... He it is who favours you with
> these commandments, using me for interpreter" (Antiq.
> 3:86-87).[226]

---

[224]Cf. MacRae, op. cit., pp. 141-142. It is probably
not significant that no rationalization is offered in the
case of the miracle of the water from the rock. Cf. Philo
Mos. I 211.

[225]As in Exodus, however, Josephus also points out that
each of these miracles was preceded by a loss of confidence
in Moses. Thus God's miracles do have the effect of fortifying
Moses' position. Cf. the conclusion to the story of the water
from the rock. The Hebrews regarded it as a gift from God,
"wherefore they also admired Moses because he was thus honored
by God and offered sacrifices to God for His providence for
them" (Antiq. 3:38).

[226]Trans. by Thackeray, Jewish Antiquities, op. cit.,
p. 359. The subordination of Moses to God is emphasized once
more in the confirmation of the high-priesthood on Aaron.

Nevertheless, Josephus does accord Moses an elevated, perhaps even divine status. Moses shares that quality which was just cited in <u>Antiquities</u> 3:85 as characteristic of God's commands: ἀρετή (cf. also <u>Antiq</u>. 1:23 cited above where God is described as the possessor of ἀρετή). Subsequent scrutiny of crucial texts where Josephus speaks of Moses' divine or semi-divine nature will show that Josephus is very cautious about calling Moses divine, usually attributing such statements to persons other than himself. Programmatic to the documentation of this point is the observation that Josephus does not mention the references to Moses as "God to Aaron" (<u>Ex</u>. 4:16) or "God to Pharaoh" (<u>Ex</u>. 7:1).[227]

Although Moses felt that he himself ought to have been worthy of the dignity (<u>Antiq</u>. 3:190) and would have given himself the position (<u>Antiq</u>. 4:27), God ruled otherwise. The miraculous destruction of Datham and his followers who oppose Aaron's priesthood is finally needed to convince the people that Aaron did not owe his position "to the favour of Moses but to the judgement of God thus clearly manifested" (<u>Antiq</u>. 4:58). God's act demonstrates that. Datham and his followers had made the same mistake as Pharaoh in regarding Moses as the opponent.

[227]In addition to the reticence that Josephus has shown in speaking the divine name (cf. <u>Antiq</u>. 2:276 and note the aversion to the term κύριος in referring to God as discussed by J.B. Fischer, "The Name Despotes in Josephus," <u>JQR</u> 49 (1958), pp. 132-138), the connection that the <u>Exodus</u> text makes between Moses' role as God and his ability to perform miracles would appear to have been contrary to Josephus' view of the clear subordination of Moses to God in miracle working. In private conversation, Professor George MacRae emphasized that the awe which Josephus has for the divine name was by no means a personal idiosyncrasy. The reticence even to pronounce the name is found in the Old Testament [cf. <u>Amos</u> 6:10 and <u>Leviticus</u> 24:16 (particularly in the LXX)], and even the initials of the names "Elohim" and "Adonai" were forbidden to be used in oaths at Qumran (cf. <u>CD</u> 15:1-2, <u>IQS</u> 6:27). This reverence affects Josephus' treatment in some striking ways. On the one hand, he frequently refrains from citing the bible directly in order to avoid using the the divine names (but see <u>Antiq</u>. 13:68), and he generally limits his vocabulary to θεός and δεσπότης and refers to the προσηγορία rather than the ὄνομα of God. On the other hand, he enhances the story of trial by ordeal of <u>Numbers</u> 5:11-

But as has already been seen in Josephus' account of
Moses' youth, Moses is the supreme possessor of military
and moral ἀρετή. While Josephus does not recount the
miracles as Moses' miracles, he does treat Moses as the
lawgiver of the Jews who possesses and displays ἀρετή,
and he documents Moses' unique status before God in his
roles as lawgiver, prophet, and general by pointing to his
ἀρετή. Indeed, Josephus' whole treatment of Moses could be
described as a recitation of his virtues, or even an aretalogy,
if it is carefully observed that it is not a recitation of
his miracles.[228]

A few of the many allusions to Moses' virtue will
suffice to show the general importance of this feature in
Josephus' account. His depiction of Moses as making the
sufferings of the people his own (Antiq. 3:5) and being
totally unconcerned about his own safety in the face of their
threats to stone him (Antiq. 3:21) demonstrates the moral
courage of Moses. This longsuffering Moses is also the
one who can answer the abuse of the multitude by taking his
stand alongside God: "God and I though vilified by you will
not cease our efforts on your behalf" (Antiq. 3:298). Again
it is Raguel, Moses' father-in-law, who leads the acclamation
of Moses' ἀρετή. When the company arrives at Sinai, Raguel
and Aaron join the people in hymns to God, "the author and
dispenser of their salvation and liberty, and they also

31 by including the divine name as part of the oath of the
ordeal. Thus it is clear that Josephus was aware of traditions
where the name had great, perhaps magical, potency. Cf. also
F. Giesebrecht, Die alttestamentliche Schätzung des Gottesnamens
und ihre religionsgeschichtliche Grundlage (Königsberg, 1901).
A. Marmorstein, The Old Rabbinic Doctrine of God (Jews' College,
Lond. Publ. #10; London, 1927). Adolf von Schlatter Die
Theologie des Judentums nach dem Bericht des Josefus (Gütersloh,
1932).

[228]Cf. chapter one section A, "The Problem of Aretalogies."

praised their general since they knew that all that had
turned out well was due to his ἀρετή." "And Raguel admired
Moses for his courage (ἀνδραγαθία), in pursuing the safety
of his friends" (Antiq. 3:65). Raguel also advises Moses to
delegate certain tasks, because he recognized that Moses'
virtue was an indispensable factor in ensuring God's continued
protection:

> "Being aware of your own virtue (ἀρετή) and how your
> service to God has worked for the salvation of the
> people, allow them to commit the arbitration of disputes
> to others" (Antiq. 3:69).

The fact that Moses takes advice and credits Raguel with the
idea is another proof of his virtue in Josephus' eyes:

> "Thus it is possible to learn of Moses' virtue (ἀρετή)
> from this as well. But we shall make other observations
> concerning it at other appropriate points of the
> writing" (Antiq. 3:74).

Josephus even suggests that Moses' virtue (ἀρετή) was an
important qualification of Aaron's so that he received the
high-priesthood (Antiq. 3:192), although he grants that Aaron
was also a man of virtue (Antiq. 3:188).

Moses' particular dignity or virtue is best seen in
Josephus' statements about him as a lawgiver, and it is in
this function that Moses approaches divine stature. To be
sure, Josephus insists that the laws are God's laws,[229] but
he also makes frequent reference to them as Moses' laws. Thus
in his extended account of the ritual laws (Antiq. 3:102-187),
Josephus regards the ordinances not only as displaying the

---

[229]Cf. particularly Antiq. 3:85-87 cited above.

232

majesty of God by their ἀρετή (cf. Antiq. 3:85 cited

above), but also as documenting Moses' semi-divine status

and his ἀρετή:

> "But one may well be astonished at the hatred which men
> have for us and which they have so persistently maintained,
> from an idea that we slight the divinity whom they
> themselves profess to venerate. For if one reflects
> on the construction of the tabernacle and looks at the
> vestments of the priest and the vessels which we use
> for the sacred ministry, he will discover that our
> lawgiver was a man of God (θεῖος ἀνήρ) and that these
> blasphemous charges brought against us by the rest of
> men are idle. In fact, every one of these objects is
> intended to recall and represent the universe (εἰς
> ἀπομίμησιν καὶ διατύπωσιν τῶν ὅλων), as he will find
> if he will but consent to examine them without prejudice
> and with understanding" (Antiq. 3:179-180).[230]

This is Josephus' strongest statement on the semi-divine

stature of Moses and the only instance where he calls Moses

a θεῖος ἀνήρ. But the passage is also one of the most

explicitly apologetic statements in the Antiquities. Josephus

makes it very clear that he is responding to anti-Semitic

polemics and is adopting the criteria of the cultured

despisers of the Jews to show that Moses measures up to their

standards for a "divine man". Thus after indulging in a

detailed allegorical exposition of the symbolic significance

of the cultic laws,[231] Josephus closes the allegory with a

---

[230]Trans. by Thackeray, Jewish Antiquities, op. cit., p.
403.

[231]There can be no doubt that here Josephus is giving
his version of a widespread allegory. Moreover, like Philo
(cf. Mos. II 88, 177-141), Josephus interpreted these laws in
terms of a favorite theme of Hellenistic philosophy of the
nature of the forms as true reflections or imitations of the
cosmic harmony. Cf. also Antiq. 3:123: μίμησις τῆς τῶν
ὅλων φύσεως and B.J. 5:212-213: εἰκὼν τῶν ὅλων. It is

clear indication that he regards these ordinances as documentation of the virtue of Moses:

> "Let these considerations be sufficient on this subject since the subject matter will provide me with frequent and ample opportunities to expatiate on the virtue (ἀρετή) of the lawgiver" (Antiq. 3:187).

This close connection between Moses' virtue and the excellence of the law also enables Josephus to maintain that the continued scrupulous observance of the law reflects the admiration which the Hebrews feel toward Moses:

> "The man of virtue (ἀρετή) was marvelous (θαυμαστός) as was his ability (ἰσχύς) to make everything he might say be believed not only in the time he lived but also now. For there is no Hebrew who does not obey his ordinances as if he were present to punish any irregularity, although it would be possible to escape detection. There are many other proofs of his more than human power" (ἡ ὑπὲρ ἄνθρωπον δύναμις: Antiq. 3:317-318).[232]

The examples of this power that Josephus adduces are not Moses' miraculous or magical performances. Moses' might and his admirable nature are documented by the respect that his laws continue to command (Antiq. 3:318-319). Thus Josephus concludes his generous praise of Moses by once again emphasizing that the basis of Moses' elevated status is his role as lawgiver:

---

probably significant, therefore, that this is the only context in which Josephus refers to Moses as a θεῖος ἀνήρ.

[232]This discussion of the "power" of Moses as a lawgiver is consistent with what Josephus defines as the peculiar "virtue" of a lawgiver in Ap. 2:153: "insight to know what is best and the ability to persuade those who are to practice the laws he establishes."

> "Thus the legislation since it is believed to be from God has caused this man to be regarded as superior to his own nature" (τῆς αὐτοῦ φύσεως κρείττονα νομίζεσθαι: Antiq. 3:320).

> "Even those who hate us confess that God is the one who established our constitution through Moses and his virtue" (διὰ Μωυσέος καὶ τῆς ἀρετῆς τῆς ἐκείνου: Antiq. 3:322).

Not only do the laws demonstrate Moses' virtue, but Moses' virtue also lends its quality to the legislation. Josephus begins his extended account of the laws of Moses (Antiq. 4:196-301) with these words:

> "I wish first to describe the constitution which was consonant with the reputation of the virtue (ἀρετή) of Moses" (Antiq. 4:196).

Josephus' version of the story of the death of Moses is also consistent with this picture. If Moses is to be accorded any kind of divine status, the basis for such consideration would have to be his possession of virtue. In his farewell speeches, Moses blesses the power (δύναμις) of God, crediting God with all the benefactions the people have received in their hours of distress (Antiq. 4:316-318). But Josephus also has Moses play his own roles of general, prophet, and paradigm of virtue one more time. Moses gives further military instructions (Antiq. 4:296-301, 305, 315). He "prophesies" (προφητεύειν) the future of the Hebrews (Antiq. 4:303, 320), and he gives a detailed lesson on the life of virtue (Antiq. 4:180-193).

In his last testament, Moses even claims for himself that at least on this occasion he is the possessor of virtue, "because souls which approach death speak with perfect

virtue" (μετ' ἀρετῆς πάσης: <u>Antiq</u>. 4:179). But as Josephus
tells it, Moses himself tried to head off the idea that his
virtue had led to his apotheosis:

> "And while he was still taking leave of Eleazar and
> conversing with Joshua, a cloud suddenly descended upon
> him and caused him to disappear in a ravine. But he
> has written in the sacred books that he died, for fear
> lest they venture to say that he had returned to the
> Deity because of his abundance of virtue" (δι' ὑπερβολὴν τῆς
> περὶ αὐτὸν ἀρετῆς: <u>Antiq</u>. 4:326).[233]

Seen from this angle, Josephus' portrait of Moses appears
to be consistent, both in his explicitly apologetic efforts
such as the <u>contra Apionem</u>, where Moses is heralded as the
paradigm of virtue with no mention of miracles, and in the
<u>Antiquities</u> where Moses' functions as a mighty general and
virtuous lawgiver are highlighted while his own role in the
performance of miracles is de-emphasized. As MacRae has
observed, Josephus believes in the miracle stories and regards
them as displays of God's providence.[234] But they are God's
acts. Josephus' portrait of Moses is painted in much more
apologetic hues which highlight those features which would

---

[233]Thackeray, <u>Josephus the Man and the Historian</u>, op. cit.,
p. 57, points out the similarities to the mode of Moses'
disappearance to Dionysius of Halicarnassus' accounts of the
apotheosis of Aeneas and Romulus (<u>Roman Antiquities</u> I 64.4;
II.56.2). The parallels are striking, but the specific
emphasis on Moses' virtue does not appear to be paralleled
in the accounts of the deaths of these figures. Cf. also
Josephus <u>Antiq</u>. 3:96-97 where when Moses does not return from
Sinai the people fear that he has "returned to the Deity"
(πρὸς τὸ θεῖον ἀνακεχωρηκέναι), which even the sober-minded
regard as possible "because of his inherent virtue" (διὰ
τὴν προσοῦσαν ἀρετήν).

[234]Op. cit., p. 142.

be especially pleasing to the eyes of an audience whose
philosophical tastes conditioned their image of the true
divine sage. Perhaps this is seen nowhere more clearly than
in Josephus' treatment of Moses than in his closing paragraph
(#327-331) of book four of the Antiquities:

> "He lived in all one hundred and twenty years and was
> ruler for a third part of that time bating one month.
> He departed in the last month of the year, which the
> Macedonians call Dystros and we Adar, on the day of the
> new moon, having surpassed in understanding (σύνεσις)
> all men that ever lived and put to noblest use the
> fruit of his reflections. In speech and in addresses to
> a crowd he found favour in every way, but chiefly
> through his thorough command of his passions (τῶν
> παθῶν αὐτοκράτωρ), which was such that he seemed to
> have no place for them at all in his soul, and only
> knew their names through seeing them in others rather
> than in himself. As general he had few to equal him,
> and as prophet none, insomuch that in all his utterances
> one seemed to hear the speech of God Himself. So the
> people mourned for him for thirty days, and never were
> Hebrews oppressed by grief so profound as that which
> filled them then on the death of Moses. Nor was he
> regretted only by those who had known him by experience,
> but the very readers of his laws have sadly felt his
> loss, deducing from these the superlative quality of
> his virtue (τὸ περιὸν αὐτοῦ τῆς ἀρετῆς). Such, then,
> be our description of the end of Moses."[235]

The adjustments in the traditional image of Moses which
Josephus makes can thus be shown to have had a consistent
tendency. Far from being merely a reproduction of the
biblical figure of Moses or a generally agglomerated portrait
composed of diverse features from Jewish tradition, Josephus'
Moses is a paradigm of the practical virtues which were so
highly prized in the sophisticated circles of Roman society

---

[235]Trans. by Thackeray, Jewish Antiquities, op. cit.,
pp. 633-635.

which cultivated the image of the ideal sage. For the
purposes of this study, one of the most telling features
of Josephus' depiction is the clear reticence to describe
his hero as a miracle worker. Although as a loyal Jew
Josephus generally defends the veracity of the biblical
miracle stories, he finds it necessary to chart an intricate
course through Jewish tradition in an attempt to present
Moses in the most favorable light before a skeptical audience.
He idealizes Moses as a supreme sage who approaches divinity
in virtue while he steers clear of those parts of the
tradition which would document Moses' elevated status on
the basis of his reputation as a miracle worker.

Within the spectrum of contemporary idealizations of Moses,
the Moses of Josephus can thus be set in close proximity to
the Moses of Philo. Both depictions aim to present the hero
of Jewish tradition as surpassing the best that the cultured
despisers of Judaism prized in their own heroes. Further
discriminations could be pursued between Philo's emphasis
on the theoretical virtues and Josephus' concentration on
the practical, but the more obvious contrast between these
idealizations taken together and the presentation of Moses
offered by Artapanus is focal to this study. While Josephus
and Philo de-emphasize the traditions which stress Moses'
role as a miracle worker, Artapanus projects such material
into the very center of his account. Furthermore, Artapanus
appears to be oblivious or unconcerned to appease any
sophisticated sensibilities by eliminating offensive elements

from the earlier tradition, choosing rather to glorify a
partisan Moses, the champion of an oppressed people.

This broad contrast represents a methodological critique
of previous scholarship on the θεῖος ἀνήρ of late antiquity
and an invitation to further discriminations. To a large
extent, the thrust of this study has been a negative
evaluation of the interpretative significance of the
generalized portrait of the θεῖος ἀνήρ which has been
extensively defended by Ludwig Bieler, among others.[236]
Indeed, the lectionary of non-Christian literature that
had been adduced by such scholars as evidence for the
general image of the θεῖος ἀνήρ has provided the point
of departure, and the success of this attempt to challenge
previous scholarship rests on the degree to which it can
demonstrate that those texts support the proposed
differentiation among the depictions of traditional heroes
who were regarded as having attained divine or semi-divine
status. In the above pages, the factor that has been
isolated for discussion is the value that is assigned to
traditions about the hero as a miracle worker for
authenticating his exalted status, and the skepticism of
miracle stories shared by pre-third century A.D. authors
who are appealing to the criteria of virtue established

---

[236]Bieler, op. cit., provides the most convenient reference
since his work is comprehensive and well-known, but the reviews
of the scholarly discussion found at the beginning of each of
the chapters of this study provide a much more comprehensive
bibliography.

by earlier philosophical discussions has furnished the
controlling norm for criticizing the synthetic portrait
of the θεῖος ἀνήρ proposed by scholars such as Bieler.[237]

On the other hand, the research which supports this
discrimination also supplements previous efforts to describe
the ways in which the recitation of the ἀρεταί of the hero
of a given tradition served important propagandistic functions
in culturally diverse settings. Thus while highlighting
the distinctions in order to provide a corrective to earlier
attempts at synthesis, this study supports the contention
that there is a general consistency among these traditions
due to the propagandistic mode. All of these figures are
charismatic in that they are endowed with divine gifts or
χαρίσματα and because their attributes and actions are
recited as the fundaments of the tradition with the central
tenets of the particular viewpoint being read back into
their lives.

It is hoped, therefore, that this review of the evidence
will have the effect of re-opening rather than closing the
discussion of "divine men" in late antiquity. Within the
spectrum of depictions of traditional heroes which Bieler,
among others, synthesized under the rubric of the θεῖος ἀνήρ,
the general propagandistic intention admits further qualifications
as to which aspect of the tradition is being propagated in a

---

[237]Cf. note #16 in chapter three below.

given setting. Even the fact that the whole range of
traditions may still be extant for a given figure does not
permit the view that a general image which is the sum of its
diverse parts is of primary interpretative value for assessing
a particular text. The general image may only exist in the
mind of the modern scholar who can assemble all of the
available traditions about a particular hero and view them
together. The alternative method proposed in this study
appears to find its most secure footing in the cases of
Socrates, Alexander the Great, and Moses where the contrast
is marked between those treatments which highlight miraculous
performances and those which are cautious of authenticating
the hero as divine on the basis of his reputation for
teratological gifts.

Thus as this chapter seeks to show, to call Moses a
θεῖος ἀνήρ because he is a miracle-working philosopher may
only impede the exegesis of the texts. In Artapanus where
Moses' capacity as a miracle worker is highlighted, the
almost complete lack of philosophical criteria is notable.
In Philo and Josephus, on the other hand, Moses is presented
as the paradigm of the philosophical virtues, at the apparent
expense of traditional stories about his teratological
prowess.

CHAPTER THREE: JESUS THE "DIVINE MAN"

Although the primary concern of this study has been to document the nature of the diversity of the ways in which charismatic figures in the concentric Hellenistic and Hellenistic Jewish spheres were authenticated as having divine status, the general significance of this research will doubtless be interpreted in terms of its applicability to the views of Jesus which were held in early Christianity. It has been a methodological objective of this analysis to avoid the circular argument of beginning with a view of the ways in which the early church understood Jesus, then turning to the broader context for parallels, and finally returning to describe the Christology of the New Testament in terms of those selected parallels. The importance of this objective and the fact that at points in this study it has been more a goal than an attainment are both heavily conditioned by the interest that this writer shares with other students of the New Testament in understanding the origins of Christianity and by the impetus that was provided for pursuing the topic by the promising work on the nature of the diversity of early Christianity that has been done by Helmut Koester,[1]

_____

[1]Perhaps the reader should be alerted that this study has been born out of the lively discussion and friendly debate among the faculty and students at Harvard concerning Professor Koester's work. It is difficult to footnote the valuable insights that have been offered in conversations in the coffee shop and in frequent conferences in the classroom and the faculty offices. But two of Professor Koester's published studies have been particularly influential. "One Jesus and Four Primitive Gospels," HTR 61 (1968), pp. 203-

James M. Robinson,[2] and Dieter Georgi.[3] Since it has
appeared to be a methodological necessity to focus the
research for this study on the larger non-Christian context,
a logical sequel to this project would be a detailed and
critical analysis of how this picture of Hellenistic patterns
of deification corresponds to the models of the development
of the early church with which modern scholars are operating.
For the present, however, a more general review of some of the
recent scholarship on this topic ought to suffice to indicate
the avenues for fresh inquiry that this study of the larger
Hellenistic context might suggest.

The first stage of the discussion must be identified by
referring to the era of gospel studies that was largely
dominated by the methods of the history of religions school.
One of the valuable contributions that this approach made to

---

247. "The Structure and Criteria of Early Christian Beliefs,"
due to be published as chapter 6 of Koester and James M.
Robinson, Trajectories through Early Christianity (Fortress
Press, 1971?). Cf. also "Häretiker im Urchristentum," RGG,
vol. 3 (1959[3]), pp. 17-21. "Häretiker im Urchristentum als
theologisches Problem," Zeit und Geschichte (Dankesgabe an
Rudolf Bultmann, hsg. v. Erich Dinkler; Tübingen, 1964),
pp. 61-76. "ΓΝΩΜΑΙ ΔΙΑΦΟΡΟΙ," HTR 58 (1965), pp. 279-318.

[2] "ΛΟΓΟΙ ΣΟΦΩΝ," Zeit und Geschichte, op. cit.,
pp. 77-96 (a revised translation of this article will appear
(as chapter 3) in Trajectories, op. cit.). "Kerygma and
History in the New Testament," The Bible in Modern Scholarship
(ed. J.P. Hyatt; New York and Nashville, 1956), pp. 114-150.

[3] Die Gegner des Paulus im 2. Korintherbrief
(Wissenschaftliche Monographien zum Alten und Neuen Testament,
Band 11; Neukirchen, 1964). "Formen religiöser Propaganda,"
Kontexte 3 (Die Zeit Jesu, ed. H.J. Schultz; Stuttgart and
Berlin, 1966), pp. 105-110.

gospel studies was the correlation of the image of Jesus in
the canonical gospels to the depictions of other men of
antiquity who were thought to have attained divine stature.
Reitzenstein provided much of the basic data for this
correlation in his wide-ranging studies of Hellenistic
miracle stories[4] and Hellenistic "mystery religions."[5]
A basic thrust of his work was the effort to demonstrate that:

> "A general conception of the θεῖος ἄνθρωπος, the
> divine man, began to be established, which bound together
> deepest modes of perception, visionary and miraculous
> powers, with a style of personal holiness. Without this
> conception, phenomena such as the preacher and miracle
> worker Apollonius of Tyana or the visionary and founder
> of a religion Alexander of Abonoteichos remain impossible
> to understand."[6]

Although the accounts of these figures who serve as the
primary paradigms of this "general conception of the divine
man" can be dated in the second and third centuries A.D., this
image of the "divine man" also provided the basis for Wetter
to describe the portrayal of Jesus in the fourth gospel in
terms of its correlation to such Hellenistic figures.[7] Wetter's

---

[4]R. Reitzenstein, Hellenistische Wundererzählungen
(Darmstadt: Wissenschaftliche Buchgesellschaft, 1963, reprint
unchanged from 1906 edition).

[5]R. Reitzenstein, Die Hellenistischen Mysterienreligionen
(Leipzig and Berlin, 1910). The third edition of this work
in 1927 is better known and is more extensive; but for the
purposes of tracing the development of this topic, it is
crucial to note that Reitzenstein had already made his basic
point in 1910. Cf. reprint of third edition, Darmstadt:
Wissenschaftliche Buchgesellschaft, 1956.

[6]Ibid., 1910 edition, p. 12. Cf. 1927 edition p. 26
where Peregrinus is also included in the list.

[7]Gilles P:son Wetter, Der Sohn Gottes:Eine Untersuchung
über den Charakter und die Tendenz des Johannes-Evangeliums
(FRLANT, n.s. 9; Göttingen, 1916), cf. p. 71.

analysis had the strength of drawing upon a broad selection
of Christian literature of the second and third centuries,
with particular attention to the apologists. While this
approach documented the efforts of those who were defending
Christianity against its cultured depisers to present Jesus
as the divine Son of God by appealing to the whole gospel
tradition, including Jesus' life, preaching, and miracles, it
was perhaps more valuable as a study of the way gospel
traditions were used by the apologists than as an exegesis
of the Gospel of John itself. Furthermore, Wetter neglected
the strong elements of criticism of the authenticating value
of miracles which are evident in the fourth gospel as well
as in early Christian apologetics.[8]

The impulse to discover a general Hellenistic image of
the "divine man" which would display the Hellenistic framework of early Christian christology was perhaps even more
marked in the study of the concept of the "divine man" of
O. Weinreich.[9] Once again, the method was to compile a list
of features which were variously ascribed to men who were
thought to have attained divine stature and to set this
conglomerate image in juxtaposition to the gospel traditions

---

[8]An excellent study of the theological turbulence which
the miracles and the issue of their value as authentication
of Jesus' divine status caused in the early church has been
made by Anton Fridrichsen, Le problème du miracle (Strasbourg,
1925), cf. particularly pp. 57-82 and p. 86 where Fridrichsen
challenges Wetter.

[9]"Antikes Gottmenschentum," Neues Jahrbuch für Wissenschaft
und Jugendbildung 2 (1926), pp. 633-651.

about Jesus. Without discriminating among the diverse gospel
portrayals of Jesus, Weinrich concludes:

> "Und doch, die Frage brennt uns allen im Herzen: Wie
> steht das Christusbild zu der antiken Welt? Was ist
> etwa antikes Erbe darin, was spontane Parallelerscheinung?
> Was Wahrheit, was Legende? Fragen leichter gestellt
> als beantwortet."[10]

The apex of this method of correlating the gospel
traditions about Jesus to a general image of the Hellenistic
divine man was reached in the mid-1930's by the studies of
Windisch[11] and Bieler[12] which were distinguished by their
thoroughness and a new level of sophistication with respect
to the diversity that they recognized in Hellenistic
portrayals of men of divine stature. Windisch, in particular,
was sensitive to contrasts in the shadings of the idealized
portrait of the "divine man" between the depictions of divine
philosophers and divine miracle workers, but his quest for
a history of religions background for the gospel image of
Jesus led him to turn to Pythagoreanism as the one place
where he believed these differing types were synthesized and
where the interpretative context of gospel materials was
most readily found.[13] Windisch enriched the discussion of
this concept by an analysis of the appropriation of Old

---

[10]Ibid., p. 650.

[11]Hans Windisch, *Paulus und Christus* (Untersuchungen z.
NT, Heft 24; Leipzig, 1934).

[12]Ludwig Bieler, ΘΕΙΟΣ ΑΝΗΡ (Wien, 1935-1936, 2 volumes).

[13]Cf. Windisch, op. cit., pp. 24-89.

Testament materials by Jews who aimed to display the heroes of
their tradition as rivals to the Greek men of divine stature.[14]
But since he regarded the synthesized or general image of the
"divine man" as the primary interpretative key to understanding
the importance of both Jesus and Paul in the early church,
the discriminations he observed were treated as of lesser
significance.[15]

Bieler also recognized the diversification in Hellenistic
views of the "divine man", and he included an analysis of
pre-Christian Jewish authors in his extensive lectionary.
But Bieler aggregated so many features into his composite
portrait of the "typical divine man" that it would be
difficult to find any hero in antiquity to whom at least
several of these qualities were not attributed, and it is
perhaps as difficult to find a pre-third century A.D.
portrayal of any figure which supplies its hero with Bieler's
complete catalog of the characteristics of the "divine man."
The image of Jesus as a "divine man" that Bieler assembled
was also a composite portrait, composed of features drawn
from all four gospels and other early Christian sources.
Thus once again, the diversity that was recognized in the
sources was treated by Bieler as of secondary importance
compared with the general conception of the "divine man"
which he believed he could identify in a wide variety of
contexts:

---

[14]Ibid., pp. 89-114.

[15]Cf. note #25 in chapter one, above.

"Es sollte eine wesentliche Aufgabe dieser Arbeit sein,
zu zeigen, dass die Antike, zumal die spätere, und das
frühe Christentum das gleiche Bild des göttlichen
Menschen kennen."[16]

In contrast with Bieler's work, which is still valuable
as an encyclopedic collection of parallels and motifs, a
study like that of Leisegang's which depends on Bieler and
stresses the archetypical features of the image of the
"divine man" displays the pitfalls of this approach.[17]
Sweeping through a vast historical panorama of about a
thousand years from the time of Pythagoras onward, Leisegang
correlates the archetypical features of the Christ portrait
of the gospels as identified by Jung to a collection of
features shared by a very disparate group of "divine men.."
The fact that the commonalty of these portrayals lies
principally in the mind of the author is perhaps best seen
from the fact that Leisegang draws his most extensive
typological correlations between the self-assertions of
Empedocles and the gospel accounts of Jesus.[18]

Such extravagance was by no means typical of the history
of religions approach, but even the more balanced and cautious
attempts to describe the ideal "divine man" in order to

---

[16]Bieler, op. cit., vol. I, p. 145.

[17]Hans von Leisegang, "Der Gottmensch als Archetypus,"
Eranos-Jahrbuch XVIII (1950: Sonderband für C.G. Jung, hsg.
v. Olga Fröbe Kapteyn: Zürich, 1950), pp. 9-45.

[18]Ibid., cf. pp. 12-20.

account for the Christ of the gospels were called into question
by the ascendency of the form critical studies of the
synoptics. Although the implications of this method were only
slowly worked into the discussion of the concept of the
"divine man," the studies of Dibelius,[19] Schmidt,[20] and
Bultmann,[21] which were published around 1920, initiated a
new stage of analysis which focused attention primarily on
the diversity in the kinds of traditions about Jesus and
attempted to situate the several modes of theological
expression in particular sociological situations of the
early church.

Dibelius stressed the variety of proclamatory uses that
the differing forms reflect, but he also drew attention to
the miracle "tales" (Novelle) which he regarded as similar
in form and function to a variety of secular (profan)
stories which were cultivated in popular Hellenistic
traditions as propaganda for a folk hero. His analysis
included the striking feature of demonstrating the contrast
in belief systems between such accounts of Jesus and those
which focused on his preaching or passion. In particular, he

---

[19]Martin Dibelius, Die Formgeschichte des Evangeliums
(Tübingen, 1919; second edition 1933 and English translation
of the second edition, From Tradition to Gospel by Bertram
Lee Woolf, New York, 1935).

[20]L. Schmidt, Der Rahmen der Geschichte Jesu (Berlin,
1919).

[21]Rudolf Bultmann, Die Geschichte der synoptischen
Tradition (FRLANT, N.F. 12; Göttingen, 1921, second edition,
1931, and English translation of the second edition,
History of the Synoptic Tradition by John Marsh, New York, 1963.

noted that the Jesus who stands at the center of these
stories is not Jesus the herald of the kingdom of God, but
Jesus the thaumaturge,[22] and thus Dibelius could describe
the response of faith that such tales evoked:

> "The content of faith in such a connection is not the
> conviction that through Christ God's call has gone out
> to all mankind, but the confidence that Jesus, the
> great miracle-worker, excelled all other thaumaturges."[23]

Dibelius de-emphasized the christological value of such
tales because he believed that they displayed little Christian
devotional reflection. But by comparing such accounts with
other miracle stories in the Hellenistic world at large, he
showed that these narratives belonged to the class of popular
and semi-literary stories that were cultivated by that
stratum of society which regarded magical and miraculous
performances as having self-convincing power for authenticating
the divine or semi-divine stature of the hero of the cult.[24]

Bultmann also recognized the importance of dealing with
the miracle narratives in the gospels against the broader
background of Hellenistic miracle stories, but his classification of this material was based on a distinction of
content, nature miracles and miracles of healing.[25]
Furthermore, he was operating on the basis of a distinction
which is less clear today between traditions of Palestinian

---

[22]Dibelius, op. cit., first edition, pp. 42-51.

[23]Ibid., second edition, p. 75, From Tradition to Gospel,
p. 79.

[24]From Tradition to Gospel, pp. 94-96.

[25]Cf. the criticisms of this classification which Dibelius
offered, Ibid., p. 54.

origin and those of Hellenistic provenance. Nevertheless, Bultmann's keen eye for the Hellenistic penetrations of Jewish culture and his sense for the way traditions are affected by their contemporary context led him to emphasize Hellenistic parallels as the proper interpretative context for gospel miracles, almost to the exclusion of Old Testament traditions.[26] In depicting the contrast between Mark and the sayings source, Q, Bultmann indicated that he regarded Mark and his sources to be much more directly under the influence of Hellenistic presentations of men of divine status. It is vital to note that Bultmann was operating with the more specific image of the "divine man" as miracle worker when he wrote:

> "In Mark he (Jesus) is a θεῖος ἄνθρωπος, indeed more; he is the very Son of God walking the earth. This mythological light in which Jesus is set by Mark is there for the most part on the author's own account but also in part on account of his material, and especially of the miracle stories. But this distinction between Mark and Q means that in Q the picture of Jesus is made essentially from the material of the Palestinian tradition, while in Mark and most of all in his miracle stories, Hellenism has made a vital contribution. So

---

[26]Op. cit., first edition, pp. 141-142. Bultmann argues convincingly that there is no simple or direct literary dependence on Old Testament accounts of miracles. Such a basic point still deserves some emphasis in the light of the attempts of some scholars to de-emphasize the Hellenistic parallels by appealing to the Old Testament. Cf. Alan Richardson, The Miracle Stories of the Gospels (London, 1941), pp. 16-17. Wm. Manson, Jesus the Messiah (London, 1943 and Philadelphia, 1946). Reginald H. Fuller, Interpreting the Miracles (London, 1963). But an emphasis on the immediate Hellenistic setting must not be allowed to obscure traces of Hellenistic interpretation of Old Testament texts.

> naturally we can rightly assume in the first place a
> Hellenistic origin for the miracle stories which Matthew
> and Luke have over and above those found in Q and
> Mark."[27]

Although Bultmann did not delineate the features of the image

of the "divine man", he bequeathed a question to subsequent

scholarship of whether Mark or his sources are presenting

Jesus as a "divine man." By drawing particular attention to

the miracle stories in this connection, he also effectively

narrowed the field of comparison suggested by the general

image of the "divine man" drafted by Reitzenstein to the more

specific figure of the divine miracle worker.

The third stage in the modern discussion of this topic

can be identified by referring to Georgi's study of Paul's

opponents in II Corinthians.[28] Georgi's analysis appears to

be a significant advance on previous work on the subject

for at least two reasons. First, it is well informed about

the fundamental diversity of first century Judaism in and

out of Palestine and thus avoids the picture of Palestinian

Judaism as a kind of monolithic norm next to which Hellenistic

Jews such as Philo, Aristobulus, and Artapanus appear as

exceptional aberrations.[29] Secondly, Georgi's work is

---

[27]Ibid., _History of the Synoptic Tradition_, p. 241. Cf.
the first edition, p. 147.

[28]_Die Gegner, op. cit._

[29]Georgi appears to have used the research of E.R.
Goodenough to particular advantage, cf. _Die Gegner, op. cit._,
p. 308. Goodenough's work must be credited with being a
major contribution to the research which has documented the
cultural complexity of Judaism of the period, rendering
obsolete the unified view of "normative Judaism" which had

distinguished by its exegetical particularity in that it
focuses primarily on that collection of Pauline correspondence
that is known as II Cor.[30] Thus when the opponents of Paul
are identified as self-proclaimed "divine men", the connotation
of that title and the catalog of features included in that
image are based primarily upon the evidence of their self-
presentation that Paul preserves.

For the purposes of this study, moreover, Georgi's
work is particularly challenging because he makes a strong
case for maintaining that these "divine men" documented
their status both by miraculous performances[31] and by
rhetorical eloquence and a set of stock arguments which show
their contacts with Jewish propagandistic circles which
imitated many of the propagandistic methods of the popular
Cynic and Stoic preachers. In Georgi's analysis, such a
combination of features is not unexpected since he stresses
the propagandistic continuum that he sees extending from

---

dominated earlier discussion under the influence of the work
of George Foote Moore, Judaism in the First Centuries of the
Christian Era (Cambridge, 1927-1930, 3 vols.).

[30]For the arguments against the unity of this epistle,
cf. Georgi, Die Gegner, op. cit., pp. 16-29, and G. Bornkamm,
"The History of the Origin of the so-called Second Letter to
the Corinthians," NTS 8 (1961-1962), pp. 258-264, translated
and abbreviated from "Die Vorgeschichte des sogenanten Zweiten
Korintherbriefes," Sitzungberichte d. Heidelberger Akademie
der Wissenschaften, Phil.-hist. Klasse (1961), no. 2.

[31]Georgi's analysis receives support at this point from
the recent study of H.D. Betz, "Eine Christus-Aretalogie
bei Paulus (2 Kor 12,7-10)," Zeitschrift für Theologie und
Kirche 66 (1969), pp. 288-305.

vulgar traditions about national heroes to the work of the
literary apologists. But against the background of the
discrimination that has been proposed in this study, such a
combination of features appears remarkable, but by no means
impossible, for the mid-first century A.D.

Perhaps the best way to indicate how the angle of
approach of this study differs slightly from, but hopefully
complements Georgi's analysis, is to raise two questions which
could only be answered by a detailed exegesis of II Cor.
that matched Georgi's study for precision. Do the features
that Georgi has identified as basic to the self-image and
christology of Paul's opponents fit together as homogeneous
elements of a consistent portrait or is there a tension
between primary and secondary features? Would an analysis
which emphasized the differentiation among the ways in which
charismatic figures were authenticated as divine in this
period alter or enhance the details of the picture of these
opponents that Georgi has reconstructed? In any case, by
his description of the theology of Paul's opponents in II Cor.,
Georgi has brought scholarship to a new level of understanding with respect to both the Pauline correspondence
and a specific example of Hellenistic religious propaganda
where the charismatic stature of the missionaries was the
primary concern.[32]

Recent discussion of the "divine man" concept has

----

[32]Georgi, _Die Gegner_, _op_. _cit_., cf. pp. 219-246.

revolved around two foci, a fresh interest in redaction
criticism and a more comprehensive attempt to chart the
development of basic patterns of theological reflection in
the early church. Obviously there is a large area of overlap
and common concern between these spheres of research, as is
well reflected in the bibliographical citations in the
respective secondary literature. But the research of the
redaction critics is centered on the description of specific
situations in the life of the early church while the second
approach is concerned to trace the dynamic growth patterns
of early Christianity by identifying the correlations between
the relatively fixed points which the redaction critics can
establish. Certainly the differentiation that this study
has emphasized with respect to the ways in which charismatic
figures were authenticated as divine in the wider Hellenistic
and Hellenistic Jewish context would suggest that if the
concept of the "divine man" is going to be used as an
interpretative key to New Testament theology,[33] it must be
understood as a comprehensive rubric, encompassing diverse
and occasionally opposing elements which should be
identified as precisely as possible in each context, rather
than as a fixed concept. This recognition that the term
θεῖος ἀνήρ is thus a conceptual umbrella only affects the
dynamic model of the patterns of growth in early Christian
theology by again drawing attention to the vital alterations

---

[33]It is not insignificant to note in this connection
that the term θεῖος ἀνηρ is not used in the New Testament.

in the images that are drafted in different contexts, but it cautions those who are analyzing a specific piece of literature against treating the "divine man" theology as an established norm which can be appealed to as an explanation of a particular outlook or by which the "purity" of other examples of the type can be evaluated.

Discussions of the theology of Mark have largely revolved around the christological question[34] since Wrede identified the so-called "messianic secret" as a key to the theological construction of the gospel.[35] Much of the recent discussion is dependent on Conzelmann's analysis of the

---

[34] A notable exception is the work of Howard C. Kee, who regards the apocalyptic-eschatological question as of central importance in Mark's Gospel. This view is advocated in his recent book, Jesus in History (New York, 1970) and will be defended at greater length in a forthcoming study of Mark. Of course, the discussion of Mark's eschatology has long been regarded as of direct relevance to the problem of the theology of the Gospel. Cf. James M. Robinson, The Problem of History in Mark (Studies in Biblical Theology, No. 21; Naperville, 1957), reviewed by H. Koester in Verkündigung und Forschung (1959) pp. 181-184. James M. Robinson, "The Problem of History in Mark Reconsidered," Union Seminary Quarterly Review 20 (1965), pp. 131-147. Cf. also W. Marxsen, Mark the Evangelist, trans. by James Boyce, Donald Juel, and Wm. Poehlmann with Roy A. Harrisville (Nashville, 1969). Hans Conzelmann, "Present and Future in the Synoptic Tradition," trans. by Jack Wilson, God and Christ (Journal for Theology and the Church, vol. 5, ed. Robert W. Funk et al.; New York, 1968), pp. 26-44. Th. J. Weeden, The Heresy that Necessitated Mark's Gospel (Unpublished doctoral dissertation, Claremont Graduate School, 1964) and "The Heresy that Necessitated Mark's Gospel," ZNW 59 (1968), pp. 145-158. The problem of which is the primary issue, eschatology or christology, may turn out to be the wrong question, but the discussion is enriched by the fact that Mark is being approached from more than one angle. Cf. also N. Perrin, "The Son of Man in the Synoptic Tradition," Biblical Research 13 (1968), pp. 3-25.

[35] William Wrede, Das Messiasgeheimnis in den Evangelien (Göttingen, 1901).

secrecy motif in Mark in which he demonstrated that Mark did
not create the "messianic secret" in an attempt to heighten
his account of Jesus powerful acts, but Mark used this notion
to control traditions about Jesus which had their own
"messianic character"[36] in order to bring them in line with
his gospel:

> "The notion of a secret obviously existed previously as
> a theological concept, and in turn enabled materials
> dissimilar (in form!) to be comprehended from a unified
> point of view. The secrecy theory is the hermeneutical
> presupposition of the genre, 'gospel.'"[37]

The contrast between the christologies of Mark and his
sources, particularly the miracle stories, is described by
Vielhauer in terms of the two ways he sees the title "Son of
God" being used in the gospel, as an eschatological royal
title and as a synonym for θεῖος ἀνήρ. [38] From the
methodological viewpoint of this study, Vielhauer's work
represents a significant advance over studies like those of
Wetter[39] or Hahn[40] in that it demonstrates the limitation of

---

[36]Philipp Vielhauer, "Erwägungen zur Christologie des
Markusevangeliums," Zeit und Geschichte (Dankesgabe an R.
Bultmann, ed. Erich Dinkler; Tübingen, 1964), p. 157, correctly
points out the term "messianic" must not be taken as a precise
reference to Jewish messianic expectations. This article is
also reprinted in a collection of Vielhauer's essays, Aufsätze
zum Neuen Testament (München, 1965), pp. 199-214.

[37]Conzelmann, op. cit., p. 43.

[38]Vielhauer, "Erwägungen zur Christologie," op. cit.,
cf. pp. 165-169.

[39]Op. cit.

[40]Cf. Vielhauer's review of F. Hahn: Christologische
Hoheitstitel, "Ein Weg zur Neutestamentlichen Christologie,"
Evangelische Theologie 28 (1965), pp. 24-72, reprinted with
minor alterations in Aufsätze zum Neuen Testament, op. cit.,
pp. 141-198.

the attempts to describe the development of christological
theologizing by focusing primarily on the various
christological titles. Vielhauer, by contrast, argues that
the diversity of christological viewpoints is best identified
by analyzing the kinds of material, such as miracle stories,
sayings, and passion narratives, which are used to give any
particular title a distinctive connotation, and he regards
the miracle stories in Mark as designating Jesus the "Son
of God" as a θεῖος ἀνήρ, for some unexplained reason
treating the second term as having a more precise referent
than the first.[41]

In his 1964 Claremont dissertation, Th. Weeden attempted
to describe the theological tensions in the gospel of Mark
in terms of an ecclesiastical struggle between Mark and his
heretical opponents.[42] Weeden's thesis deserves attention
primarily because it is a comprehensive effort to show the
theological issues at stake in the several editorial features
of Mark's gospel which Wrede had treated as apologetic. In
particular, he shows the theological impact and strategic
arrangement of the commands to silence (Mk 1:24-25, 34, 44;

---

[41]It should be emphasized, however, that Vielhauer is
treating the term θεῖος ἀνήρ as a conceptual link with the
Hellenistic thought world, and he does not regard it as a
title. Thus it would be unfair to accuse him of regarding
θεῖος ἀνήρ as a technical term. Nevertheless, his description of the material is more helpful than his use of the
term which remains vague. Cf. note #45 below. Cf. also
A.D. Nock, Early Gentile Christianity and its Hellenistic
Background (New York, 1964), pp. 45-46.

[42]The Heresy that Necessitated Mark's Gospel, op. cit.,
cf. also ZNW 59 (1968), op. cit.

3:12; 5:43; 7:36), and he documents the progression of the
depiction of the incorrect understanding of Jesus by pointing
out how Mark describes the disciples as moving from
imperceptivity, to misunderstanding, and finally to
abandonment of the suffering Jesus.[43] Furthermore he sees
the contrasting viewpoints in terms of the discontinuity
between a triumphalist christology of glory which would
ensure a lofty status for the disciples and a theology of
the cross which emphasizes the suffering of Jesus and his
followers. Following the suggestions of Georgi and Koester,[44]
Weeden correlates the triumphalist christology which Mark
appears to ascribe to the disciples to the θεῖος ἀνήρ
viewpoint of Paul's opponents in II Cor.[45]

---

[43]Cf. also H.J. Ebeling, Das Messiasgeheimnis und die
Botschaft des Markusevangelium (Zeitschrift für d. N.T.
Wissenschaft, Beiheft 19; Berlin, 1939). Alfred Kuby, "Zur
Konzeption des Markus-Evangeliums," ZNW 49 (1958), pp. 52-
64. Joseph Tyson, "The Blindness of the Disciples," JBL 80
(1961), pp. 261-268. Leander E. Keck, "Mark 3: 7-12 and
Mark's Christology," JBL 84 (1965), pp. 341-358.

[44]Cf. Koester, "Häretiker," RGG, op. cit., pp. 17-21
and Georgi, Die Gegner, op. cit., pp. 210-218, and cf. Koester,
"One Jesus and Four Gospels," op. cit., p. 233, note 106.

[45]The identification of the theological tradition
which is controlled by the "messianic secret" as a "θεῖος
ἀνήρ christology" appears to have gained acceptance among
many scholars who still disagree on Mark's own theology. Cf.
also J. Schreiber, "Die Christologie des Markusevangeliums,"
ZThK 58 (1961), pp. 154-183. U. Luz, "Das Geheimnismotif
und die Markinische Christologie," ZNW 56 (1965), pp. 9-30.
S. Schulz, Die Stunde der Botschaft (Hamburg, 1967), pp. 64-
79. Heinz-Dieter Knigge, "The Meaning of Mark," Interpretation
22 (1968), pp. 53-70. R.H. Fuller, review of G. Minette De
Tillesse, Le secret messianique dans l'evangile de Marc
(Lectio Divina 47; Paris, 1968) in CBQ 31 (1969), pp. 109-112.

Weeden's analysis, however, appears to have over-
simplified the complex process of the growth of gospel
traditions by reading Mark too directly in terms of Paul's
struggles with his opponents in II Cor., as analyzed by
Georgi. Without correlating specific traits of Mark's
"opponents" to the wider scope of Hellenistic and Hellenistic
Jewish propagandistic traditions as Georgi has done for
II Cor., Weeden short-circuits his analysis of the "divine
man" theology he sees behind Mark by drawing correlations
almost exclusively between Mark's "opponents" and Paul's.
The assumption, which from the viewpoint of this study would
appear misinformed, appears to be that the "θεῖος ἀνήρ"
was a fixed concept, with Georgi's description of Paul's
opponents furnishing the normative example. Consequently,
Weeden highlights all the possible similarities between the
two sets of "opponents" as well as between the ways Paul and
Mark use the theology of the cross to combat such heresies.
Unfortunately Weeden draws these correlations by frequent
recourse to terms like "pneumatic" and "exalted,"[46] categories
which could, but in his analysis do not, admit significantly
diverse interpretations. Even the most complex features of
Markan gospel traditions appear to be reduced to ad hoc
appropriations which can be explained by the conflict
situation. Thus the apocalyptic material in chapter 13 is

---

[46]Cf. The Heresy that Necessitated Mark's Gospel, op. cit.,
pp. 88-89, pp. 210-214.

merely used by Mark to counter the pneumatics, in analogy to
the way Paul uses the eschatological reservation in
I Thessalonians 4 and I Corinthians 15.[47] The immense
block of miracle stories in the first eight chapters is
merely a device to document the process by which the
disciples were misled:

> "Waving the red flag of θεῖος ἀνήρ christology, as he
> does, by introducing Jesus as the Son of God, saturating
> the first half of his Gospel with wonder-working
> activities of Jesus, and interspersing his own
> summaries on this θεῖος ἀνήρ activity (1:32 ff, 3:7ff;
> 6:53ff), Mark intends the reader to draw the only
> conclusion possible: Peter makes a confession to a
> θεῖος ἀνήρ Christ."[48]

Arguing from Mark's silence on the presence of any of the
disciples at the crucifixion, Weeden maintains that Mark was
striking a cryptic blow at the Petrine tradition and thus at
the opponents by the sudden conclusion of the Gospel in
16:8, where:

> "he intentionally suggests by the response of the women
> that Peter and the disciples never received the news
> from the angel about the empty tomb and the angel's
> confirmation that Jesus would appear to them again in
> the 'end time' at Galilee. As a result, the tradition
> which Peter and the disciples handed down was erroneous
> and defective, and so also, by implication, was the
> position of Mark's opponents."[49]

---

[47]Ibid., pp. 40-90, here Weeden opposes Conzelmann,
"Geschichte und Eschaton nach Mc 13," ZNW 50 (1959), pp. 210-
221, cf. "Present and Future in the Synoptic Tradition,"
op. cit.

[48]ZNW 59 (1968), p. 148.

[49]The Heresy that Necessitated Mark's Gospel, op. cit.,
p. 172.

Leander Keck must be credited with a more cautious
attempt to describe precisely what kind of understanding of
Jesus Mark was seeking to control with his own christology.[50]
Keck also refers to the theology Mark was correcting as a
θεῖος ἀνήρ christology, but he finds its particular focus
in the miracle stories. Furthermore, he criticizes Vielhauer
and Schreiber for not discriminating between those miracle
stories which reflect this outlook and those which do not.[51]
Keck is operating with a distinction between a group of
Palestinian traditions which he suggests are closely related
to the message of Jesus in its native setting and a cycle of
miracle stories which focuses on the "sovereign Jesus" with
little attention to his teachings:

> "The former stands under the rubric, 'the strong man'
> (3:37); the latter under the stamp of the hellenistic
> θεῖος ἀνήρ whose divine power is manifested on earth."[52]

Keck's analysis is striking in that it avoids a generalized
portrait of Jesus as a "divine man" by emphasizing the
features which have been seen as crucial to the particular
image of the charismatic figure as miracle worker. Furthermore, he discovers this image to be transmitted by the
specific block of gospel traditions which Dibelius identified
form critically as tales or Novellen. Keck correctly points

---

[50]L. Keck, "Mark 3: 7-12 and Mark's Christology," JBL 84
(1965), pp. 341-358.

[51]Ibid., notes 61 and 69.

[52]Ibid., pp. 350-351.

262

out that Dibelius missed the christological force of these
stories by discounting them as "secular" (profan). But Keck
clouds the precision of his analysis by suggesting that the
best way to describe this christology is to correlate it
to the image of the θεῖος ἀνήρ as described by Bieler.[53]

The methodological difficulties of Keck's analysis,
namely his confidence in the Hellenistic/Palestinian distinction and the correlation of the more specific identification of the view of Jesus as the superior thaumaturge to
Bieler's generalized concept, are recognized and directly
challenged by T.A. Burkill.[54] The problem of appealing to
Bieler's model is obvious from the difficulty that Bieler
himself had in integrating miracle working as a feature of
his "divine man". Bieler had to insist that the miracles of
the θεῖος ἀνήρ, "even if they may have ever so close a
similarity to sorcery as far as content and form, are not
magic and sorcery but theurgy and often actually an immediate
outflow of divine power."[55]

But it is the very nature of these "tales" to be
cultivated in circles where such distinctions are largely
ineffective. As Dibelius puts it:

"there is a certain relationship of kind between the

[53]Ibid., pp. 351-352.

[54]"Mark 3: 7-12 and the Alleged Dualism in the Evangelist's
Miracle Material," JBL 87 (1968), pp. 409-417.

[55]Bieler, op. cit., vol. I, p. 141, cf. Keck, op. cit.,
pp. 350-351, note 67.

Gospel Tales and the non-Christian miracle stories, and
thus a certain approximation to the literature of 'the
world', not, of course, to fine literature, but to
popular literature and indeed to the writing of the
people."[56]

Cautious clarifications about what is or is not "magical"[57]
were not characteristic of the society that authenticated
its charismatic heroes as divine on the basis of their
miraculous performances. Thus the introduction of the
categories of magic as distinguished from theurgy, which the
neo-Platonists may have found helpful,[58] does not advance
the understanding of the christological thrust of these
miracle stories in their original setting. The contrast
between this type of authentication of divine stature and
that of Philo's Moses or Lucian's Demonax, for example, is
highlighted by the fact that both Dibelius and Burkill find
many of the most striking parallels between gospel traditions
and non-Christian accounts of magical-miraculous performances
by examining these miracle "tales" in particular.[59]

In a paper delivered on March 29, 1969 at a meeting of
the Hermeneutical Project of the Institute for Antiquity and

---

[56]From Tradition to Gospel, op. cit., p. 93.

[57]Cf. footnote 126 in the previous chapter.

[58]Cf. Bieler, op. cit., vol. I, pp. 86-87.

[59]Burkill points to his earlier study of Mark, Mysterious
Revelation (Ithaca, 1963), where he attempts to correlate
such features to similar magico-religious notions which he
found to be widespread and cutting through racial and national
barriers. Certainly more work is needed on this subject,
but cf. also S. Eitrem, Some Notes on the Demonology of the
New Testament (Symbolae Osloenses, Fasc. Suppl. 12; Oslo,
1950).

Christianity in Claremont, California, Dieter Georgi
discussed "The Form-critical Assessment of Miracle Stories."[60]
Georgi treated those stories identified as Novellen or
"tales" by Dibelius, but which he classifies with the more
descriptive title of "novelistic miracle stories,"[61] as
betraying a new stage in the development of early Christian
theology:

> "This development indicated a certain change in theology
> that I should define as an adoption of a 'θεῖος ἀνήρ
> theology' from Hellenistic Jewish missionary theology.
> The major contribution this change caused in the area of
> miracle-stories was the creation of the Christian
> novelistic miracle-story."[62]

Several aspects of this analysis merit appreciative
notice. First of all, Georgi indicates that he is not
referring to a fixed concept of the θεῖος ἀνήρ by describing
this material as pointing to a θεῖος ἀνήρ theology. The
indefinite article must not be overlooked since it calls for
exegetical specificity with respect to the precise
identification of the theology of the novelistic miracle
stories, no matter how the general significance of the term
θεῖος ἀνήρ is conceived. The importance of this methodological caution has also been underlined by the perceptive
studies of Hans Dieter Betz which document the diversity of

---

[60]I am indebted to James M. Robinson for supplying me
with a copy of this paper.

[61]Ibid., pp. 2-3. In the face of much disagreement about
the nomenclature for the categories of miracle stories, such
an attempt to use more neutral descriptive language is to be
welcomed.

[62]Ibid., p. 6.

theological options which may be considered under the

θεῖος ἀνήρ   rubric.[63]

Secondly Georgi suggests that Mark 4:35-6:56, with some

exceptions, may have been the first major collection of

miracle stories,[64] although he does not spell out the

redactional details. Here again Georgi is at the frontier

of the discussion along with Koester and Robinson in seeking

to describe the theological framework in which such

collections were made.[65] Notably this section is dominated

by six of the ten stories that Dibelius has classified as

"tales" (4:35-41; 5:1-20; 5:21-43 - two stories woven

---

[63]"Jesus as Divine Man," Jesus and the Historian (Essays
in honor of Ernest Cadman Colwell, ed. F.T. Trotter;
Philadelphia, 1968), pp. 114-133. While attending to the
necessary discriminations, however, Betz appears to attempt
to bring materials that are fundamentally diverse on several
levels under the θεῖος ἀνήρ umbrella when he concludes, "As
a result, the Gospels and their source materials represent
five different versions of the Divine Man Christology"
(p. 129). From the point of view of this study, "The
Divine Man Christology" which can encompass the christologies
of the four gospels and the pre-gospel miracle cycles would
have to be too broad a concept to have much specific
interpretative value. Nevertheless, Betz is very keen at
making correlations between such gospel traditions and a vast
range of Hellenistic materials. This is particularly clear
in his forthcoming article, "Gottmensch", which is due to be
published in the Reallexicon für Antike und Christentum
and which he kindly allowed this writer to consult in its
manuscript form.

[64]"The Form-Critical Assessment of the Miracle Stories,"
op. cit., p. 6. Note that Dibelius, From Tradition to Gospel,
op. cit., p. 73 is willing to regard the tales of Mk 4:35-
5:43 as constituting a cycle.

[65]Cf. especially, Koester, "One Jesus and Four Gospels,"
op. cit., pp. 230-236.

together, perhaps by the pre-Markan collector; 6:35 - 44;
6:45 - 52).[66]

For the present purpose, the specificity of the framework
of understanding displayed in the novelistic miracle
stories as described by Dibelius and Georgi and the distance
of such a depiction of Jesus from the accounts of the heroes
of the philosophical traditions call for special comment.
Much more extensive study is needed of these stories, but
even a quick review supports Dibelius' contention that here
Jesus is presented as the superior thaumaturge. The positive
value of features which must be regarded as magical-miraculous
can not be denied. In Mark 1:40 - 45, for example, the
details of thaumaturgic technique involved in the dramatic
emotional displays which accompanied such an act
(ἐμβριμήσασθαι: 1:43) have been analyzed by Bonner and Bevan
in terms of their correlation to other accounts of magical-
miraculous feats.[67] Similarly in Mark 5:41 and 7:34, Jesus

---

[66]The other four stories that fall into this category
are: Mk 1: 40 - 45, 7:32 - 37; 8:22 - 26; 9:14 - 29. Georgi,
however, classifies Mk 6:45 - 52 as an epiphany-story which
differs slightly from the novelistic miracle story by its
esoteric character and its interest in the appearance of the
divine being rather than in the merger of the divine and the
human, cf. "The Form-Critical Assessment of the Miracle
Stories," op. cit., p. 3.

[67]Campbell Bonner, "Traces of Thaumaturgic Technique in
the Miracles," HTR 20 (1927), pp. 171-181. Edwyn Bevan,
"Note on Mark 1:41 and John 11:33, 38," JTS 33 (1932),
pp. 186-188. Note that MSD reads ὀργισθείς, which both
Bonner and Fuller regard as the better reading, cf. R. Fuller,
Interpreting the Miracles (London, 1963), p. 49, "the wonder
worker has to work up his emotions in preparation for the
difficult deed of healing." Alan Richardson, The Miracle
Stories of the Gospels (London, 1941), p. 60 also regards MSD
as having preferred reading, but thinks it intended to show
"divine anger against sin." But the context does not appear

is reported to have performed miracles by uttering the semitic words, _Talitha cumi_ and _Ephphatha_. The inclusion of such details of the technique of miracle working is seen by Dibelius as a primary characteristic of this form, and the preservation of foreign words and phrases may show that such stories were used as a kind of handbook to Christian miracles and magic.[68] In Mark 7:33 and 8:23, these stories also include the novelistic feature of Jesus performing healing by means of spittle, accompanied in the first instance by the groaning sighs of the thaumaturge (7:34),[69] and in the second by details of the stages of recovery.

Dibelius doubted the edifying value of these tales and described the "faith" in Jesus evoked by these miracles as a

---

to support that connotation. F. Mussner, _The Miracles of Jesus_, trans. by Albert Wimmer (Notre Dame, 1968), p. 35, suggests that Jesus is angry at "the injustice done to the lepers by the Jews." But such attempts to explain what Jesus was angry at have missed the point of the emotional frenzy of the wonder worker.

[68]Cf. Dibelius, _From Tradition to Gospel_, op. cit. H.D. Betz, _Lukian von Samasota und das N.T._ (T.U. #76; Berlin, 1961), p. 154, where Betz brings in a variety of examples from magical practice.

[69]Cf. Bonner, op. cit., pp. 171-174. In addition to the notes of rage (1:41) and groaning (7:34), the possibility of translating ἐπιτιμᾶν as "roaring" [cf. H.C. Kee, "The Terminology of Mark's Exorcism Stories,: NTS 14 (1967-1968), pp. 237-238] ought not be overlooked, particularly in 4:39 where the wind is "rebuked" and 8:25 where an unclean spirit is "rebuked." Kee's study shows that it is necessary to allow for more direct semitic influence on the miracle stories, including those stories that can be form-critically described as tales and those which are less marked by novellistic details. Certainly the cultural and religious syncretism involved in the cultivation of magical stories would argue against any rigid Hellenistic/Jewish dichotomy.

268

belief that Jesus "excelled all other thaumaturges."[70] To
be sure, "faith" (πίστις) in this context is directed toward
Jesus the miracle worker (cf. Mk 4:40; 5:34) and is even the
means by which Jesus' power (δύναμις) may be appropriated
(Mk 5:30). Thus lack of faith is displayed in a lack of
confidence or fear (Mk 4:40; 5:36), and when the followers
of Jesus are unable to cast out demons as he did,[71] Jesus
reprimands the "faithless generation" and performs the
exorcism after having evoked a response of faith (Mk 9:19,
23-24). But while Dibelius is correct that such faith is
not connected with any of Jesus' edifying teachings or with
the significance of his passion, the christological value
of these performances must not be underrated since they
evoke the numinous religious response of awe and wonder
(cf. Mk 4:41; 5:20, 42; 6:51; 7:37).

Magical elements and the response of wonder are, of
course, by no means limited to the novelistic miracle
stories; and the complex questions of the redaction history
of Mark can not be simply resolved by assuming that this

---

[70]From Tradition to Gospel, op. cit., p. 79.

[71]The possibility that this inability of the disciples
was introduced by Mark as a criticism of the christological
thrust of the miracle stories has been suggested by Koester,
"One Jesus and Four Gospels," op. cit., p. 233. Whether this
note thus serves to curb the authenticating value of such
acts or to heighten Jesus' performance, the kind of faith
or lack of it adduced in the text is correlated to the power
to work miracles. Cf. James M. Robinson, "Kerygma and
History," op. cit., pp. 128-129, for a discussion of such
faith with reference to John's Gospel and I Cor. 13:2.

list of tales constituted the evangelist's miracle source or accounts for all the theological tensions of the Gospel by itself.[72] Nevertheless, since Dibelius, Keck, and Georgi have pointed to these stories as transmitting a particular christological viewpoint which stands in tension with that of the Gospel itself, it is important to note that here it is the magical-miraculous performances of Jesus that authenticate his charismatic status. Thus if this Jesus is to be compared with other figures of the period who were depicted as having attained divine status, it must be carefully observed that the basis of Jesus' elevated status in these stories is dramatically different from that of Philo's Moses or that of the other heroes of the philosophical traditions.

Redaction studies of the Gospel of John have attained a broader level of consensus, at least with respect to the existence of a pre-gospel cycle of miracles, than is true for Mark. Scholars have long been drawn to attempt to describe the composition of the fourth gospel by suggesting sources of various descriptions. The difficulty of

---

[72]In particular, notice should be taken of the tensions associated with the titles, "Son of God" and "Christ." Cf. Koester, "One Jesus and Four Gospels," op. cit., p. 232, note 103. Cf. also, Koester, "The Structure and Criteria of Early Christian Beliefs," op. cit. For the present it can be observed that in one of the novelistic miracle stories, Jesus is called the "Son of the Most High God" by a demoniac (Mk 5:7) which corresponds to a similar confession of him as "Son of God" by the unclean spirits in Mk 3:11, which appears to be a Markan summary. The real crux of interpretation, however, remains Mark's account of the confrontation at Caesarea Philippi where Peter confesses Jesus as the Christ.

maintaining any strictly literary dependence was demonstrated
by E. Schweizer's critique of the earlier source theories
of Spitta, Wendt, Faure and Hirsch in which he showed that
their hypothetical sources could not be distinguished from
the evangelist's work on the basis of stylistic
characteristics.[73] Furthermore the possibility that the
synoptics served as a literary source was effectively
squelched by the work of Gardner-Smith and Goodenough.[74]

The most massive attempt to describe the sources of the
Gospel of John was Rudolf Bultmann's commentary which first
appeared in 1941.[75] The storm of criticism that has surrounded

---

As Robinson observes, this is "the gordian knot that must be
resolved if we are to understand the Marcan composition."
James M. Robinson, "On the Gattung of Mark (and John),"
Jesus and Man's Hope (Papers delivered at the Pittsburgh
Festival of the Gospels, vol. I; Pittsburgh, 1970), pp. 105-
106.

[73]Eduard Schweizer, Ego Eimi: Die religionsgeschichtliche
Herkunft und theologische Bedeutung der johanneischen
Bildreden, zugleich ein Beitrag zur Quellenfrage des vierten
Evangeliums (FRLANT, n.s. #38, entire series, #56; Göttingen,
1939).

[74]P. Gardner-Smith, Saint John and the Synoptic Gospels
(Cambridge, 1938). E.R. Goodenough, "John a Primitive
Gospel," JBL 64 (1945), pp. 145-182. C.H. Dodd, The Inter-
pretation of the Fourth Gospel (Cambridge, 1953), p. 419,
grants Gardner-Smith's point and gives it further support
in his book, Historical Traditions in the Fourth Gospel
(Cambridge, 1963). The point is also conceded by C.K. Barrett,
The Gospel According to St. John (London, 1962), p. 34,
although he thinks John knew Mark and perhaps Luke. John A.
Bailey, The Traditions Common to the Gospels of Luke and
John (Supplements to Novum Testamentum #7; Leiden, 1963),
believes John knew Luke and Mark, but grants that any
dependence was minimal.

[75]Das Evangelium des Johannes: Kritisch-exegetisher
Kommentar über das Neue Testament begründet von H.A.W. Meyer,

this work would constitute a study in itself, but two phases
of the scholarly response merit particular scrutiny.

The negative criticism of Bultmann's commentary is
usually identified with the studies of Ruckstuhl and Noack.[76]
In his arsenal of weapons for attacking Bultmann, Ruckstuhl
included an expansion of Schweizer's list of stylistic
characteristics which documents the literary unity of the
Gospel, but Ruckstuhl moved beyond Schweizer in concluding
that this evidence disproved any attempt to separate sources
and even precluded the possibility of the existence of such
written sources.[77] By focusing on the difficulties of
identifying any particular Old Testament textual tradition in
the fourth gospel, Noack expanded on Ruckstuhl's analysis
to maintain that the evangelist used nothing but oral

Abt. 2 (Göttingen, 1941, 19th edition 1968. Ergänzungsheft,
1957. Bultmann mentions his use of the work of Alexander
Faure, "Die alttestamentlichen Zitate im 4. Evangelium und
die Quellenscheidungs-Hypothese," ZNW 21 (1922), pp. 99-121.
But as Robinson has recently shown ("The Johannine
Trajectory," op. cit.), Bultmann's critics have frequently
been inaccurate in maintaining that Bultmann adopted Faure's
view. Bultmann disagrees with Faure on the issue that is
fundamental to Faure's thesis, the inclusion of Old
Testament citations in the source.

[76]E. Ruckstuhl, Die Literarische Einheit des Johannes-
evangeliums (Studia Friburgensia, n.f. Heft #3; Freiburg,
1951). B. Noack, Zur johanneischen Tradition, Beiträge zur
Kritik an der literarkritischen Analyse des vierten
Evangeliums (Publiciations de la Société des Sciences et des
Letters d'Aarhus, Série de Théologie #3; København, 1954).

[77]Cf. the balanced review of the debate by D. Moody
Smith, "The Sources of the Gospel of John: an assessment of
the Present State of the Problem," NTS 10 (1963-1964),
pp. 336-351.

sources, even depending on his memory for Old Testament citations.[78]

A much more threatening note of negative criticism of Bultmann's work has been sounded by Ernst Käsemann, whose perspective on the fourth gospel promises to furnish a major counterpoint in Johannine studies for some time. Unlike Ruckstuhl and Noack, Käsemann confronts Bultmann's analysis on its own terms. He shares Bultmann's sensitivity to the growth of gospel traditions and his awareness that the earlier written and oral traditions have undergone some modifications, including stylistic adaptations, in their incorporation into the Gospel. But Käsemann's view of the theological interpretation of the evangelist himself differs markedly from Bultmann's, and thus his assessment of the relationship between the Gospel and the possible sources is also in significant disagreement with Bultmann's. Käsemann identifies the crux of his interpretation by focusing on Jn. 1:14, a verse which Bultmann assigned to a pre-gospel hymn but which Käsemann regards as functioning as a commentary on the hymn and central to the theology of the Gospel.[79] The crucial issue is how this verse is to be interpreted in

---

[78]Cf. also C. Goodwin, "How did John treat his Sources?" JBL 73 (1954), pp. 61-75.

[79]Ernst Käsemann, "The Structure and Purpose of the Prologue to John's Gospel," New Testament Questions of Today, trans. by W.J. Montague (Philadelphia, 1969), pp. 138-167. [First published in German in Libertas Christiana, Friedrich Delekat zum 65. Geburtstag, ed. E. Wolf and W. Mathias (München, 1957), pp. 75-99.]

the theology of the whole Gospel.

Bultmann situated this verse, which he regarded to be taken from tradition, in the interpretative framework of the Gospel by emphasizing that for the evangelist its import would have been found in the first element, "The word became flesh." The confession "and we beheld his glory" is only to be understood in the shadow of the scandal of incarnation:

> "In purer Menschlichkeit ist er der Offenbarer. Gewiss, die Seinen sehen auch seine δόξα (v. 14b); und wäre sie nicht zu sehen, so könnte ja von Offenbarung nicht die Rede sein. Aber das ist die Paradoxie, die das ganze Evg. durchzieht, dass die δόξα nicht neben der σάρξ oder durch sie, als durch ein Transparent, hindurch zu sehen ist, sondern nirgends anders als in der σάρξ und dass der Blick es aushalten muss, auf die σάρξ gerichtet au sein, ohne sich beirren zu lassen, - wenn er die δόξα sehen will. Die Offenbarung ist also in einer eigentümlichen Verhülltheit da."[80]

Käsemann, however, defends the converse of this position. The presupposition of the fourth gospel is not the messianic secret or the hiddenness of the revelation but the display of divine presence:

> "Flesh for the Evangelist here is nothing else but the possibility for the Logos, as the Creator and Revealer, to have communication with men. 14a takes up 10a and makes the transition to what follows. The theme, for which this transitional phrase prepares the way, is stated in 14c: 'We beheld his glory.' This theme is at the same time that of the whole Gospel which is concerned exclusively throughout with the presence of God in Christ."[81]

In his study of John 17,[82] Käsemann extends this line of

---

[80]Bultmann, Johannes, op. cit., pp. 40-41.

[81]"The Prologue to John's Gospel," op. cit., p. 159.

[82]The Testament of Jesus: A Study of the Gospel of John in the Light of Chapter 17, trans. by Gerhard Krodel

interpretation, punctuating his analysis with a series of
provocative comments.

> "While Paul and the Synoptics also know the majesty of
> the earthly Jesus, in John the glory of Jesus determines
> his whole presentation so thoroughly from the very
> outset that the incorporation and position of the passion
> narrative of necessity becomes problematical. Apart
> from a few remarks that point ahead to it, the passion
> comes into view in John only at the very end. One is
> tempted to regard it as being a mere postscript which
> had to be included because John could not ignore this
> tradition nor yet could he fit it organically into his
> work."[83]

In a reference to the earlier studies of F.C. Baur, Wetter,
and Hirsch, Käsemann maintains that recent scholarship has
slighted the "liberal interpretation which characterizes the
Johannine Christ as God going about on the earth."[84]

> "John is, to our knowledge, the first Christian to use
> the earthly life of Jesus merely as a backdrop for the
> Son of God proceeding through the world of men and as
> the scene of the inbreaking of the heavenly glory. Jesus
> is the Son of Man because in him the Son of God comes
> to man."[85]

It is significant to note that Käsemann allows that John
drew upon miracle traditions, but he suggests that John's
very principle of selection was his interest in maximizing
Jesus' glory.

> "The presence of the miracles narrated by John cannot
> be explained by John's faithfulness toward the
> traditions. John took up that tradition freely. It was

(Philadelphia, 1968), from the German _Jesu letzter Wille nach
Johannes_ 17 (Tübingen, 1966).

[83]_Ibid._, p. 7.

[84]_Ibid._, pp. 8-9.

[85]_Ibid._, p. 13.

not accidental that he omitted demon exorcisms as not being illustrative enough of Jesus' glory and that he selected the most miraculous stories of the New Testament."[86]

Thus the tension between the evangelist's view and the understanding of Jesus implied in the miracle stories is completely relaxed. The only danger is that the miracles themselves might become the focus of interest.

"It is indeed correct to point out that John attacks a craving for miracles. This is not done, however, on the basis of a criticism of miracles in general, but in the interest of his one and only theme, namely, his christology. His dominant interest which is everywhere apparent is that Christ himself may not be overshadowed by anything, not even by his gifts, miracles and works."[87]

In contrast to these negative criticisms of Bultmann's understanding of _John_, many scholars have responded positively to his description of the "Signs Source" or "Miracles Source"[88] while remaining less convinced about the other sources he identified.[89] After granting that stylistic criteria do not provide an adequate basis for isolating such a source or proving its integrity, scholars who share Bultmann's basic conception of the theological tensions in

---

[86]Ibid., p. 22, cf. also p. 35 where Käsemann refers to "the tradition miracle stories which John took up."

[87]Ibid., p. 21.

[88]The term "miracle source" appears to be more satisfactory since it corresponds to the understanding of such acts that the source itself appears to imply, while the performances appear to have been re-interpreted by the evangelist as "signs".

[89]Cf. D. Moody, Smith, "The Sources of the Gospel of John," op. cit., pp. 342-343.

the fourth gospel appear to want to take his delineation of
the source in one of two directions, either expanding it to
include most of the narrative material in the gospel so that
it becomes an extended "narrative source", or focusing more
specifically on the miracle stories themselves as the heart
of a source or at least as a cycle of stories which presents
Jesus in the light of being a mighty miracle worker.

The approach of those who argue that Bultmann's description of the source must be expanded appears to be
conditioned by an understanding of it as a "narrative source"
which showed many similarities in form and content to the
material in the synoptics. Thus arguing from the analogy
with the synoptics, they suggest that a "narrative source"
would probably also include an account of the passion. This
approach was given some impetus by Haenchen's suggestions
that the source may have been "a Gospel of a non-synoptic
type"[90] or "a sort of crude version of the gospel of Mark."[91]
Haenchen has not yet spelled out the contrasts with the
Markan gospel except to suggest that John was dealing, often
from memory, with a gospel tradition that was used in his
own church and which stressed the visibility of the
revelation of God in Jesus without recourse to the theme of

---

[90]Ernst Haenchen, "Johanneische Probleme," ZThK 55
(1959), p. 54. [Reprinted in Gott und Mensch (Tübingen,
1965), p. 113.]

[91]Ernst Haenchen, "Aus der Literatur zur Johannesevangelium
1929-1956," Th.R., n.s. 23 (1955-1956), pp. 303-304.

the messianic secret.[92]   D. Moody Smith also presses the point
that a narrative source would have included a passion and a
resurrection story:

> "If there had been such a document, designed to evoke
> belief on the basis of Jesus' miraculous signs, would it
> have omitted the greatest sign of all, namely Jesus'
> resurrection? A resurrection story would have demanded
> a passion story also. ... It could be suggested that
> the narrative source included a passion-resurrection
> report, in which case it would be more appropriately
> styled an Urevangelium (Wellhausen, Wilkens, and Haenchen)
> than a semeia-source."[93]

The most extensive effort to expand Bultmann's source
is that of Robert T. Fortna.[94]   In his study, the definition
of the source as "the narrative source" and the argument
from analogy with the synoptic gospels circumscribe the area
of discussion so that several of Fortna's arguments appear
to merely be points on his methodological circle. For
example, in defining his source as "the narrative source,"
Fortna is using an inclusive category largely derived from
an image of Mark as a whole. Then having understood that
similar forms may bear similar theological outlooks, Fortna
can argue that a "narrative source" may be said to end

---

[92]Ibid., Cf. also "Der Vater, der mich gesandt hat,"
NTS 9 (1962-1963), p. 208. [Reprinted in Gott und Mensch
(Tübingen, 1965), p. 68.]

[93]D. Moody Smith, The Composition and Order of the
Fourth Gospel: Bultmann's Literary Theory (New Haven and
London, 1965), pp. 112-113.

[94]Robert T. Fortna, The Gospel of Signs: A Reconstruction
of the Narrative Source underlying the Fourth Gospel (Society
for New Testament Studies Monograph Series #11; Cambridge,
1970).

consistently with a passion narrative. But the definition
begs the question of the similarity of the source to the
Gospel of Mark. If the source were defined as a "collection
of miracles," for example, it would be comparable to the
pre-gospel cycle of miracles still recognizable in Mark, and
the burden of proof would be on the scholar who aims to show
that such "miracle collections" would end in a passion
narrative.

Again when Fortna tallies the synoptic parallels to
discover that, "every one of the parallels is to be found in
our source, rather than in the Johannine portions,"[95] the
observation is less noteworthy in the light of the fact that
synoptic parallelism has been used as a criterion of inclusion
for the source.[96] This circular argument is particularly
risky since Fortna uses it to include the passion narrative
material in the process of offering a more detailed
description of the source which Haenchen had called a
"coarsened Mark,"[97] and which Fortna calls the Gospel of
Signs.[98] But what kind of genre is a "coarsened Mark?" If

---

[95]Ibid., p. 87.

[96]Ibid., cf. p. 56 on Jn 6:2-3 and p. 57 on Jn 6:5 and
p. 79 for a few random samples.

[97]Ibid., p. 109. Cf. also Robinson's criticisms of
Fortna's Arguments for the unity of the source. "The
Johannine Trajectory," op. cit.

[98]Ibid., cf. pp. 221-223. Cf. also Robert T. Fortna,
"Source and Redaction in the Fourth Gospel's Portrayal of
Jesus' Signs," JBL 89 (1970), pp. 151-166.

it may be accepted that the genre "gospel" was the creation of Mark the evangelist,[99] the reader is at a loss to understand which stage in the development of the synoptic traditions offers a genuine parallel to this "narrative source."[100]

A further illustration of this problem is found in the fact that when Fortna tries to identify the christology of his source by correlating it to accounts of "divine men," he finds the concept useful in describing the kind of "Messiah" that could be presented on the basis of the performance of miraculous feats, but he is less able to account for the function of the passion narrative in such a context, except as a prelude to the resurrection.[101]

Among those scholars who are willing to accept Bultmann's contention that John drew on a source for his miracle stories, however, there appears to be a minimal agreement that, regardless of how extensive the narrative material may have been, the focus of the source or cycle of stories was found in the miracles themselves as pointing to a particular understanding of Jesus. The strongest evidence for the existence of such a source is also to be found in connection with the miracle stories themselves, i.e. the

---

[99]Cf. Marxsen, op. cit., pp. 107-150.

[100]Cf. Robinson, "The Johannine Trajectory," p. 15 of the manuscript, "Fortna's reasoning seems to rest ultimately on the assumption that the Johannine Source must have been of the Synoptic type, but this is precisely what is not to be assumed but rather proved."

[101]Cf. Fortna, The Gospel of Signs, op. cit., pp. 228-234.

evidence of a numbered list. In <u>Jn</u> 2:11, the changing of
the water into wine is called the "first of the miracles"
(ἡ ἀρχῆ τῶν σημείων)   and <u>Jn</u> 4:54 refers to the healing of
the ruler's son as "the second miracle" (δεύτερον σημεῖον)
which would seem to suggest that the intervening signs which
John mentions in 2:23 and 4:45 were not included in this
list.[102] Furthermore those who have accepted the possibility
of the existence of such a source appear to agree that its
theological climax and conclusion appears to be found in
<u>Jn</u> 20:31-32, where attention is focused on the miracles and
an enumeration is implied:

> "Now Jesus did many other miracles (σημεῖα) before his
> disciples which are not written in this book; these
> however, were written down in order that you may believe
> that Jesus is the Christ, the Son of God."[103]

If at least a minimalist position may be held to the
effect that John incorporated a traditional cycle of miracle
stories into his gospel, the first observation that must be
made is that most, if not all, of those miracle accounts can
be classified form-critically as "tales" or "novelistic
miracle stories" according to Dibelius' description of that
form. Dibelius himself described several of these accounts
as tales, including the changing of water into wine (2:1ff),

------

[102]Robinson, "The Johannine Trajectory," op. cit.,
backs this observation with an analysis of the redactional
"seams" that show where John was adjusting his account to
fit in the source material.

[103]Cf. Koester, "One Jesus and Four Gospels," op. cit.,
p. 231.

the healing of the official's son (4:46ff), the healing of a thirty-eight year illness at the Bethzatha pool (5:2ff), the healing of the blind man at the pool of Siloam (9:1ff) and the raising of Lazarus (11:1ff).[104] Georgi agrees and adds the account of the feeding of the multitude (6:1ff) to his catalog of novelistic miracle stories.[105] All of these stories fall within the miracle source as described by both Bultmann and Fortna. In addition, James Brashler, a graduate student at Claremont, has attempted to show that all of the miracle stories that Fortna has included in his source still show enough traits of this form to suggest that "the miracle source was a collection of Novelistic Miracle Stories designed to convince those who read or heard them that Jesus was a θεῖος ἀνήρ in whom one should believe."[106]

Perhaps the generalization is a bit premature both because of the tenuous character of the current state of redaction studies and because of the difficulty of pressing all of the stories into this mold,[107] but it is apparent that

---

[104]From Tradition to Gospel, op. cit., p. 72.

[105]"The Form-Critical Assessment of the Miracle Stories," op. cit., p. 3.

[106]James Brashler, "A Form-Critical Analysis of the Miracle Stories in Fortna's Reconstructed 'Gospel of Signs,'" Course paper: Claremont Graduate School and University Center, 1969. I am grateful to the author for allowing me to examine this unpublished paper.

[107]A good case in point is John 6:15-25, the story of the walking on the water, which both Bultmann and Fortna include in the source. Brashler, op. cit., p. 26, admits that as it stands the account is form-critically an epiphany

form-critical analysis must be applied more rigourously to
the Johannine material to identify the particular theological
freight that a form is carrying and to avoid the confusion
created by using a literary category like "narrative material"
which is too inclusive.

Even by limiting the analysis to those stories Dibelius
identified as "tales", it becomes clear that a rather
specific image of Jesus, the miracle worker, can still be
identified in the Johannine material, an image which stands
in contrast to John's christology. In particular, attention
should be drawn to the traces of thaumaturgic technique which
correspond directly to features of the novelistic miracle
stories in Mark. In Jn 11:33, the report that Jesus "was
enraged in his spirit and stirred himself up" (ἐνεβριμήσατο
τῷ πνεύματι καὶ ἐτάραξεν ἑαυτόν)   must be compared with
the rage of the thaumaturge (also ἐμβριμοῦσθαι)   in Mark
1:43.[108] Again the report in Jn 9:6 that Jesus cured the
man born blind by first anointing his eyes with clay made
wet by spittle should be correlated with the reports of

---

story, but he looks for hints of a novelistic miracle story
lying behind this section. It would appear that the functions
of these two forms may have been quite similar (cf. note #66
above), but objective controls as to John's editorializing
of such traditional material appear to still be elusive.
More form critical and literary studies are clearly called
for in this area.

[108]Cf. Bonner and Bevan, op. cit., and the textual
problem in Mark (note #67 above). Cf. also Jn 11:43 where
the loud cry may be thaumaturgic, cf. Fortna, The Gospel
of Signs, op. cit., p. 83.

healing with spittle which are found in the novelistic miracle stories in <u>Mark</u> (7:33; 8:23).

Similarly the continual dialectic in <u>John</u> concerning the nature of faith seems best understood when it is realized that the evangelist is critical of the faith in Jesus which is based on the miracles alone. This is an elusive issue since the instances where "believing" is specifically mentioned in verses that have been attributed to the source (cf. 2:11; 4:53; 20:31) correspond to the recognized pattern of Johannine style of using only the verb and never the noun. But even if these summaries betray the hand of the evangelist,[109] it seems clear that he was consciously opposing a faith based on miracles. This can be observed both from direct criticisms of such belief [cf. 2:23-24, "many believed (πιστεύειν) in his name when they saw his signs which he did; but Jesus did not trust himself to them;" 4:48;[110] 6:26] as well as by the fact that some of the Jews who saw his miracles and believed in him (πιστεύειν)

---

[109]The question of Johannine style is still heavily debated and this observation of the consistent use of the verb "to believe" instead of the noun "belief" is not intended as a means of taking sides in that discussion. But before the reader decides that such usage represents John's semitic outlook, he should consult, E.C. Colwell, <u>The Greek of the Fourth Gospel</u> (Chicago, 1931).

[110]Contrast Jesus' response in 2:23-24 with his openness to the Samaritans who believe because of his word, <u>Jn</u> 4:39-42. Cf. the evidence that the word of Jesus in 4:48 is a redactional insertion, Fortna, <u>The Gospel of Signs</u>, op. cit., p. 41, and Robinson, "The Johannine Trajectory," op. cit., p. 12 of the manuscript.

precipitate his death by reporting the signs to the Pharisees
(Jn 11:45-53).[111]

This does not mean that John did not believe in the
miracles. Käsemann is probably correct in maintaining over
against Bultmann that the miracles are not merely symbolic
for John, but Käsemann has failed to take adequate notice
of the reticence that John displays at allowing the miracles
to serve as a primary basis for faith.[112] As a result, his
provocative analysis of the Gospel has muddied the waters
of interpretation at a crucial point by attributing to John
the very christological viewpoint that the evangelist was
apparently seeking to control.[113]

Käsemann's analysis, however, has contributed to the
discussion by pointing out the possible triumphalist
tendencies of Johannine christology and by demonstrating the
hazards of reading the fourth gospel through the glasses of
Paul's theology of the cross. Doubtless this debate will
continue for years to come. But from the perspective of this
study, it is crucial to note that even if Käsemann were

---

[111]Cf. Jürgen Becker, "Wunder und Christologie," NTS 16
(1969-1970), p. 143. This article is a sober and precise
response to Käsemann.

[112]Käsemann, The Testament of Jesus, op. cit., pp. 21-22.

[113]Cf. Günther Bornkamm, "Zur Interpretation des
Johannes-Evangeliums: Eine Auseinandersetzung mit Käsemann's
Schrift Jesu letzter Wille nach Johannes 17," Ev. Th. 28
(1968), pp. 8-25. [Reprinted in Geschichte und Glaube,
Gesammelte Aufsätze, 3 (1968), pp. 104-121.]

basically correct that John intends to display Jesus as "God going about on the earth," the fourth gospel as it now stands would still have to be seen as reflecting a disagreement as to whether the miracles serve as primary authentication of that status. Since Käsemann appeals to earlier liberal scholarship on the fourth gospel, which aimed to show the correlation between this Jesus and such "divine men" as Hercules, it is germane to note again that when Simon reviewed the supposed parallels that liberal scholarship found in the Cynic and Stoic idealizations of Hercules, he observed that Jesus' miracles were specifically without parallel in those traditions.[114] Against the backdrop of Hellenistic portrayals of charismatic figures as analyzed in this study, the turbulence created in John by the appropriation of novelistic miracle stories does not appear exceptional. In fact, the debate recorded by Plutarch in roughly the same era provides evidence of a very similar disagreement as to whether Socrates' δαιμόνιον was divine because it furnished him with a miraculous power or because it allowed him to face death with an indeflectible purpose.[115]

This discrimination should also be tested against the complex questions of tradition and redaction in Luke-Acts.

---

[114]Marcel Simon, Hercule et le Christianisme (Paris, 1955), p. 64.

[115]Cf. de genio Socratis 580-582, discussed in notes #55-56 and text ad loc of chapter one above.

In fact, since both modes of trumphalist theology which have
been analyzed in this study stand in immediate juxtaposition
in Luke-Acts, the discrimination might provide a fruitful
avenue of approach to this literature. On the one hand,
miraculous and magical traditions concerning the heroes are
apparently counted as authenticating their stature. Jesus
is the "man attested to you by God with mighty works and
wonders and signs" (Acts 2:22). Even Peter's shadow is
lieved to have healing power (Acts 5:15), and handker-
chiefs and aprons which had touched Paul's body could effect
cures (Acts 19:11). On the other hand, the author is
clearly aware of certain literary conventions of Hellenistic
historiography and molds his account at crucial points to
appeal to more cultured tastes. Thus it is not a mere
coincidence that Hadas and Smith find the Gospel of Luke to
be the closest approximation in the New Testament to the
"literary aretalogy" of a sage that they believed developed
in the Hellenistic world under the influence of Plato's
account of the martyrdom of Socrates.[116] Furthermore, the
highly contrived speech of Paul on the Areopagus (Acts 17)
is apparently the author's attempt to display the hero as
capable of cultured discourse on the nature of God, although
he admits that the philosophical audience took offense as

---

[116]Moses Hadas and Morton Smith, Heroes and Gods (New
York, 1965), pp. 161-195. Cf. chapter one above, notes
#10-14. Cf. also Koester, "One Jesus and Four Gospels,"
op. cit., p. 235, and H. Conzelmann, The Theology of Saint
Luke, trans. by Geoffrey Buswell (London, 1960).

soon as the miraculous note of the resurrection was introduced.
Both of these modes of presentation can be discussed under
the general rubric of the glorification of charismatic
heroes, but an awareness of their disparity might provide a
point of departure for analyzing how the author attempts
his synthesis.[117]

In addition to redaction studies of particular books,
current discussion of presentations of Jesus as a "divine
man" is also being influenced by the more dynamic model of
the development of early Christian theology which is being
set forth by Koester and Robinson.[118] While their approach
is firmly grounded in the critical exegesis of early
Christian texts, it marks a new stage in the methodology of
the study of the literature of the period because it
presents a model which is essentially kinetic, reflecting
the vital growth processes of early Christian theological
reflection, focusing on the fundamental diversity that was
characteristic of the period, and drawing attention to the

---

[117]One example that would merit additional scrutiny is
the author's critique of magicians (Acts 8, Simon Magus;
Acts 13, Bar Jesus; Acts 19, the seven sons of Sceva and the
Christian magicians). It is difficult to see how these
practitioners differ phenomenologically from the apostles
as depicted in several of the stories. In Acts 13, Paul
produces belief in the proconsul by showing superiority of
power over Bar Jesus. In these contexts, there seems to be
no critique of the faith generated by such performances,
although there is a tendency to give God the credit. Cf.
A.D. Nock, "Paul and the Magus," The Beginnings of
Christianity (ed. F.J. Foakes-Jackson and Kirsop Lake), vol. V
(London, 1933), pp. 164-188.

[118]Cf. particularly the essays collected in the forthcoming
volume, Trajectories through early Christianity, op. cit.

changes and moderations in each of those developmental

patterns. Since such an approach concentrates on describing

the processes of growth rather than on isolating fixed

concepts, it creates certain terminological problems with

respect to the previously accepted jargon of the discipline,

which might be compared with the difficulty of explaining

trigonometric concepts in arithmetic categories. Perhaps

this problem of reformulation and the difficulty of finding

metaphors which are adequate for the model can be seen most

dramatically in Robinson's programmatic statement:

> "In Koester's terminology, how is it that both Mark and
> John, independently of each other, represent the shift
> from the aretalogy type to the kerygma type of Gospel?
> . . . The suggestion that comparable positions on a
> trajectory, the movemental equivalent to a common _Sitz
> im Leben_, could explain the comparable forms of Mark
> and John is an illustration of the way in which the
> recasting of New Testament research into trajectory
> patterns could recast old problems in such a way as to
> point to new solutions. The historian's task is not
> merely to continue to study the history of specific
> dependencies and influences of one fixed point on
> another fixed point, but perhaps more basically, to
> orient attention to the history of the morphological
> stages in the development of early Christianity, as it
> was borne along the conveyor belt upon which the whole
> Hellenistic world was moving. Such a reorientation of
> scholarly investigation may be the precondition for
> the possibility of a more adequate grasp of the history
> of primitive Christianity in the coming generation."[119]

Among the several "trajectory patterns" that Koester

and Robinson have analyzed, they have grouped the traditions

that emphasize the remarkable accomplishments and glorious

traits of the charismatic heroes of early Christianity under

---

[119]"The Johannine Trajectory," _op. cit._, pp. 29-30 in
the manuscript.

the comprehensive rubric of θεῖος ἀνήρ. [120] Once again,
the "trajectory" approach gives such a term a particular
connotation which must be carefully noted, since it is clear
from Koester and Robinson's methodological orientation that
no fixed concept would be adequate to explain all of the
points on the continuum. But the specific force that such
a term has in their approach is likely to be misunderstood
by other students of the New Testament since, as this chapter
has shown, many scholars have been operating under the false
impression that the term θεῖος ἀνήρ was a fixed concept in
the Hellenistic world.

While this study has been primarily an analysis of the
differentiation that existed in the non-Christian Hellenistic
world with respect to the ways in which charismatic figures
were authenticated as divine, perhaps it may prove to have
some value for suggesting avenues of approach to early
Christian literature. The terms "θεῖος ἀνήρ" and "aretalogy"
have only been used with great caution since it has been
argued that phenomena which ought to be differentiated have
frequently been imprecisely lumped together in scholarship
by appeals to these locutions. Nevertheless, a review of the
texts that have been discussed would show that they share a
general propagandistic intent of documenting the glorious
features or even divine stature of the charismatic figure

---

[120]Cf. particularly Koester, "One Jesus and Four Gospels,"
op. cit., and "The Structures and Criteria of Early
Christian Beliefs," op. cit.

who serves as a focus of the particular tradition. Whatever
terms may be chosen to describe this commonalty, great
care must be exercised to identify precisely which features
are regarded as verifying this status in a given context.

From this perspective, it ought to be possible to
undertake a detailed study of the theological traditions of
early Christianity that were primarily inspired by the image
of the "sovereign Jesus", in typological contrast to those
outlooks which viewed him primarily as the suffering, the
teaching, or the revealing Jesus. One possible method for
such a study would be to begin with those traditions which
have been described by Georgi, Koester and Robinson as viewing
Jesus through the prism of the "divine man" and to attempt
to identify the shadings in the image of Jesus that are
projected upon various points in the spectrum of texts. At
one pole, the novelistic miracle stories seem to paint
Jesus in the hues of the divine miracle worker. Apparently
the opponents of Paul in II Cor. portrayed Jesus (and
themselves) as both miracle worker and sage. And in Luke's
Gospel, the image of Jesus is clearly shaded in the direction
that he becomes the paradigm of the Christian virtues,
especially piety. Against the non-Christian background that
this study has described, such variations in the spectrum of
this christological outlook could perhaps yield more data
about the cultural diversity of early Christianity.

To choose yet another metaphor for describing the dynamic
interaction of traditions, it might be fruitful to compare

the process to the confluence of the tributaries of a river.
Because of the greater availability of literary sources,
the most clearly defined stream of tradition that this study
has identified is that of the depiction of the heroes of
moral virtue in the philosophical traditions. Whether the
figure in question is Plato's Socrates, Dio of Prusa's
Diogenes, Plutarch's Alexander, or Philo's Moses, the
elevated or even divine status of the charismatic figure
rests upon his characterization as a sage and possessor of
virtue who can serve as a paradigm for moral edification.
The second stream is fed by diverse accounts of popular
heroes and can still be recognized primarily in smaller
units of tradition or stories which were occasionally
preserved in literary works or which somehow survived the
ravages of time. These heroes of the popular romantic
legends of pseudo-Callisthenes and Artapanus and of the
syncretistic circles that collected magical and miraculous
tales are remembered with awe for their possession of
miraculous powers which defy sensibility, and such figures
serve as a focus for nationalistic or personal hopes for the
conquest of oppressive forces. When the streams of these
modes of propaganda begin to merge, as they do increasingly
in the later Hellenistic period, a turbulence is created,
particularly at the points where more sophisticated authors
such as Seneca, Plutarch, Dio of Prusa and Lucian attempt to
prevent the pollution of the philosophical stream of tradition
by the currents of popular idealizations which carry the

crass features of the magicians and miracle workers. Even
an author like Philostratus can be seen in the third century
A.D. as still conscious of such philosophical tastes,
although he is trying to show that his hero Apollonius of
Tyana was both a philosopher and a miracle worker.

The literature of early Christianity is merely a
microcosm of this Hellenistic process, both reflecting and
contributing to the confluence of traditions. Early
accounts of Jesus as a mighty miracle worker, particularly
as collected in cycles of novelistic miracle stories, are
partially diverted from developing into full-blown
characterizations by their incorporation into the canonical
gospels.[121] But as in other Hellenistic contexts, the
stream of traditions depicting the charismatic figure as a
miracle worker does not flow smoothly into Christian
literature, but creates a turbulence which can still be
detected in the final editions of the gospels.

---

[121]The thrust of such material was not, however,
completely contained as is best seen in the kinds of stories
found in the apocryphal acts and infancy gospels. Cf.
Koester, "One Jesus and Four Gospels," op. cit., pp. 234-236.

BIBLIOGRAPHY

Aly, W. "Aretalogoi." PW, Suppl. vol. VI (1935). Pp. 13-15.

Anderson, A.R. "Heracles and His Successors." Harvard Studies in Classical Philology, 39 (1928). Pp. 7-58.

Arnim, H. von. Leben und Werke des Dio von Prusa. Berlin: 1898.

Arnim, Johannes von. Stoicorum veterum fragmenta. Stuttgart: B.G. Teubner, 1964 (second edition). [First edition vols. I-IV, 1921-1924.]

Barrett, C.K. "Christianity at Corinth." Bulletin of the John Rylands Library, 46 (1964). Pp. 269-297.

Barrett, C.K. The Gospel According to St. John. London: SPCK, 1962.

Barrett, C.K. The Holy Spirit and the Gospel Tradition. New York: The Macmillan Company, 1947.

Becker, Jürgen. "Wunder und Christologie." NTS, 16 (1969-1970). Pp. 130-148.

Bergman, Jan. Ich Bin Isis; Studien zum memphitischen Hintergrund der griechischen Isisaretalogien. Uppsala: Berlingska Boktryckeriet, 1968. (Acta Universitatis Upsaliensis, Historia Religionum 3.)

Betz, Hans Dieter. "Eine Christus-Aretalogie bei Paulus (2 Kor. 12,7-10)." ZThK, 66 (1969). Pp. 288-305.

Betz, Hans Dieter. "Gottmensch." Article due to be published in RAC.

Betz, Hans Dieter. "Jesus as Divine Man." Jesus and the Historian. Festschrift for E.C. Colwell, ed. F. Thomas Trotter. Philadelphia: Westminster, 1968. Pp. 114-133.

Betz, Hans Dieter. Lukian von Samosata und das Neue Testament. Berlin: Akademie-Verlag, 1961. (TU, 76.)

Bevan, Edwyn. "Note on Mark 1:41 and John 9:33,38." JTS, 33 (1932). Pp. 186-188.

Bieler, Ludwig. ΘΕΙΟΣ ΑΝΗΡ. Wien: Buchhandlung Oskar Höfels, 1935-1936, 2 vols. [Reprinted unaltered, Darmstadt: Wissenschaftliche Buchgesellschaft, 1967.]

Bieneck, Joachim. Sohn Gottes als Christusbezeichnung der Synoptiker. Zürich: Zwingli-Verlag, 1951. (Abhandlungen zur Theologie des Alten und Neuen Testaments, 21.)

Bogaert, Pierre. Apocalypse de Baruch. Paris: Editions du Cerf, 1969. (Sources Chretiennes, 144,145.)

Bompaire, Jacques. Lucien écrivain. Paris: De Boccard, 1958. (Bibliothèque des Ecoles francaises d' Athènes et de Rome, 190.)

Bonner, Campbell. "Traces of Thaumaturgic Technique in the Miracles." HTR, 20 (1927). Pp. 171-181.

Bonnet, Hans. Reallexicon der Ägyptischen Religionsgeschichte. Berlin: Walter De Gruyter & Co., 1952.

Bornkamm, Günther. "The History of the Origin of the so-called Second Letter to the Corinthians." NTS, 8 (1961-1962). Pp. 258-264.

Bornkamm, Günther. "Zur Interpretation des Johannes-Evangeliums: Eine Auseinandersetzung mit Käsemanns Schrift Jesu letzter Wille nach Johannes 17." EvTh 28 (1968). Pp. 8-25. [Reprinted in Geschichte und Glaube, I, Gesammelte Aufsätze, 3 (1968). Pp. 104-121.]

Botte, Bernard. "La vie de Moïse par Philon." Moïse, l'homme de l' alliance. Paris: Desclée & Cie., 1955. Pp. 55-62. (Special Issue of Cahiers Sioniens.)

Bousset, W. and H. Gressmann. Die Religion des Judentums im späthellenistischen Zeitalter. Tübingen: J.C.B. Mohr (Paul Siebeck), 1966 (fourth edition). (Handbuch zum Neuen Testament, 21.)

Brandon, S.G.F. Jesus and the Zealots. Cambridge: Manchester University Press, 1967.

Brashler, James. "A Form-Critical Analysis of the Miracle Stories in Fortna's Reconstructed 'Gospel of Signs'." Unpublished course paper: Claremont Graduate School and University Center, 1969.

Braun, Martin. History and Romance in Graeco-Oriental Literature. Oxford: Blackwell, 1938.

Bréhier, Émile. Les idées philosophique et religieuses de Philon d'Alexandrie. Paris: Librarie Philosophique, 1925. (Etudes de philosophie medievale, 8.)

Brown, Raymond E. The Gospel According to John. Vol. I.
New York: Doubleday and Co., 1966. (The Anchor Bible.)

Brown, Raymond E. "The Gospel Miracles." New Testament
Essays. New York: Image Books, 1968. Pp. 218-245. [Reprinted
from The Bible in Current Catholic Thought, ed. John L.
McKenzie. New York: Herder & Herder, 1963.]

Brown, Raymond E. "The Kerygma of the Gospel according to
John: The Johannine view of Jesus in Modern Studies."
Interpretation, 21 (1967). Pp. 387-400.

Brownlee, William H. "John the Baptist in the New Light of
Ancient Scrolls." Interpretation, 9 (1955). Pp. 71-90.

Bruce, F.F. Biblical Exegesis in the Qumran Texts. Grand
Rapids: Wm. B. Eerdmans, 1959.

Budge, E.A. Wallis. Alexander the Great. London: C.J. Clay
and Sons, 1896.

Bultmann, Rudolf. Das Evangelium des Johannes. Abt. II of
Kritisch-exegetischer Kommentar über das Neue Testament.
Founded by H.A.W. Meyer. Göttingen: Vandenhoeck und
Ruprecht, 1941. [19th edition 1968 with Ergänzungsheft,
1957.]

Bultmann, Rudolf. Die Geschichte der synoptischen Tradition.
Göttingen: Vandenhoeck, 1921. (FRLANT, N.F., 12.) [Second
edition, 1931 and English translation of the second
edition by John Marsh, History of the Synoptic Tradition.
New York: Harper and Row, 1963.]

Bultmann, Rudolf. "The Stoic Ideal of the Wise Man."
Primitive Christianity (trans. by R.H. Fuller). New York:
Meridian Books, 1956. Pp. 135-145.

Burkert, Walter. Weisheit und Wissenschaft. Nürnberg: Hans
Carl, 1962. (Erlanger Beiträge zur Sprach- und Kunstwissenschaft, 10.)

Burkill, T.A. "Mark 3:7-12 and the Alleged Dualism in the
Evangelist's Miracle Material." JBL, 87 (1968). Pp. 409-
417.

Burkill, T.A. Mysterious Revelation. Ithaca: Cornell University
Press, 1963.

Burkill, T.A. "The Notion of Miracle." ZNW, 50 (1959). Pp.
33-48.

296

Campbell, C. Studies in Magical Amulets. Ann Arbor: University of Michigan, 1950. (University of Michigan Studies, Humanistic Series, vol. 49.)

Carmignac, Jean. Christ and the Teacher of Righteousness (trans. by Katharine Greenleaf Pedley). Baltimore: Helicon Press, 1962.

Case, Shirley Jackson. Experience with the Supernatural in Early Christian Times. New York: The Century Co., 1929.

Caster, M. Lucien et la pensée religieuse de son temps. Paris: Société d' édition 'Les Belles Lettres,' 1937.

Cerfaux, Lucien. "Influence des mystères sur le Judaisme Alexandrin avant Philon." Le Muséon, 37 (1924). Pp. 28-88.

Charles, R.H. The Apocrypha and Pseudeipgrapha of the Old Testament. 2 vols. Oxford: Clarendon Press, 1913.

Cohn, Leopold. "An Apocryphal Work Ascribed to Philo of Alexandria." JQR, 10: old series (1898). Pp. 277-332.

Collins, John and William Poehlmann. "Artapanus." Unpublished Paper from New Testament Seminar 201, Harvard Divinity School, April 6, 1970.

Colwell, Ernest Cadman. The Greek of the Fourth Gospel. Chicago: University of Chicago Press, 1931.

Conzelmann, Hans. "Die Mutter der Weisheit." Zeit und Geschichte. Dankesgabe an Rudolf Bultmann, ed. Erich Dinkler. Tübingen: J.C.B. Mohr, 1964. Pp. 225-234.

Conzelmann, Hans. "Present and Future in the Synoptic Tradition" (trans. by Jack Wilson). God and Christ, ed. Robert W. Funk et al. New York: Harper and Row, 1968. Pp. 26-44. (Journal for Theology and the Church, vol. V.)

Cox, A.S. "To do as Rome does." Greece and Rome, 12 (1965), pp. 85-96.

Cross, F.M. Jr. The Ancient Library of Qumran. Garden City, New York: Anchor Books, 1961. [Revised edition]

Crusius, O. "Aretalogoi." PW, vol. II (1896). Pp. 670-672.

Dalbert, Peter. Die Theologie der Hellenistisch-Jüdischen Missionsliteratur unter Ausschluss von Philo und Josephus. Hamburg-Volksdorf: Reich, 1954. (Theologische Forschung: Wissenschaftliche Beiträge zur Kirchlich-Evangelischen Lehre, 4.)

Davey, F.N. "Healing in the New Testament." The Miracles and
the Resurrection. London: SPCK, 1964. Pp. 50-63. (SPCK
Theological Collections, 3.)

Deissmann, A. Light from the Ancient East (trans. by Lionel
R.M. Strachan). New York: George H. Doran, 1927.

Deissner, Kurt. Das Idealbild des Stoischen Weisen. Griefswald:
L. Bamberg, 1930.

Delling, G. "Josephus und das Wunderbare." NT, 2 (1958).
Pp. 291-309.

Denis, Albert-Marie. Introduction aux pseudépigraphes grecs
d'ancien testament. Leiden: E.J. Brill, 1970. (Studia
in Veteris Testamenti pseudeipgrapha, 1.)

De Vogel, C.J. Greek Philosophy: A Collection of Texts.
Vol. III: The Hellenistic-Roman Period. Leiden: E.J. Brill,
1959.

De Witt, Norman Wentworth. Epicurus and His Philosophy.
Minneapolis: University of Minnesota Press, 1954.

Dibelius, Martin. Die Formgeschichte des Evangeliums.
Tübingen: Mohr, 1919. [Second edition 1933.]

Dibelius, Martin. From Tradition to Gospel (trans. from
second German edition by Bertram Lee Woolf). New York:
Charles Scribner's Sons, 1935.

Dibelius, Martin. Gospel Criticism and Christology. London:
Ivor Nicholson & Watson, 1935.

Dibelius, Martin. "The Structure and Literary Character of
the Gospels." HTR, 20 (1927). Pp. 151-170.

Diels, Hermann. Die Fragmente der Vorsokratiker. 7.Auflage
hsg. v. Walther Kranz. Berlin: Weidmansche Verlagsbuchhandlung,
1954.

Dodd, C.H. Historical Tradition in the Fourth Gospel. Cambridge:
Cambridge University Press, 1963.

Dodd, C.H. The Interpretation of the Fourth Gospel. Cambridge:
Cambridge University Press, 1953.

Dodds, Eric Robertson. The Greeks and the Irrational.
Berkeley: University of California Press, 1959. (Sather
Classical Lectures, 25.)

Driver, G.R. The Hebrew Scrolls. London: Oxford University Press, 1951.

Dudley, Donald R. A History of Cynicism. London: Methuen & Co., 1937.

Dupont-Sommer, A. The Essene Writings from Qumran. Cleveland and New York: Meridian Books, 1962.

Dupont-Sommer, A. "Exorcismes et guérisons dans les écrits de Qumran." Suppl. to Vetus Testamentum VII. Leiden: E.J. Brill, 1960. Pp. 251-253.

Ebeling, H.J. Das Messiasgeheimnis und die Botschaft des Markusevangeliums. Berlin: Töpelmann, 1939. (BZNW, 19.)

Edelstein, Emma J. and Ludwig. Asclepius. Two volumes. Baltimore: The Johns Hopkins Press, 1945. (Publications of the Institute of the History of Medicine, The Johns Hopkins University: Second Series, Texts and Documents, volume 2.)

Edward, William A. The Suasoriae of Seneca the Elder. Cambridge: Cambridge University Press, 1928.

Eisler, R. ΙΗΣΟΥΣ ΒΑΣΙΛΕΥΣ ΟΥ ΒΑΣΙΛΕΥΣΑΣ. Heidelberg: C. Winter, 1929-1930, two volumes.

Eissfeldt, Otto. The Old Testament (trans. by Peter R. Ackroyd). New York: Harper and Row, 1965.

Eitrem, S. Some Notes on the Demonology in the New Testament. Oslo: A.W. Brøgger, 1950. (Symbolae Osloenses, Fasc. Supplet., 12.)

Farmer, W.R. Maccabees, Zealots, and Jospehus. New York: Columbia University Press, 1956.

Fascher, Erich. Kritik am Wunder. Berlin: Evangelische Verlangsanstalt, 1960. (Aufsätze und Vorträge zur Theologie und Religionswissenschaft, 13.)

Fascher, Erich. ΠΡΟΦΗΤΗΣ. Giessen: A. Töpelmann, 1927.

Faure, Alexander. "Die alttestamentlichen Zitate im 4. Evangelium und die Quellenscheidungs-Hypothese." ZNW, 21 (1922). Pp. 99-121.

Feldman, Louis H. "Hellenizations in Josephus' Portrayal of Man's Decline." Religions in Antiquity. Essays in Memory of Erwin Ramsdell Goodenough, ed. Jacob Neusner. Leiden: E.J. Brill, 1968. Pp. 336-353. ((Studies in the History of Religions, 14.)

Fensham, F.C. "'Camp' in the New Testament and Milḥmah." *Revue de Qumran*, 4 (1963-1964). Pp. 557-562.

Festugière, A.J. "À propos des arétalogies d'Isis." *HTR*, 42 (1949). Pp. 209-234.

Festugière, A.J. *Epicurus and his Gods* (trans by C.W. Chilton). Oxford: Blackwell, 1955.

Festugière, A.J. "Sur une nouvelle édition du 'De vita Pythagorica' de Jamblique." *Revue des Études Grecques*, 50 (1937). Pp. 470-494.

Fiebig, Paul. *Jüdische Wundergeschichten des neutestamentlichen Zeitalters*. Tübingen: J.C.B. Mohr, 1911.

Fischel, Henry A. "Studies in Cynicism and the Ancient Near East: The Transformation of a *Chria*." *Religions in Antiquity*. Essays in Memory of Erwin Ramsdell Goodenough, ed. Jacob Neusner. Leiden: E.J. Brill, 1968. Pp. 372-411. (Studies in the History of Religions, 14.)

Fischer, J.B. "The Name *Despotes* in Josephus." *JQR*, 49 (1958). Pp. 132-138.

Fisher, Loren. "Can this be the Son of David?" *Jesus and the Historian*. Festschrift for E.C. Colwell, ed. F. Thomas Trotter. Philadelphia: Westminster, 1968. Pp. 82-96.

Flusser, D. "Healing through the Laying on of Hands in a Dead Sea Scroll." *Israel Exploration Journal*, 7 (1957). Pp. 107-108.

Fortna, Robert T. *The Gospel of Signs*: A Reconstruction of the Chief Narrative Source Underlying the Fourth Gospel. Cambridge: Cambridge University Press, 1970. (Monograph Series of the Society for New Testament Studies, 11.)

Fortna, Robert T. "Sources and Redaction in the Fourth Gospel's Portrayal of Jesus' Signs." *JBL*, 89 (1970). Pp. 151-166.

Freudenthal, J. *Hellenistische Studien*: Heft 1 & 2: *Alexander Polyhistor*. Breslau: Verlag von H. Skutsch, 1875.

Fridrichsen, Anton. *Le problème du miracle*. Strasbourg: Librarie Istra, 1925.

Fuller, Reginald H. *Interpreting the Miracles*. London: SCM, 1963.

Fuller, Reginald H. Review of B. Minette De Tillesse, Le
secret messianique dans l'evangile de Marc (Lectio
Divina, 47; Paris: Editions du Cerf, 1968). CBQ, 31
(1969). Pp. 109-112.

Gager, John G. The Figure of Moses in Greek and Roman Pagan
Literature. Unpublished Doctoral Dissertation: Harvard
University, 1968.

Gardner-Smith, P. Saint John and the Synoptic Gospels.
Cambridge: Cambridge University Press, 1938.

Gaster, M. The Samaritans. London: Milford, 1925.

Georgi, Dieter. "The Form-Critical Assessment of the Miracle
Stories." Unpublished paper delivered at a meeting of
The Hermeneutical Project of the Institute for Antiquity
and Christianity, Claremont, California, March 29, 1969.

Georgi, Dieter. "Formen religiöser Propaganda." Die Zeit
Jesu, ed. H.J. Schultz. Stuttgart & Berlin: Kreuz-Verlag,
1966. (Kontexte, 3.) Pp. 105-110.

Georgi, Dieter. Die Gegner des Paulus im 2. Korintherbrief.
Neukirchen-Vluyn: Neukirchener Verlag, 1964. (Wissenschaftliche Monographien zum Alten und Neuen Testament,
11.)

Georgi, Dieter. "Zur Frage der Chronologie." Die Geschichte
der Kollekte des Paulus für Jerusalem. Hamburg-Bergstedt:
Herbert Reich-Evangelischer Verlag, 1965. Pp. 91-96.
(Theologische Forschung, 38.)

Giesebrecht, Friedrich. Die alttestamentliche Schätzung des
Gottesnamens und ihre religionsgesichtliche Grundlage.
Königsberg: Thomas & Oppermann, 1901.

Goodenough, Erwin R. By Light, Light. New Haven: Yale University
Press, 1935.

Goodenough, Erwin R. An Introduction to Philo Judaeus. New
Haven: Yale University Press, 1940.

Goodenough, Erwin R. Jewish Symbols in the Greco-Roman Period.
Vols. 1-12. New York: Pantheon Books, 1953-1965. (Bollingen
Series, 37.)

Goodenough, Erwin R. "John a Primitive Gospel." JBL, 64
(1945). Pp. 145-182.

Goodenough, Erwin R. "Philo's Exposition of the Law and his
De vita Mosis." HTR, 26 (1933). Pp. 109-125.

Goodenough, Erwin R. "The Political Philosophy of Hellenistic
Kingship." Yale Classical Series. Vol. I, ed. Austin M.
Harmon. New Haven: Yale University Press, 1928.

Grant, Robert M. Miracle and Natural Law in Graeco-Roman
and Early Christian Thought. Amsterdam: North Holland
Publishing Company, 1952.

Groos, Karl. Review of Kurt Deissner, Das Idealbild des
Stoischen Weisen. Deutsche Literaturzeitung, 51 (1930).
Pp. 1688-1696.

Gross, K. "Apollonius von Tyana." RAC, vol. I (1950). Pp.
529-533.

Grundmann, Walter. "δύναμαι/δύναμις." TDNT, vol. II. Pp.
284-317.

Hadas, Moses. Hellenistic Culture. New York: Columbia
University Press, 1959.

Hadas, Moses and Morton Smith. Heroes and Gods: Spiritual
Biographies in Antiquity. New York: Harper and Row, 1963.

Hadas, Moses. Three Greek Romances. New York: Anchor, 1953.

Haenchen, Ernst. "Aus der Literatur zum Johannesevangelium,
1929-1956." ThR, n.s., 23 (1955-1956). Pp. 295-335.

Haenchen, Ernst. "Faith and Miracle." Studia Evangelica.
Edited by K. Aland, F.L. Cross, J. Danielou, H. Riesenfeld
and W.C. van Unnik. Berlin: Akademie-Verlag, 1959. Pp.
495-498. (TU, 73.)

Haenchen, Ernst. "Johanneische Probleme." ZThK, 55 (1969).
Pp. 19-54. [Reprinted in Gott und Mensch. Tübingen: J.C.B.
Mohr, Paul Siebeck, 1965. Pp. 78-113.]

Haenchen, Ernst. "Der Vater der mich gesandt hat." NTS, 9
(1962-1963). Pp. 208-216. [Reprinted in Gott und Mensch.
Tübingen: J.C.B. Mohr, Paul Siebeck, 1965. Pp. 68-77.]

Hahn, Ferdinand. Christologische Hoheitstitel; ihre Geschichte
im frühen Christentum. Götingen: Vandenhoeck & Ruprecht,
1963. (FRLANT, 83.) [English Translation: The Titles of
Jesus in Christology; Their History in Early Christianity.
New York: World Publishing, 1969.]

Halévy, M.A. Moïse. Paris: Les Éditions Rieder, 1927. (Judaisme,
6).

Hamilton, W. "The Myth in Plutarch's De genio." The Classical Quarterly, 28 (1934). Pp. 175-182.

Harrington, Daniel Joseph. Text and Biblical Text in Pseudo-Philo's Liber Antiquitatem Biblicarum. Unpublished Doctoral Dissertation, Harvard University, October, 1969.

Headlam, A.C. "Theudas." Hastings Dictionary of the Bible. Vol. IV (1903). P. 750.

Heinemann, I. "Moses." PW, vol. XVI (1935). Pp. 359-375.

Hengel, Martin. Judentum und Hellenismus. Tübingen: J.C.B. Mohr, 1969. (Wissenschaftliche Untersuchungen zum Neuen Testament, 10.)

Hengel, Martin. Nachfolge und Charisma: Eine exegetisch-religionsgeschichtliche Studie zu Mt 8:21f. und Jesu Ruf in die Nachfolge. Berlin: Töpelmann, 1968. (BZNW, 34.)

Hengel, Martin. Die Zeloten: Untersuchungen zur Jüdischen Freiheitsbewegung in der Zeit von Herodes I bis 70 n. Chr. Leiden: E.J. Brill, 1961. (Arbeiten zur Geschichte des Spätjudentums und Urchristemtums, 1.)

Herzog, Rudolf. Die Wunderheilungen von Epidauros. Leipzig: Dietrich'sche Verlagsbuchhandlung, 1931. (Philologus, Supplementband 22, Heft 3.)

Hicks, R.D. Stoic and Epicurean. New York: Charles Scribner's Sons, 1910.

Holstad, Ragnar. Cynic Hero and Cynic King. Uppsala: Carl Bloms, 1948.

Hornsby, H.M. "The Cynicism of Peregrinus Proteus." Hermathea, 48 (1933). Pp. 65-84.

Jacoby, Felix. Die Fragmente der Griechischen Historiker. Leiden: E.J. Brill, 1957 ff.

Jaeger, Werner. Aristotle (trans. R. Robinson). Oxford: Clarendon, 1948

Jaeger, Werner. Early Christianity and Greek Paideia. Cambridge: Belknap Press, 1961.

James, M.R. The Biblical Antiquities of Philo. London: SPCK, 1917.

Jeremias, Joachim. The Eucharistic Words of Jesus (trans. by Norman Perrin). New York: Scribner's, 1966.

Jeremias, Joachim. "Μωυσῆς." TDNT, vol. IV. Pp. 848-873.

Jonge, M. de. "The Use of the Word 'Anointed' in the Time of Jesus." NT, 8 (1966). Pp. 132-148.

Käsemann, Ernst. "The Structure and Purpose of the Prologue to John's Gospel." New Testament Questions of Today (trans. by W.J. Montague). Philadelphia: Fortress Press, 1969. Pp. 138-167.

Käsemann, Ernst. The Testament of Jesus (trans. by Gerhard Krodel). Philadelphia: Fortress Press, 1968.

Kallas, James. The Significance of the Synoptic Miracles. London: SPCK, 1961.

Keck, Leander E. "Mark 3:7-12 and Mark's Christology." JBL, 84 (1965). Pp. 341-358.

Kee, Howard Clark. Jesus in History, an Approach to the Study of the Gospels. New York: Harcourt, Brace & World, Inc., 1970.

Kee, Howard Clark. "The Terminology of Mark's Exorcism Stories." NTS, 14 (1967-1968). Pp. 232-246.

Keller, Ernst and Marie-Luise. Miracles in Dispute (trans. by Margaret Kohl). Philadelphia: Fortress Press, 1969.

Keller, O. Rerum Naturalium Scriptores Graeci Minores, vol. I: Paradoxographi Antigonus, Apollonius, Phlegon, Anonymus Vaticanus. Lipsiae: Teubner, 1897.

Kern, O. "Epimenides." PW, vol VI (1909). Pp. 173-178.

Klein, Günter. Wunderglaube und Neues Testament. Wuppertal-Barmen: Jugenddienst-Verlag, 1960. (Das Gespräch, 28.)

Knigge, Heinz-Dieter. "The Meaning of Mark." Interpretation, 22 (1968). Pp. 53-70.

Knox, Wilfred L. "The 'Divine Hero' Christology in the New Testament." HTR, 41 (1948). Pp. 229-249.

Knox, Wilfred L. "The Divine Wisdom." JTS, 38 (1937). Pp. 230-231.

Knox, Wilfred L. "Jewish Liturgical Exorcism." HTR. 31 (1938). Pp. 191-203.

Knox, Wilfred L. Some Hellenistic Elements in Primitive Christianity. London: Oxford University Press, 1944. (Schweich Lectures of the British Academy, 1942.)

Koester, Helmut. "ΓΝΩΜΑΙ ΔΙΑΦΟΡΟΙ." HTR, 58 (1965). PP. 279-318.

Koester, Helmut. "Häretiker im Urchristentum." RGG, vol. III (1959³). Pp. 17-21.

Koester, Helmut. "Häretiker im Urchristentum als theologisches Problem." Zeit und Geschichte. Tübingen: J.C.B. Mohr, Paul Siebeck, 1964. Pp. 61-76. (Dankesgabe an Rudolf Bultmann, hsg. v. Erich Dinkler.)

Koester, Helmut. "One Jesus and Four Primitive Gospels." HTR, 61 (1968). Pp. 203-247.

Koester, Helmut. Review of James M. Robinson, The Problem of History in Mark. Verkündigung und Forschung (1959). Pp. 181-184.

Koester, Helmut. "The Structure and Criteria of Early Christian Beliefs." Due to be published as chapter 6 of Trajectories through Early Christianity. Philadelphia: Fortress Press, 1970 (?).

Kraabel, Alf Thomas. Judaism in Western Asia Minor under the Roman Empire. Unpublished Doctoral Dissertation: Harvard University, 1968.

Kuby, Alfred. "Zur Konzeption des Markus-Evangeliums." ZNW, 49 (1958). Pp. 52-64.

Kuhn, Karl Georg. Konkordanz zu den Qumrantexten. Göttingen: Vandenhoeck & Ruprecht, 1960.

Kuhn, Karl Georg. "Nachträge zur Konkordanz zu den Qumrantexten." Revue de Qumran, 4 (1963-1964). Pp. 163-234.

Labriolle, Pierre. La réaction païenne; Étude sur la polémique antichrétienne du Ier au VIe siècle. Paris: l'Artisan du Livre, 1942.

Lattimore, R. "Portents and Prophecies in Connection with the Emperor Vespasian." The Classical Journal, 29 (1933). Pp. 441ff.

Leisegang, Hans. "Der Gottmensch als Archetypus." Uranos Jahrbuch, 18 (Jung Festschrift, hsg. v. Olga Fröbe Kapteyn). Zürich: Rhein-Verlag, 1950. Pp. 9-45.

Levy, Isidore. Recherches sur les sources de la légende de Pythagore. Paris: Leroux, 1926. (Bibliotheque de l'école des hautes études, sc. rel, 42.)

Lowe, Herbert. "Deamons and Spirits (Jewish)." Encyclopedia
of Religion and Ethics (ed. James Hastings). New York:
Charles Scribner's Sons, 1914. Vol. IV. Pp. 612-615.

Luz, Ulrich. "Das Geheimnismotiv und die Markinische Christologie."
ZNW, 56 (1965). Pp. 9-30.

McCasland, S.V. "Portents in Josephus and the Gospels."
JBL, 51 (1932). Pp. 323-335.

MacDonald, John. The Theology of the Samaritans. London:
SCM Press, 1964.

McGinley, Laurence J. Form Criticism of the Synoptic Healing
Narratives. Woodstock: Woodstock College Press, 1944.

MacKay, B.S. "Plutarch and the Miraculous." Miracles:
Cambridge Studies in their Philosophy and History (ed.
Charles F.D. Moule). London: A.R. Mowbray, 1965. Pp. 93-
111.

MacMullen, Ramsay. Enemies of the Roman Order. Cambridge:
Harvard University Press, 1966.

MacRae, George W. "The Ego-Proclamation in Gnostic Sources."
The Trial of Jesus. Cambridge Studies in honour of C.F.D.
Moule, ed. E. Bammel. London: SCM, 1970. Pp. 122-134.
(Studies in Biblical Theology, second series, 13.)

MacRae, George W. "The Fourth Gospel and Religionsgeschichte."
CBQ, 32 (1970). Pp. 13-24.

MacRae, George W. "Miracle in The Antiquities of Josephus."
Miracles: Cambridge Studies in their Philosophy and History
(ed. Charles F.D. Moule). London: A.R. Mowbray, 1965.
Pp. 127-147.

Manson, W. Jesus the Messiah. London: Hodder and Stoughton
Lt., 1943. [Republished, Philadelphia: The Westminster
Press, 1946.]

Marcus, R. "Divine Names and Attributes in Hellenistic Jewish
Literature." Proceedings of the American Academy for
Jewish Research (1931-1932).

Marmorstein, Arthur. The Old Rabbinic Doctrine of God. London:
Oxford University Press, 1927. (Jews' College, London,
Publ., 10.)

Marxsen, Willi. Mark the Evangelist (trans. by James Boyce,
Donald Juel, William Poehlmann with Roy A. Harrisville).
Nashville: Abingdon Press, 1969.

Meeks, Wayne A. "Moses as God and King." Religions in Antiquity. Essays in Memory of Erwin Ramsdell Goodenough, ed. Jacob Neusner. Leiden: E.J. Brill, 1968. Pp. 354-371. (Studies In the History of Religions, 14.)

Meeks, Wayne A. The Prophet-King: Moses Traditions and the Johannine Christology. Leiden: E.J. Brill, 1967. (Suppl. to Novum Testamentum, 14.)

Michel, Otto. "Studien zu Josephus: Apokalyptische Heilsansagen im Bericht des Josephus (B.J. 6,290f, 293-95); ihre Umdeutung bei Josephus." Neotestamentica et Semitica. Studies in honour of Matthew Black, eds. E. Earle Ellis and Max Wilcox. Edinburgh: T.&T. Clark, 1969. Pp. 240-244.

Milik, J.T. Ten Years of Discovery in the Wilderness of Judaea (trans. by John Strugnell). Naperville Ill.: Allenson, 1959. (Studies in Biblical Theology, 26.)

Moore, George Foote. Judaism in the First Centuries of the Christian Era. Cambridge: Harvard University Press, 1927-1930, 3 vols.

Morenz, Siegfried. "Vespasian: Heiland der Kranken." Würzburger Jahrbuch für die Altertümswissenschaft, vol. IV, no. 2 (1949-1952). Pp. 370-378.

Mussner, Franz. The Miracles of Jesus (trans. by Albert Wimmer). Notre Dame: University of Notre Dame, 1968.

Nilsson, Martin P. Geschichte der Griechischen Religion. Band II: Die Hellenistische und Römische Zeit. München: C.H. Beck'sche Verlagsbuchhandlung, 1961.

Noack, B. Zur johanneischen Tradition, Beiträge zur Kritik an der literarkritischen Analyse des vierten Evangeliums. København: Rosenkilde Og Bogger, 1954. (Publications de la Société des Sciences et des Letters d'Aarhus, Série de Théologie, 3.)

Nock, Arthur Darby. "Alexander of Abonuteichos." The Classical Quarterly, 22 (1928). Pp. 160-162.

Nock, Arthur Darby. Conversion. London: Oxford Paperbacks #30, 1961.

Nock, Arthur Darby. "Deification and Julian." Journal of Roman Studies, 47 (1957). Pp. 115-123.

Nock, Arthur Darby. Early Gentile Christianity and its
Hellenistic Background. New York: Harper and Row, 1964.
(Harper Torchbooks, the Cloister Library, TB 111.)

Nock, Arthur Darby. "Paul and the Magus." The Beginnings
of Christianity (ed. F.J. Foakes-Jackson and Kirsop Lake).
Vol. V. London: Macmillan & Co., 1933. Pp. 164-188.

Nock, Arthur Darby. Review of H. Jonas, Gnosis und spätantiker
Geist. Gnomon, 12 (1936). Pp. 605-612.

Nock, Arthur Darby. "Studies in the Graeco-Roman Beliefs
of the Empire." Journal of Hellenic Studies, 45 (1925).
Pp. 84-101.

Oxyrhynchus Papyri, The. Part XI, ed. with translation and
notes by B.P. Grenfell & A.S. Hunt. London: Oxford
University Press, 1915.

Peek, W. Der Isishymnus von Andros und verwandte Texte.
Berlin: 1930.

Perels, Otto. Die Wunderüberlieferung der Synoptiker in
ihrem Verhältnis zur Wortüberlieferung. Stuttgart-Berlin:
W. Kohlhammer, 1934. (Beiträge zur Wissenschaft vom
Alten und Neuen Testament, vierte Folge, Heft 12, der
ganzen Sammlung, Heft 64.)

Perrin, Norman. "The Son of Man in the Synoptic Tradition."
Biblical Research, 13 (1968). Pp. 3-25.

Petzke, Gerd. Die Traditionen über Apollonius von Tyana und
das Neue Testament. Leiden: E.J. Brill, 1970. (Studia ad
Corpus Hellenisticum Novi Testamenti, 1.)

Pfister, F. "Epiphanie." PW, Suppl. IV (1924). Pp. 277-323.

Poehlmann, William and E. Jeff Miller. "Pseudo Eupolemus."
Unpublished paper delivered in New Testament Seminar 201,
Harvard Divinity School, April 27, 1970.

Rad, Gerhard von. Old Testament Theology (trans. by D.M.G.
Stalker). Vol. I. New York: Harper and Row, 1962.

Ramsey, A.M. Christianity and the Supernatural. London:
Athlone Press, 1963. (Ethel M. Wood Lectures, 1963.)

Rappaport, Salomo. Agada und Exegese bei Josephus. Wien:
Alexander Kohut Memorial Foundation, 1930.

Reitzenstein, Richard. Die Hellenistischen Mysterienreligionen. Leipzig & Berlin: B.G Teubner, 1910. [Third edition, 1927, reprinted, Darmstadt: Wissenschaftliche Buchgesellschaft, 1956.]

Reitzenstein, Richard. Hellenistische Wundererzälungen. Darmstadt: Wissenschaftliche Buchgesellschaft, 1963, an unaltered reprint from 1906 edition.

Richardson, Alan. The Miracle Stories of the Gospels. London: SCM Press, 1941.

Riemann, Paul Alfonso. Desert and Return to Desert in the Pre-exilic Prophets. Unpublished Doctoral Dissertation, Harvard University, 1964.

Ringgren, H. Word and Wisdom. Lund: Ohlssons, 1947.

Robertson, Jerry. "Ezekiel the Tragedian." Unpublished paper prepared for New Testament Seminar 201, Harvard Divinity School, May 8, 1970.

Robinson, James M. "The Johannine Trajectory." Due to be published as chapter 7 of Trajectories through early Christianity. Philadelphia: Fortress Press, 1970 (?).

Robinson, James M. "Kerygma and History in the New Testament." The Bible in Modern Scholarship. Papers read at the 100th meeting of the Society of Biblical Literature, December 28030, 1964, ed. Philip Hyatt. Nashville: Abingdon Press, 1965. Pp. 114-150.

Robinson, James M. "ΛΟΓΟΙ ΣΟΦΩΝ." Zeit und Geschichte. Tübingen: J.C.B. Mohr, Paul Siebeck, 1964. Pp. 77-96. (Dankesgabe an Rudolf Bultmann, hsg. v. Erich Dinkler.) [A revised English translation of this article will appear as chapter 3 of Trajectories through Early Christianity. Philadelphia: Fortress Press, 1971 (?).]

Robinson, James M. "On the Gattung of Mark (and John)." Jesus and Man's Hope. Papers delivered at the Pittsburgh Festival of the Gospels, ed. David G. Buttrick. Pittsburgh: Pittsburgh Theological Seminary, vol. I, 1970. Pp. 99-129.

Robinson, James M. The Problem of History in Mark. Naperville: Allenson, 1957. (Studies in Biblical Theology, 21.)

Robinson, James M. "The Problem of History in Mark Reconsidered." Union Seminary Quarterly Review, 20 (1965). Pp. 131-147.

Robinson, James M. "The Recent Debate on the 'New Quest'."
Journal of Bible and Religion, 30 (1962). Pp. 198-208.

Rose, H.J. "Herakles and the Gospels." HTR, 31 (1938).
Pp. 113-142.

Roth, C. The Historical Background of the Dead Sea Scrolls.
Oxford: Blackwell, 1959.

Ruckstuhl, E. Die Literarische Einheit des Johannesevangeliums.
Freiburg: Paulusverlag, 1951. (Studia Friburgensia, n.f.,
3.)

Rudberg, Gunnar. "Zum Diogenes-Typus." Symbolae Osloenses,
Fasc. 14 (Oslo, 1935). Pp. 1-18.

Rudberg, Gunnar. "Zur Diogenes-Tradition." Symbolae Osloenses,
Fasc. 14 (Oslo, 1935). Pp. 22-43.

Schlatter, Adolf von. Die Theologie des Judentums nach dem
Bericht des Josefus. Gütersloh: C. Bertelsmann, 1932.

Schreiber, Johannes. "Die Christologie des Markusevangeliums."
ZThK, 58 (1961). Pp. 154-183.

Schulz, Siegfried. Die Stunde der Botschaft. Hamburg:
Furche-Verlag, 1967.

Schweizer, E. Ego Eimi ... Die religionsgeschichtliche
Herkunft und theologische Bedeutung der johanneischen
Bildreden, zugleich ein Beitrag zur Quellenfrage des
vierten Evangeliums. Götingen: Vandenhoeck und Ruprecht,
1939. (FRLANT, a.s. 38, entire series 56.)

Simon, Marcel. Hercule et le christianisme. Strasbourg:
Publications de la faculté des lettres de l'université
de Strasbourg, 1955.

Smith, Dwight Moody, Jr. The Composition and Order of the
Fourth Gospel: Bultmann's Literary Theory. New Haven and
London: Yale University Press, 1965.

Smith, Dwight Moody, Jr. "The Sources of the Gospel of John:
An Assessment of the Present State of the Problem." NTS,
10 (1963-1964). Pp. 336-351.

Smith, Morton. "The Account of Simon Magus in Acts 8."
Harry Austryn Wolfson, Jubilee Volume: English Section II.
Jerusalem: American Academy for Jewish Research, 1965.
Pp. 735-749.

Smith, Morton. "Palestinian Judaism in the First Century." Israel: Its Role in Civilization, ed. Moshe Davis. New York: Harper and Bros., 1956. Pp. 67-81.

Strugnell, John. "Notes on the Text and Metre of Ezekiel the Tragedian's 'Exagoge'." HTR, 60 (1967). Pp. 449-457.

Sweet, J.P.M. "The Theory of Miracle in the Wisdom of Solomon." Miracles: Cambridge Studies in their Philosophy and History (ed. Charles F.D. Moule). London: A.R. Mowbray, 1965. Pp. 115-126.

Taeger, Fritz. Charisma: Studien zur Geschichte des Antiken Herrscherkultes. Stuttgart: W. Kohlhammer, vol. I, 1957, vol. II, 1960.

Talmon, Shemaryahu. "The 'Desert Motif' in the Bible and in Qumran Literature." Biblical Motifs. Studies and Texts, vol. III, ed. Alexander Altmann. Cambridge: Harvard University Press, 1966. Pp. 31-63.

Tcherikover, V. and A. Fuks. Corpus Papyrorum Judaicarum. Vol. I. Cambridge: Harvard University Press, 1957.

Tcherikover, V. Hellenistic Civilization and the Jews (trans. by S. Applebaum). Philadelphia: Jewish Publication Society, 1959.

Tcherikover, V. "The Ideology of the Letter of Aristeas." HTR, 51 (1958). Pp. 59-85.

Tcherikover, V. "Jewish Apologetic Literature Reconsidered." Eos, 48,3 (1956). Pp 169-193.

Teeple, Howard M. The Mosaic Eschatological Prophet. Philadelphia: Society of Biblical Literature, 1957. (JBL Monograph series, 10.)

Thackeray, H. St. John. Josephus the Man and the Historian. New York: Jewish Institute of Religion Press, 1929. (The Hilda Stich Stroock Lectures of the Jewish Institute of Religion.)

The Miracles and the Resurrection: Studies by I.T. Ramsey, G.H. Boobyer, F.N. Davey, M.C. Perry, Henry J. Cadbury. London: SPCK, 1964. (SPCK Theological Collections, 3.)

Toynbee, Arnold J. A Study of History. Vol. VI. London: 1939.

Turowski, Edmund. Die Widerspiegelung des stoischen Systems bei Philon von Alexandria. Leipzig: Universitätsverlag, 1927.

311

Tyson, Joseph. "The Blindness of the Disciples." JBL, 80
(1961). Pp. 261-268.

Usener, Hermann (ed.). Epicurea. Lipsiae: B.G. Teubner, 1887.

Vermes, Geza. "La figure de Moïse au tournant des deux
testaments." Moïse, l'homme de l'alliance. Paris: Desclée &
Cie., 1955. Pp. 63-92. (Special Issue of Cahiers Sioniens.)

Vielhauer, Philipp. "Erwägungen zur Christologie des Markus-
evangeliums." Zeit und Geschichte. Tübingen: J.C.B. Mohr,
Paul Siebeck, 1964. Pp. 155-169. (Dankesgabe an Rudolf
Bultmann, ed. Erich Dinkler.) [Reprinted in Aufsätze zum
Neuen Testament. München: Chr. Kaiser Verlag, 1965. Pp.
199-214.]

Vielhauer, Philipp. "Ein Weg zur Neutestamentlichen Christologie?"
Review of F. Hahn, Christologische Hoheitstitel.
Evangelische Theologie, 28 (1965). Pp. 24-72. [Reprinted
with minor alterations in Aufsätze zum Neuen Testament.
München: Chr. Kaiser Verlag, 1965. Pp. 141-198.]

Walter, Nikolaus. Der Thoraausleger Aristobulos. Berlin:
Akademie-Verlag, 1964. (TU, 86.)

Weeden, Th. J. The Heresy that Necessitated Mark's Gospel.
Unpublished Doctoral Dissertation: Claremont Graduate
School, 1964.

Weeden, Th. J. "The Heresy that Necessitated Mark's Gospel."
ZNW, 59 (1968). Pp. 145-168.

Weinreich, O. "Antikes Gottmenschtum." N. Jahrbuch für
Wissenschaft und Jugendbildung, 2 (1926). Pp. 633-651.

Weinreich, O. Antike Heilungswunder. Giessen: Töpelmann,
1909. (Religionsgeschichtliche Versuche und Vorarbeiten,
Band 8, Heft 1.)

Weinreich O. Gebet und Wunder. Stuttgart: Verlag von W.
Kohlhammer, 1929. [Reprint from the Festschrift Genethliakon
Wilhelm Schmid. Stuttgart: Verlag von W. Kohlhammer, 1929.
Pp. 169-464. (Tübinger Beiträge zur Altertumswissenschaft,
5.)]

Weinreich, O. Menekrates Zeus und Salmoneus. Stuttgart: Verlag
von W. Kohlhammer, 1933.

Wendland, Paul. Die Hellenistisch-römische Kultur. Tübingen:
J.C.B. Mohr, 1912 (second edition). (Handbuch zum Neuen
Testament, I,2.)

Wendland, Paul. "ΣΩΤΗΡ." ZNW, 5 (1904). Pp. 335-353.

Wetter, Gillis P:son. Der Sohn Gottes: Eine Untersuchung
über den Charakter und die Tendenz des Johannes-Evangeliums.
Göttingen: Vandenhoeck & Ruprecht, 1916. (FRLANT, n.s.,
9.)

Wieder, N. "The 'Law-Interpreter' of the Sect of the Dead
Sea Scrolls: the second Moses." Journal of Jewish Studies,
4 (1953). Pp. 158-175.

Windisch, Hans. Paulus und Christus. Leipzig: J.C. Hinrichs'sche
Buchhandlung, 1934. (Untersuchungen zum Neuen Testament, 24.)

Wolfson, H.A. "Albinus and Plotinus on Divine Attributes."
HTR, 45 (1952). Pp. 115-130.

Wrede, William. Das Messiasgeheimnis in den Evangelien.
Göttingen: Vandenhoeck & Ruprecht, 1963, reprint unaltered
from 1901 edition.

Yadin, Y. The Scroll of the War of the Sons of Light against
the Sons of Darkness. London: Oxford University Press,
1962.

Yarbro, Adela and Daniel Fraikin. "The Fragments of Aristobulus."
Unpublished paper prepared for New Testament Seminar 201,
Harvard Divinity School, May 28, 1970.

Zeller, Edward. Greek Philosophy (trans. by Sarah F. Alleyne
and Evelyn Abbott). New York: Henry Holt & Co., 1886.

ΑΠΟΛΛΩΝΙΟΥ

ΙΣΤΟΡΙΑΙ ΘΑΥΜΑΣΙΑΙ.

I. Βώλου· Ἐπιμενίδης Κρὴς λέγεται ὑπὸ τοῦ πατρὸς
καὶ τῶν ἀδελφῶν τοῦ πατρὸς ἀποσταλεὶς εἰς ἀγρόν, πρόβατον
ἀγαγεῖν εἰς τὴν πόλιν, καταλαβούσης αὐτὸν νυκτὸς παραλλάξαι
τῆς τρίβου καὶ κατακοιμηθῆναι ἔτη ἑπτὰ καὶ πεντήκοντα, καθάπερ ἄλλοι τε πολλοὶ εἰρήκασιν, ἔτι δὲ καὶ Θεόπομπος ἐν ταῖς
ἱστορίαις ἐπιτρέχων τὰ κατὰ τόπους θαυμάσια. Ἔπειτα συμβῆ-
ναι ἐν τῷ μεταξὺ χρόνῳ, τοὺς μὲν οἰκείους τοῦ Ἐπιμενίδου
ἀποθανεῖν, αὐτὸν δὲ ἐγερθέντα ἐκ τοῦ ὕπνου ζητεῖν ἐφ' ὃ
ἀπεστάλη πρόβατον, μὴ εὑρόντα δὲ πορεύεσθαι εἰς τὸν ἀγρόν
(ὑπελάμβανεν δὲ ἐγηγέρθαι τῇ αὐτῇ ἡμέρᾳ ἧπερ ἔδοξεν κεκοι-
μῆσθαι), καὶ καταλαβὼν τὸν ἀγρὸν πεπραμένον καὶ τὴν σκευὴν
ἠλλαγμένην ἀπαίρειν εἰς τὴν πόλιν. Καὶ εἰσελθὼν εἰς τὴν οἰκίαν ἐκεῖθεν πάντα ἔγνω, ἐν οἷς καὶ τὰ περὶ τοῦ χρόνου καθ'
ὃν ἀφανὴς ἐγένετο. Λέγουσι δὲ οἱ Κρῆτες, ὥς φησιν ὁ Θεόπομπος, ἔτη βιώσαντα αὐτὸν ἑκατὸν πεντήκοντα καὶ ἑπτὰ ἀποθανεῖν.
Λέγεται δὲ περὶ τοῦ ἀνδρὸς τούτου καὶ ἄλλα οὐκ ὀλίγα παράδοξα.

II. Ἀριστέαν δὲ ἱστορεῖται τὸν Προκοννήσιον ἔν τινι
γναφείῳ τῆς Προκοννήσου τελευτήσαντα ἐν τῇ αὐτῇ ἡμέρᾳ καὶ
ὥρᾳ ἐν Σικελίᾳ ὑπὸ πολλῶν θεωρηθῆναι γράμματα διδάσκοντα,

APOLLONIUS'

MARVELOUS TALES

I. According to Bolus, Epimenides the Cretan was
reported to have been sent by his father and brothers
into the country in order to bring back a sheep into the
city. When night overtook him, he deviated from the path
and went to sleep for 57 years, exactly as many others have
said. And even Theopompus touches on the marvels at places
in his history. Then, in the mean time, Epimenides'
relatives died; but when he woke up from his sleep, he
continued to seek the sheep for which he had been sent.
And although he did not find it, he proceeded to the farm.
(And he supposed that he had awakened on the same day in
which he believed he had fallen asleep.) And when he
arrived at the farm and found it sold and the style of
dress changed, he departed for the city. And when he had
arrived home, thence he knew everything, even including
the things that had happened around the time when he had
disappeared. And the Cretans say, as Theopompus reports,
that when he had lived 157 years, he died. And not a few
other amazing things are told about this man.
II. It is reported that in the same day and hour when
Aristeas of Proconnesius died in a certain fuller's shop
of Proconnesius, he was seen by man teaching letters in Sicily.

314

ὅθεν πολλάκις αὐτῷ τοῦ τοιούτου συμβαίνοντος καὶ περιφανοῦς
γιγνομένου διὰ πολλῶν ἐτῶν καὶ πυκνότερον ἐν τῇ Σικελίᾳ φαν-
ταζομένου οἱ Σικελοὶ ἱερόν τε καθιδρύσαντο αὐτῷ καὶ ἔθυσαν
ὡς ἥρωϊ.
    III. Περὶ δὲ Ἑρμοτίμου τοῦ Κλαζομενίου τοιαῦτά τινα
μυθολογεῖται. Φασὶν γὰρ αὐτοῦ τὴν ψυχὴν ἀπὸ τοῦ σώματος
πλαζομένην ἀποδημεῖν ἐπὶ πολλὰ ἔτη καὶ κατὰ τόπους γινομένην
προλέγειν τὰ μέλλοντα ἀποβήσεσθαι, οἷον ὄμβρους μεγάλους
καὶ ἀνουβρίας, ἔτι δὲ σεισμούς τε καὶ λοιμοὺς καὶ παραπλήσια,
τοῦ σωματίου κειμένου, τὴν δὲ ψυχὴν καθάπερ εἰς ἔλυτρον διὰ
χρόνων τινῶν εἰσερχομένην διεγείρειν τὸ σῶμα. Τοῦτο δὲ αὐτοῦ
πολλάκις ποιοῦντος καὶ τῆς γυναικὸς ἐντολὰς ὑπ᾿ αὐτοῦ ἐχούσης,
ὅτε μέλλοι χωρίζεσθαι, μηδένα θιγεῖν τοῦ σωματίου μήτε τινα
τῶν πολιτῶν μήτ᾿ ἄλλον ἄνθρωπον, εἰσελθόντες τινὲς εἰς τὴν
οἰκίαν καὶ ἐκλιπαρήσαντες τὸ γύναιον ἐθεώρησαν χαμαὶ κείμενον
γυμνὸν τὸν Ἑρμότιμον ἀκίνητον. Οἱ δὲ πῦρ λαβόντες κατέκαυ-
σαν αὐτόν, οἰόμενοι τῆς ψυχῆς παραγενομένης καὶ μηκέτι ἐχούσης ὅπου εἰσδύσεται παντελῶς στερήσεσθαι τοῦ ζῆν, ὅπερ καὶ
συνέπεσεν. Τὸν μὲν οὖν Ἑρμότιμον Κλαζομένιοι τιμῶσι μέχρι
τοῦ νῦν καὶ ἱερὸν αὐτοῦ καθίδρυται, εἰς ὃ γυνὴ οὐκ εἰσέρχεται
διὰ τὴν προειρημένην αἰτίαν.

Since this sort of thing happened often in his case and
he became famous over a period of many years and was seen
rather frequently in Sicily, the Silicians built a temple
and sacrificed to him as a hero.
    III. Such myths as these are related about Hermotimus
of Clazomenae. For they say that his soul wandered from
his body and was abroad for many years. And when it was
at a place, it would predict the things which were about to
happen such as great rains and droughts, and again earthquakes and plagues and similar things, while his body lay
resting. And after a certain time, his soul re-entered,
as into a shell, and revived the body. But after he had
done this several times and his wife had his command that
when he was due to be separated no one was to touch the body,
whether he be one of the citizens or another man, some
men, having entered his house and earnestly entreated his
wife, saw Hermotimus lying naked on the ground motionless.
And they seized fire and burned him, because they thought
that since his soul was standing by and had no place where
it could enter, it would be utterly deprived of life, which
is indeed what happened. But the people of Clazomenae are
still honoring Hermotimus and consecrating his temple into
which his wife does not enter on account of the guilt which
has been previously mentioned.

IV. Ἄβαρις δὲ ἐξ Ὑπερβορέων ἦν μὲν καὶ αὐτὸς τῶν
θεολόγων, ἔγραφε δὲ καὶ χρησμοὺς τὰς χώρας περιερχόμενος,
οἵ εἰσιν μέχρι τοῦ νῦν ὑπάρχοντες. Προέλεγεν δὲ καὶ οὗτος
σεισμοὺς καὶ λοιμοὺς καὶ τὰ παραπλήσια καὶ τὰ γιγνόμενα κατ'
οὐρανόν. Λέγεται δὲ τοῦτον εἰς Λακεδαίμονα παραγενόμενον
εἰρηκέναι τοῖς Λάκωσι κωλυτήρια θῦσαι τοῖς θεοῖς, καὶ ἐκ
τούτου ὕστερον ἐν Λακεδαίμονι λοιμὸς οὐκ ἐγένετο.

V. Τὰ δὲ περὶ Φερεκύδην τοιαῦτά τινα ἱστορεῖται. Ἐν
Σκύρῳ ποτὲ τῇ νήσῳ διψῶντα ὑδάτιον αἰτῆσαι παρά τινος τῶν
γνωρίμων, πιόντα δὲ καὶ προειπεῖν σεισμὸν ἐσόμενον ἐν τῇ νήσῳ
μετὰ τρίτην ἡμέραν. Τούτου δὲ συμβάντος μεγάλην δόξαν αὐτὸν ἀπενέγκασθαι. Πάλιν δὲ εἰς Σάμον πορευόμενον εἰς τῆς
Ἥρας ἱερὸν ἰδεῖν πλοῖον εἰς τὸν λιμένα καταγόμενον, καὶ
εἰπεῖν τοῖς συνεστῶσιν, ὡς οὐκ εἰσελεύσεται ἐντὸς τοῦ λιμένος.
Ἔτι δὲ λέγοντος αὐτοῦ καταρραγῆναι γνόφον καὶ τέλος ἀφανισ-
θῆναι τὴν ναῦν.

VI. Τούτοις δὲ ἐπιγενόμενος Πυθαγόρας, Μνησάρχου υἱός,
τὸ μὲν πρῶτον διεπονεῖτο περὶ τὰ μαθήματα καὶ τοὺς ἀριθμούς,
ὕστερον δέ ποτε καὶ τῆς Φερεκύδου τερατοποιΐας οὐκ ἀπέστη.
Καὶ γὰρ ἐν Μεταποντίῳ πλοίου εἰσερχομένου φορτίον ἔχοντος
καὶ τῶν παρατυχόντων εὐχομένων σωστὸν κατελθεῖν διὰ τὸν

IV. Abaris the Hyperborean was, himself, one of those
who discourse on the gods, and as he traveled around the
territories, he also recorded oracles, some of which are
still extant. And he also used to predict earthquakes and
plagues and similar things and things which happen by the
favor of heaven. And it is said that when he came to
Lacedaemon, he told the Laconians to offer a preventative
sacrifice and because of this a plague did not take place
in Lacedaemon.

V. Such things as these are recorded of Pherecydes.
Once on the island of Skyros when he was thirsty, he
requested water from a notable person. When he had drunk,
he predicted there would be an earthquake on the island
after three days. And when this happened, great glory was
accorded to him. Again when he was coming into Samos into
the temple of Hera, he saw a boat coming into the harbor
to land, and he said to those standing with him that it
would not come within the harbor. And while he was still
speaking, a dark cloud rushed down, and the ship disappeared
completely.

VI. Although Pythagoras the son of Mnesarchus came
after these and at first labored dilligently at mathematics
and numbers, subsequently he did not refrain from the
wonderworking of Pherecydes. For once in Metapontus when
a boat entered bearing a cargo and those who were present
were praying that it might be safe on account of the

φόρτον, ἑστῶτα τοῦτον εἰπεῖν "νεκρὸν τοίνυν φανήσεται ὑμῖν
σῶμα ἄγον τὸ πλοῖον τοῦτο." Πάλιν δ' ἐν Καυλωνίᾳ, ὥς φησιν
'Αριστοτέλης . . . γράφων περὶ αὐτοῦ πολλὰ μὲν καὶ ἄλλα λέγει
καί, τὸν ἐν Τυρρηνίᾳ, φησιν, δάκνοντα θανάσιμον ὄφιν αὐτὸς
δάκων ἀπέκτεινεν. Καὶ τὴν γινομένην δὲ στάσιν τοῖς Πυθαγορεί-
οις προειπεῖν. Διὸ καὶ εἰς Μεταπόντιον ἀπῆρεν ὑπὸ μηδενὸς
θεωρηθείς, καὶ ὑπὸ τοῦ Κόσα ποταμοῦ διαβαίνων σὺν ἄλλοις
ἤκουσε φωνὴν μεγάλην ὑπὲρ ἄνθωπον "Πυθαγόρα χαῖρε." Τοὺς
δὲ παρόντας περιδεεῖς γενέσθαι. 'Εφάνη δέ ποτε καὶ ἐν Κρότωνι
καὶ ἐν Μεταποντίῳ τῇ αὐτῇ ἡμέρᾳ καὶ ὥρᾳ. 'Εν θεάτρῳ δὲ καθή-
μενός ποτε ἐξανίστατο, ὥς φησιν 'Αριστοτέλης, καὶ τὸν ἴδιον
μηρὸν παρέφηνε τοῖς καθημένοις εἰς χρυσοῦν. Λέγεται δὲ περὶ
αὐτοῦ καὶ ἄλλα τινὰ παράδοξα. 'Ημεῖς δὲ μὴ βουλόμενοι μετα-
γραφέων ἔργον ποιεῖν αὐτοῦ τὸν λόγον καταπαύσομεν.

cargo, as he stood there he said this, "It shall now be
evident to you that this ship is bearing a dead body."
And (this happened) again in Kaulonia as Aristotle
reports ... who in writing about him says many and various
things and reports that in Tyrrhenia he himself bit a deadly
biting serpent and killed it. And he also predicted the
division which took place among the Pythagoreans. And
consequently he departed for Metapontus without being
observed by anyone, and as he passed over the Cosa river
with others, he heard a great supra-human voice say,
"Hail Pythagoras!" And those who were with him were in
great fear. And once he appeared both in Croton and
Metapontus on the same day and hour. Once while he was
seated in the theater, he stood up, as Aristotle reports,
and he showed his thigh to be golden to those who were
seated. And some other miraculous things are told about
him. But since we do not wish to produce a work of the
transcribers, we will end the report.

Appendix II: Artapanus on Moses (P.E. IX: 27: cf. pp. 150 ff)

ΚΕΦΑΛΑΙΟΝ ΚΖ'

'Αρταπάνου, περὶ τοῦ αὐτοῦ.

'Αρταπάνος δέ φησιν ἐν τῇ περὶ 'Ιουδαίων, 'Αβραὰμ τελευ-
τήσαντος, καὶ τοῦ υἱοῦ αὐτοῦ Μεμφασθενὼθ, ὁμοίως δὲ καὶ τοῦ
βασιλέως τῶν Αἰγυπτίων, τὴν δυναστείαν παραλαβεῖν τὸν υἱὸν
αὐτοῦ Παλμανώθην. (2) Τοῦτον δὲ τοῖς 'Ιουδαίοις φαύλως προσ-
φέρεσθαι· καὶ πρῶτον μὲν τὴν Κεσσὰν οἰκοδομῆσαι, τό τε ἐπ'
αὐτῇ ἱερὸν καθιδρύσασθαι, εἶτα τὸν ἐν 'Ηλιουπόλει ναὸν κατασκευάσαι. (3) Τοῦτον δὲ γεννῆσαι θυγατέρα Μέρριν, ἣν Χενεφρῇ τινι κατεγγυῆσαι, τῶν ὑπὲρ Μέμφιν τόπων βασιλεύοντι·
πολλοὺς γὰρ τότε τῆς Αἰγύπτου βασιλεύειν. Ταύτην δὲ στεί-
ραν ὑπάρχουσαν ὑποβαλέσθαι τινὸς τῶν 'Ιουδαίων παιδίον, τοῦτο
δὲ Μώυσον ὀνομάσαι· ὑπὸ δὲ τῶν 'Ελλήνων αὐτὸν ἀνδρωθέντα
Μουσαῖον προσαγορευθῆναι. (4) Γενέσθαι δὲ τὸν Μώυσον τοῦτον
'Ορφέως διδάσκαλον. 'Ανδρωθέντα δ' αὐτὸν πολλὰ τοῖς ἀνθρώποις
εὔχρηστα παραδοῦναι· καὶ γὰρ πλοῖα, καὶ μηχανὰς πρὸς τὰς λι-
θοθεσίας, καὶ τὰ Αἰγύπτια ὅπλα, καὶ τὰ ὑδρευτικὰ καὶ πολεμικὰ
καὶ τὴνφιλοσοφίαν ἐξευρεῖν. "Ετι δὲ τὴν πόλιν εἰς λς' νομοὺς
διελεῖν, καὶ ἑκάστῳ τῶν νομῶν ἀποτάξαι τὸν θεὸν σεφθήσεσθαι,
τά τε ἱερὰ γράμματα τοῖς ἱερεῦσιν· εἶναι δὲ καὶ αἰλούρους

CHAPTER 27
Artapanus, concerning the same (Moses)

In his book "Concerning the Jews," Artapanus says
that when Abraham had died and his son Mempsasthenoth (!)
and likewise the king of the Egyptians, Palmenothis his
son inherited the sovereignty. (2) This king behaved
badly toward the Jews. And first he built Kessa and
founded a temple there. Then he constructed the temple
in Heliopolis. (3) He fathered a daughter Merris, whom he
betrothed to a certain Chenephres, a ruler of the regions
above Memphis. For at that time there were many rulers of
Egypt. Since she was barren, she adopted a child of one of
the Jews, and named him Mousos. But when he had become a man,
he was called Musaeus by the Greeks. (4) And this Mousos
was the teacher of Orpheus. And when he had become a man
he provided men with many useful things. For he invented ships,
and devices for laying stones, and Egyptians arms, and
implements for drawing water and for warfare, and philosophy.
He also divided the state into 36 Nomes and prescribed the
god to be worshipped by each Nome, and gave the sacred letters
to the priests, and the gods were cats and dogs and

317

318

καὶ κύνας καὶ ἴβεις· ἀπονεῖμαι δὲ καὶ τοῖς ἱερεῦσιν ἐξαίρε-
τον χώραν. (5) Ταῦτα δὲ πάντα ποιῆσαι χάριν τοῦ τὴν μοναρ-
χίαν βεβαίαν τῷ Χενεφρῇ διαφυλάξαι· πρότερον γὰρ ἀδιατάκτους
ὄντας τοὺς ὄχλους ποτὲ μὲν ἐκβάλλειν, ποτὲ δὲ καθιστάνειν
βασιλεῖς, καὶ πολλάκις μὲν τοὺς αὐτούς, ἐνιάκις δὲ ἄλλους.
(6) Διὰ ταῦτα οὖν τὸν Μώυσον ὑπὸ τῶν ἱερέων ἰσοθέου τιμῆς
καταξιωθέντα προσαγορευθῆναι Ἑρμῆν διὰ τὴν τῶν ἱερῶν γραμμά-
των ἑρμηνείαν. (7) Τὸν δὲ Χενεφρῆν ὁρῶντα τὴν ἀρετὴν τοῦ
Μωύσου φθονῆσαι αὐτῷ, καὶ ζητεῖν αὐτὸν ἐπ᾽ εὐλόγῳ αἰτίᾳ τινὶ
ἀνελεῖν. Καὶ δή ποτε τῶν Αἰθιόπων ἐπιστρατευσαμένων τῇ Αἰγύπ-
τῳ, τὸν Χενεφρῆν ὑπολαβόντα εὑρηκέναι καιρὸν εὔθετον πέμψαι
τὸν Μώυσον ἐπ᾽ αὐτοὺς στρατηγὸν μετὰ δυνάμεως· τὸ δὲ τῶν
συγγενῶν αὐτῷ συστῆσαι πλῆθος, ὑπολαβόντα ῥᾳδίως αὐτὸν διὰ
τὴν τῶν στρατιωτῶν ἀσθένειαν ὑπὸ τῶν πολεμίων ἀναιρεθήσεσθαι.
(8) Τὸν δὲ Μώυσον ἐλθόντα ἐπὶ τὸν Ἑρμουπολίτην ὀνομαζόμενον
νομόν, ἔχοντα περὶ δέκα μυριάδας γεωργῶν, αὐτοῦ καταστρατεῦσαι·
πέμψαι δὲ στρατηγοὺς τοὺς προκαθεδουμένους τῆς χώρας, οὓς δὴ
πλεονεκτεῖν ἐπιφανῶς κατὰ τὰς μάχας. Λέγει δέ φησιν Ἡλιουπολίτας γενέσθαι τὸν πόλεμον τοῦτον ἔτη δέκα. (9) Τοὺς οὖν
περὶ τὸν Μώυσον διὰ τὸ μέγεθος τῆς στρατιᾶς πόλιν ἐν τούτῳ
κτίσαι τῷ τόπῳ, καὶ τὴν ἴβιν ἐν αὐτῷ καθιερῶσαι διὰ τὸ ταύτην

ibises. He also designated a selected precinct of land for
the priests. (5) And he did all these things in order to keep
the monarchy safe for Chenephres. For since the masses had
previously been unordered, they would at one time depose
kings and at another set them up, and frequently they did
this to the same people, but sometimes to others. (6) For
these reasons, therefore, Mousos was beloved of the masses.
And because he was regarded by the priests as worthy of
being honored like a god, he was called Hermes because of
his interpretation of the sacred letters. (7) But when
Chenephres saw Mousos' prowess, he envied him and sought to
murder him on some plausible charge. And thus when the
Ethiopians invaded Egypt, Chenephres, supposing that he had
found an opportune moment, sent Mousos against them as the
commander of an army. But he enrolled a host of farmers,
supposing that he would easily be killed by the enemy
because of the weakness of his troops. (8) But when Mousos
came to the Nome which is named Hermopolis with about
100,000 peasants, he set up camp there. And he sent
commanders to occupy the land in advance and they were
remarkably successful in their battles. And he says that
the Heliopolitans say that this battle lasted 10 years.
(9) Because of the magnitude of the army, those close to
Mousos founded a city at this place and dedicated the ibis

βλάπτοντα ζῷα τοὺς ἀνθρώπους ἀναιρεῖν· προσαγορεῦσαι δὲ
αὐτὴν Ἑρμούπολιν. (10) Οὕτω δὴ τοὺς Αἰθίοπας, καίπερ ὄντας πολεμίους στέρξαι τὸν Μώυσον, ὥστε καὶ τὴν περιτομὴν
τῶν αἰδοίων παρ' ἐκείνου μαθεῖν· οὐ μόνον δὲ τούτους, ἀλλά
καὶ τοὺς ἱερεῖς ἅπαντας.
    (11) Τὸν δὲ Χενεφρῆν, λυθέντος τοῦ πολέμου, λόγῳ μὲν
αὐτὸν ἀποδέξασθαι, ἔργῳ δὲ ἐπιβουλεύειν. Παρελόμενον γοῦν
αὐτοῦ τοὺς ὄχλους τοὺς μὲν ἐπὶ τὰ ὅπια τῆς Αἰθιοπίας πέμψαι,
προφυλακῆς χάριν τοῖς δὲ προστάξαι τὸν ἐν Διὸς πόλει ναὸν
ἐξ ὀπτῆς πλίνθου κατεσκευασμένον καθαιρεῖν ἕτερον δὲ λίθινον
κατασκευάσαι, τὸ πλησίον ὄρος λατομήσαντας· τάξαι δὲ ἐπὶ
τῆς οἰκοδομίας ἐπιστάτην Ναχέρωτα. (12) Τὸν δὲ, ἐλθόντα
μετὰ Μωύσου εἰς Μέμφιν πυθέσθαι παρ' αὐτοῦ. εἴ τι ἄλλο ἐστὶν
εὔχρηστον τοῖς ἀνθρώποις, τὸν δὲ φάναι γένος τῶν βοῶν διὸ
τὸ τὴν γῆν ὑπὸ τούτων ἀροῦσθαι· τὸν δὲ Χενεφρῆν προσαγορεύ-
σαντα ταῦρον Ἄπιν, κελεῦσαι ἱερὸν αὐτοῦ τοὺς ὄχλους καθιδρύσασθαι, καὶ τὰ ζῷα τὰ καθιερωθέντα ὑπὸ Μωύσου κελεύειν ἐκεῖ
φέροντας θάπτειν, κατακρύπτειν θέλων τὰ τοῦ Μωύσου ἐπινοήματα.
(13) Ἀποξενωσάντων δὲ αὐτὸν τῶν Αἰγυπτίων, ὁρκωμοτῆσαι τοὺς
φίλους, μὴ ἐξαγγεῖλαι τῷ Μωύσῳ τὴν ἐπισυνισταμένην αὐτῷ ἐπιβουλὴν, καὶ προβαλέσθαι τοὺς ἀναιρήσοντας αὐτόν. (14) Μηδενὸς

in it because this bird kills animals which harm men. And
they called it the city of Hermes. (10) Thus although they
were enemies, the Ethiopians loved Mousos with the result
that they even learned the practice of circumcision of
genitalia from him; and not only they, but all the priests.
    (11) When the war was ended, Chenephres welcomed him
in word, but in deed he contrived against him. At any rate,
he took away his troops, sending some to the boundaries of
Ethiopia as a safety precaution, and he commanded others to
destroy the temple in Disopolis which was constructed of
baked brick and to build another of stone, once they had
quarried the neighboring mountain. And he commanded that
Nacheros be the building foreman. (12) But when he had
entered Memphis with Mousos, he inquired of him whether
there was anything else which is useful for men, and he
said, the breed of oxen because the earth is tilled by means
of them. And Chenephres having called the bull Apis,
commanded the troops to erect his temple and commanded that
the animals which Mousos had consecrated be brought there and
buried, because he wished to conceal Mousos' inventions.
(13) Once the Egyptians had been alienated from him, he
swore his friends to secrecy not to tell Mousos the plot
that was being laid against him; and he appointed his
executioners. (14) But when noe one obeyed, Chenephres

δ' ὑπακούσαντος, ὀνειδίσαι τὸν Χενεφρῆν Χανεθώθην τὸν μάλιστα
προσαγορευόμενον ὑπ' αὐτοῦ, τὸν δὲ ὀνειδισθέντα ὑποσχέσθαι
τὴν ἐπίθεσιν, λαβόντα καιρόν. (15) Ὑπὸ δὲ τοῦτον τὸν καιρὸν τῆς Μέρριδος τελευτησάσης, ὑποσχέσθαι τὸν Χενεφρῆν τῷ
τε Μωύσῳ καὶ τῷ Χανεθώθη τὸ σῶμα ὥστε διακομίσαντας εἰς τοὺς
ὑπὲρ Αἴγυπτον τόπους θάψαι, ὑπολαβόντα τὸν Μώυσον ὑπὸ τοῦ
Χανεθώθ ἀναιρεθήσεσθαι. (16) Πορευομένων δὲ αὐτῶν τὴν ἐπιβουλὴν τῷ Μωύσῳ τῶν συνειδότων ἐξαγγεῖλαί τινα, τὸν δὲ φυλάσ-
σοντα αὐτὸν τὴν μὲν Μέρριν θάψαι, τὸν δὲ ποταμὸν, καὶ τὴν ἐν
ἐκείνῳ πόλιν Μερόην προσαγορεῦσαι· (τιμᾶσθαι δὲ τὴν Μέρριν
ταύτην ὑπὸ τῶν ἐγχωρίων οὐκ ἔλαττον ἢ τὴν Ἶσιν.) (17) Ἀάρωνα
δὲ τὸν τοῦ Μωύσου ἀδελφὸν τὰ περὶ τὴν ἐπιβουλὴν ἐπιγνόντα συμ-
βουλεῦσαι τῷ ἀδελφῷ εἰς τὴν Ἀραβίαν, τὸν δὲ πεισθέντα, ἀπὸ
Μέμφεως τὸν Νεῖλον διαπλεύσαντα, ἀπαλλάσσεσθαι εἰς τὴν Ἀραβίαν. (18) Τὸν δὲ Χανεθώθην πυθόμενον τοῦ Μωύσου τὴν φυγὴν,
ἐνεδρεύειν ὡς ἀναιρήσοντα. Ἰδόντα δὲ ἐρχόμενον σπάσασθαι
τὴν μάχαιραν ἐπ' αὐτόν, τὸν δὲ Μώυσον προκαταχήσαντα τήν τε
χεῖρα κατασχεῖν αὐτοῦ, καὶ σπασάμενον τὸ ξίφος, φονεῦσαι τὸν
Χανεθώθην. (19) Διεκδρᾶναι δὲ εἰς τὴν Ἀραβίαν, καὶ Ῥαγου-
ήλῳ τῷ τῶν τόπων ἄρχοντι συμβιοῦν, λαβόντα τὴν ἐκείνου θυγατέρα. Τὸν δὲ Ῥαγουῆλον βούλεσθαι στρατεύειν ἐπὶ τοὺς Αἰγυπτίους, κατάγειν βουλόμενον τὸν Μώυσον, καὶ τὴν δυναστείαν τῇ

reproached Chanethothes whom he named in particular, and
having been reproached he promised to make an assault
when he got a chance. (15) About this time Merris died,
and Chenephres charged Mousos and Chanethothes to tranport
the body to the regions beyond Egypt for burial, figuring
that Mousos would be killed by Chanethothes. (16) But as
they traveled, one of those who was aware of the plot
reported it to Mousos. And being on his guard, he buried
Merris himself; and he named the river and the city at
that spot Meroe. (And this Merris is honored by the
inhabitants no less than Isis.) (17) And when he had
learned of the plot, Mousos' brother Aaron advised his
brother to flee to Arabia. And being persuaded, he sailed
across the Nile from Memphis to escape into Arabia. (18)
But when Chanethothes learned of Mousos' flight, he lay
in wait to kill him. And when he saw him coming, he drew
his sword against him, but Mousos having overtaken him first,
mastered him, and drawing his sword, he killed Chanethothes.
(19) And he escaped into Arabia, and dwelt with Raguel the
ruler of the region, having married his daughter. But
Raguel wished to wage war against the Egyptians, thinking
he would restore Mousos and procure the sovereignty for

τε θυγατρὶ καὶ τῷ γαμβρῷ κατασκευάσαι, τὸν δὲ Μώϋσον ἀποκω-
λῦσαι στοχαζόμενον τῶν ὁμοφύλων· τὸν δὲ Ῥαγουῆλον διακωλύ-
οντα στρατεύειν τοῖς "Αραψι προστάξαι λῃστεύειν τὴν Αἴγυπτον.
(20) Ὑπὸ δὲ τὸν αὐτὸν χρόνον καὶ Χενεφρῆν πρῶτον ἁπάντων ἀνθρωπων ἐλεφαντιάσαντα μεταλλάξαι· τούτῳ δὲ τῷ πάθει
περιπεσεῖν διὰ τὸ τοὺς Ἰουδαίους προστάξαι σινδόνας ἀμφιέν-
νυσθαι, ἐρεᾶν δ' ἐσθῆτα μὴ ἀμπέχεσθαι, ὅπως ὄντες ἐπίσημοι
κολάζωνται ὑπ' αὐτοῦ. (21) Τὸν δὲ Μώϋσον εὔχεσθαι τῷ θεῷ,
ἤδη ποτὲ τοὺς λαοὺς παῦσαι τῶν κακοπαθειῶν· ἱλασκομένου δ'
αὐτοῦ, αἰφνιδίως φησὶν ἐκ τῆς γῆς πῦρ ἀναφθῆναι, καὶ τοῦτο
κάεσθαι, μήτε ὕλης μήτε ἄλλης τινὸς ξυλείας οὔσης ἐν τῷ
τόπῳ· τὸν δὲ Μώϋσον, δείσαντα τὸ γένος φεύγειν, φωνὴν δ'
αὐτῷ θείαν εἰπεῖν, στρατεύειν ἐπ' Αἴγυπτον, καὶ τοὺς Ἰουδαίους διασώσαντα, εἰς τὴν ἀρχαίαν ἀγαγεῖν πατρίδα. (22) Τὸν
δὲ θαρρήσαντα δύναμιν πολεμίαν ἐπάγειν διαγνῶναι τοῖς Αἰγυπτίοις, πρῶτον δὲ πρὸς Ἀαρῶνα τὸν ἀδελφὸν ἐλθεῖν. Τὸν δὲ
βασιλέα τῶν Αἰγυπτίων, πυθόμενον τὴν τοῦ Μωϋσου παρουσίαν
καλέσαι πρὸς αὐτὸν, καὶ πυνθάνεσθαι ἐφ' ὅτῳ ἥκοι· τὸν δὲ
φάναι, προστάξαι αὐτῷ τὸν τῆς οἰκουμένης Δεσπότην ἀπολῦσαι
τοὺς Ἰουδαίους. (23) Τὸν δὲ πυθόμενον εἰς φυλακὴν αὐτὸν
καθεῖρξαι νυκτὸς δὲ ἐπιγενομένης τάς τε θύρας αὐτομάτως
ἀνοιχθῆναι τοῦ δεσμωτηρίου, καὶ τῶν φυλάκων οὒ μὲν τελευτῆσαι,

his daughter and son-in-law. But Mousos prevented it,
taking thought for his own people. But Raguel hindering
him from fighting with the Arabs commanded brigandry against
Egypt.
(20) About the same time Chenephres died, having been
the first of all men to have elephantiasis. This disease
fell upon him because he commanded that the Jews wear linen
and not be dressed in woolen clothing in order that since
they were conspicuous they might be punished by him.
(21) But Mousos prayed to God that even now he might put
an end to the sufferings of the people. Since God was
appeased, suddenly, it is said, a fire was kindled from the
earth, and it blazed although there was neither wood nor
any other kindling in the place. And because he was alarmed,
Mousos began to flee, but a divine voice commanded him to
advance with an army against Egypt and when he had rescued
the Jews to lead them to their ancient homeland. (22) And
he took courage and determined to lead a hostile force against
the Egyptians, but first he went to his brother Aaron.
And when the king of the Egyptians learned of Mousos'
coming, he summoned him before him and inquired why he had
come. And he said because the Lord of the world had
commanded him to set the Jews free. (23) And when he
learned this, the king confined him in prison. But when
night came, the doors of the prison opened of their own
accord, and some of the guards died, while some were

τινὰς δὲ ὑπὸ τοῦ ὕπνου παρεθῆναι, τά τε ὅπλα κατεαγῆναι.
(24) Ἐξελθόντα δὲ τὸν Μώυσον, ἐπὶ τὰ βασίλεια ἐλθεῖν,
εὑρόντα δὲ ἀνεῳγμένας τὰς θύρας εἰσελθεῖν, καὶ ἐνθάδε τῶν
φυλάκων παρειμένων τὸν βασιλέα ἐξεγεῖραι. Τὸν δὲ ἐκπλαγέντα
ἐπὶ τῷ γεγονότι κελεῦσαι τῷ Μώυσῳ τὸ τοῦ πέμψαντος αὐτὸν θεοῦ
εἰπεῖν ὄνομα, διαχλευάσαντα αὐτόν. (25) Τὸν δὲ, προσκύψαντα
πρὸς τὸ οὖς εἰπεῖν, Ἀκούσαντα δὲ τὸν βασιλέα, πεσεῖν ἄφωνον,
διακρατηθέντα δὲ ὑπὸ τοῦ Μωύσου πάλιν ἀναβιῶσαι. (26) Γράψαντα
δὲ τοὔνομα εἰς δέλτον, κατασφραγίσασθαι, τῶν δὲ ἱερέων τὸν
ἐκφαυλίσαντα τὰ ἐν τῇ πινακίδι γεγραμμένα μετὰ σπασμοῦ τὸν
βίον ἐκλιμπάνειν. (27) Εἰπεῖν τε τὸν Βασιλέα σημεῖόν τι
αὐτῷ ποιῆσαι, τὸν δὲ Μώυσον, ἣν εἶχε ῥάβδον ἐκβαλόντα, ὄφιν
ποιῆσαι· πτοηθέντων δὲ πάντων, ἐπιλαβόμενον τῆς οὐρᾶς ἀνε-
λέσθαι, καὶ πάλιν ῥάβδον ποιῆσαι. (28) Προελθόντα δὲ μικρὸν,
τὸν Νεῖλον τῇ ῥάβδῳ πατάξαι, τὸν δὲ ποταμὸν, πολύχουν γενό-
μενον, κατακλύζειν ὅλην τὴν Αἴγυπτον· (ἀπὸ τότε δὲ καὶ τὴν
κατάβασιν αὐτοῦ γίνεσθαι·) συναγαγὸν δὲ τὸ ὕδωρ ἀποζέσαι,
καὶ τὰ ποτάμια διαφθεῖραι ζῷα, τούς τε λαοὺς διὰ τὴν δίψαν
φθείρεσθαι. (29) Τὸν δὲ βασιλέα τούτων γενομένων τῶν τερά-
των, φάναι μετὰ μῆνα τοὺς λαοὺς ἀπολύσειν, ἐὰν ἀποκαταστήσῃ
τὸν ποταμόν· τὸν δὲ Μώυσον πάλιν τῇ ῥάβδῳ πατάξαντα τὸ ὕδωρ

beset with sleep and their weapons were broken. (24) And
Mousos went out and came to the palace, and he found the
doors opened, and he entered. Here also the guards were
relaxed, and he roused the king. And he was astounded and
commanded Mousos to tell him the name of the god who had
sent him. (25) And he leaned over and spoke into his ear,
and when the king had heard it, he fell down mute, but
Mousos held him up and revived him again. (26) And he wrote
the name on a tablet and sealed it, and one of the priests
who scorned what was written on the tablet died in a
convulsion. (27) The king told him to do some sign for
him, and Mousos took the rod which he had and made it into
a serpant. And when they were all terrified, he grasped the
tail and picked it up and made it into a rod again. (28)
And he proceded a little farther and struck the Nile with
his rod and the river became flooded and deluged all of
Egypt. (From this time its inundation began.) And the
gathered waters stank, and the river animals perished, and
the people were perishing of thirst. (29) And when these
wonders had been wrought, the king said that he would
release the people after a month, if he would restore
the river. And Mousos again struck the water with his rod

συστεῖλαι τὸ ῥεῦμα. (30) Τούτου δὲ γενομένου, τὸν βασιλέα
τοὺς ἱερεῖς ὑπὲρ Μέμφιν καλέσαι, καὶ φάναι αὐτοὺς ἀναιρτήσειν
καὶ τὰ ἱερὰ κατασκάψειν, ἐὰν μὴ καὶ αὐτοι τερατουργήσωσι τοὺς
δὲ τότε διά τινων μαγγάνων καὶ ἐπαοιδῶν δράκοντα ποιῆσαι καὶ
τὸν ποταμὸν μεταχπῶσαι. (31) Τὸν δὲ βασιλέα φρονηματισθέντα
ἐπὶ τῷ γεγονότι, πάσῃ τιμωρίᾳ καὶ κολάσει καταικίζειν τοὺς
Ἰουδαίους. Τὸν δὲ Μώυσον ταῦτα ὁρῶντα ἄλλα τε σημεῖα καὶ
πατάξαντα τὴν γῆν τῇ ῥάβδῳ ζῷόν τι πτηνὸν ἀνεῖναι, ὃ λυμή-
νασθαι τοὺς Αἰγυπτίους, πάντα τε ἐξελκωθῆναι τὰ σώματα. Τῶν
δὲ ἰατρῶν μὴ δυναμένων ἰᾶσθαι τοὺς κάμνοντας, οὕτω πάλιν
ἀνέσεως τυχεῖν τοὺς Ἰουδαίους. (32) Πάλιν τε τὸν Μώυσον
βάτραχον διὰ τῆς ῥάβδου ἀνεῖναι, πρὸς δὲ τούτοις ἀκρίδας καὶ
σκνίπας· διὰ τοῦτο δὲ καὶ τοὺς Αἰγυπτίους τὴν ῥάβδον ἀνατι-
θέναι εἰς πᾶν ἱερόν, ὁμοίως δὲ καὶ τῇ Ἴσιδι, διὰ τὸ τὴν γῆν
εἶναι Ἴσιν, παιομένην δὲ τῇ ῥάβδῳ, τὰ τέρατα ἀνεῖναι. (33)
Τοῦ δὲ βασιλέως ἔτι ἀφρονουμένου, τὸν Μώυσον χάλαζάν τε καὶ
σεισμοὺς διὰ νυκτὸς ἀποτελέσαι, ὥστε τοὺς τὸν σεισμὸν φεύ-
γοντας ἀπὸ τῆς χαλάζης ἀναιρεῖσθαι, τούς τε τὴν χάλαζαν
ἐκκλίνοντας ὑπὸ τῶν σεισμῶν διαφθείρεσθαι. Συμπεσεῖν δὲ
τότε τὰς μὲν οἰκίας πάσας, τῶν τε ναῶν τοὺς πλείστους.
(34) Τελευταῖον τοιαύταις συμφοραῖς περιπεσόντα τὸν βασιλέα τοὺς Ἰουδαίους ἀπολῦσαι· τοὺς δὲ χρησαμένους παρὰ τῶν

and reduced the flood. (30) When this happened, the
king called the priests from above Memphis and threatened
to kill them and destroy the temples unless they also
performed some wonders. And then they made a serpent by
certain magical means and incantations. (31) But when the
king had become arrogant about what had happened, he
maltreated the Jews with every kind of vengeance and
punishment. And Mousos saw these acts and did still more
signs and struck the earth with his rod to bring up a
winged creature to distress the Egyptians. And all of them
broke out in body sores. And it was because their physicians
were unable to cure the sufferers that the Jews gained
relief once more. (32) And again Mousos brought up frogs
by means of his rod and also locusts and lice. And for
this reason the Egyptians dedicate the rod in every temple
and similarly to Isis, because the earth is Isis and when
smitten by the rod she sent up the wonders. (33) But since
the king was still being heedless, Mousos sent hail and
earthquakes by night so that those who were fleeing from the
earthquake were killed by the hail while those who avoided
the hail were destroyed by the earthquakes. And at that
time, all of the houses and most of the temples were
destroyed. (34) Finally after having endured such
calamities, the king released the Jews. And having

Αἰγυπτίων πολλὰ μὲν ἐκπώματα, οὐκ ὀλίγον δὲ ἱματισμὸν ἄλλην
τε παμπληθῆ γάζαν, διαβάντας τοὺς κατὰ τὴν Ἀραβίαν ποτα-
μοὺς, καὶ διαβάντας ἱκανὸν τόπον, ἐπὶ τὴν Ἐρυθρὰν τριταίους
ἐλθεῖν θάλασσαν. (35) Καὶ Μεμφίτας μὲν λέγειν ἔμπειρον ὄντα
τὸν Μώυσον τῆς χώρας, τὴν ἄμπωτιν τηρήσαντα διὰ κηρᾶς τῆς
θαλάσσης τὸ πλῆθος περαιῶσαι· Ἡλιουπολίτας δὲ λέγειν ἐπι-
καταδραμεῖν τὸν βασιλέα μετὰ πολλῆς δυνάμεως, ἅμα καὶ τοῖς
καθιεπωμένοις ζώοις, διὰ τὸ τὴν ὕπαρξιν τοὺς Ἰουδαίους τῶν
Αἰγυπτίων χρησαμένους διακομίζειν. (36) Τῷ δὲ Μωύσῳ θείαν
φωνὴν γενέσθαι πατάξαι τὴν θάλασσαν τῇ ῥάβδῳ· τὸν δὲ Μώυσον
ἀκούσαντα ἐπιθίγειν τῇ ῥάβδῳ τοῦ ὕδατος, καὶ οὕτω τὸ μὲν νᾶμα
διαστῆναι, τὴν δὲ δύναμιν διὰ ξηρᾶς ὁδοῦ πορεύεσθαι. (37)
Συνεμβάντων δὲ τῶν Αἰγυπτίων καὶ διωκόντων φησὶ πῦρ αὐτοῖς
ἐκ τῶν ἔμπροσθεν ἐκλάμψαι, τὴν δὲ θάλασσαν πάλιν τὴν ὁδὸν
ἐπικλῦσαι· τοὺς δὲ Αἰγυπτίους ὑπό τε τοῦ πυρὸς καὶ τῆς πλημ-
μυρίδος πάντας διαφθαρῆναι. (38) Τοὺς δὲ Ἰουδαίους διαφυ-
γόντας τὸν κίνδυνον, τριάκοντα ἔτη ἐν τῇ ἐρήμῳ διατρῖψαι,
βρέχοντος αὐτοῖς τοῦ θεοῦ κριμνον ὅμοιον ἐλύμῳ, χιόνι παρα-
πλήσιον τὴν χρόαν.(39)Γεγονέναι δέ φησι τὸν Μώυσον μακρὸν,
πυρράκτην πολιὸν, κομήτην, ἀξιωματικόν. Ταῦτα δὲ πρᾶξαι
περὶ ἔτη ὄντα ὀγδοήκοντα ἐννέα.

appropriated many drinking vessels, and not a few clothes,
and a great deal of other treasures from the Egyptians,
they crossed the rivers on the Arabian side and passed
through a broad area to come to the Red Sea on the third
day. (35) To be sure, the Memphites say that Mousos was
experienced in this area and having awaited the ebb, he
conducted the people through the sea when it was dry. But
the Heliopolitans say that the king rushed down with a great
army and also with the consecrated animals because the
Jews had appropriated and were carrying off the property of
the Egyptians. (36) But the divine voice came to Mousos
telling him to strike the sea with his rod. And when
Mousos heard this he touched the water with the rod and thus
the streat divided and the host passed via a dry path.
(37) But when the Egyptians came upon them and pursued
them, it is said a fire shone out upon them from the front
and the sea again overflowed the path. And the Egyptians
were all destroyed by the fire and the flood. (38) But
having escaped the danger, the Jews spent 40 years in the
desert, while God rained down meal upon them like millet,
similar in color to snow. (39) And it is said that Mousos
was tall and ruddy, venerable, with long hair, dignified.
And he did these things when he was about 89 years old.